ADVANCES IN DEVELOPMENTAL PSYCHOLOGY
Volume 1

Edited by

MICHAEL E. LAMB
University of Utah

ANN L. BROWN
University of Illinois

LAWRENCE ERLBAUM ASSOCIATES, PUBLISHERS

1981   Hillsdale, New Jersey

Lawrence Erlbaum Associates, Inc., Publishers
365 Broadway
Hillsdale, New Jersey 07642

ISSN 0275-3049

ISBN 0-89859-103-1

Printed in the United States of America

Contents

List of Contributors

Thomas M. Achenbach, *Departments of Psychology and Psychiatry, University of Vermont, Burlington, Vermont*

Douglas Derryberry, *Department of Psychology, University of Oregon, Eugene, Oregon*

S. Shirley Feldman, *Department of Psychology, Stanford University, Stanford, California*

Randall C. Flanery, *Department of Psychology, University of Wisconsin, Madison, Wisconsin*

Janice Gruendel, *Department of Psychology, Yale University, New Haven, Connecticut*

Ellen Markman, *Department of Psychology, Stanford University, Stanford, California*

Sharon Churnin Nash, *Department of Psychology, Stanford University, Stanford, California*

Katherine Nelson, *Department of Psychology, Graduate Center of the City University of New York, New York*

D. W. Rajecki, *Department of Psychology, Purdue University of Indianapolis, Indianapolis, Indiana*

Mary Klevjord Rothbart, *Department of Psychology, University of Oregon, Eugene, Oregon*

Editorial Consultants

Preface

With this volume, we introduce a new series designed, as the name implies, to survey in thoughtful detail important new strides in developmental psychology. In selecting the chapters to appear in this volume, we first identified those researchers whose recent work has provided or promises to provide new understanding of the processes and course of development across the life span. Each of the researchers so identified was then invited to prepare a manuscript describing the research and its theoretical implications. These manuscripts were reviewed by the editors and several consultant experts and were then revised by the authors in the light of this feedback. As a result, the chapters present exceptionally valuable perspectives on those aspects of developmental psychology exhibiting significant recent progress.

Readers might find it valuable if we articulated the philosophy that guided the preparation of this volume and will guide the preparation of later volumes in the series. First and foremost, the "advances" worthy of treatment in our series must involve methodologically appropriate empirical work that has clear and significant implications for the understanding and conceptualization of developmental process. The processes we wish to elucidate are not those that were central to "experimental child psychology"—they are processes that facilitate explanations of *development across the life span*. The emphasis on heuristically significant endeavors is evident in each of the chapters in this volume. The authors all present theoretical frameworks that provide testable predictions whose verification or refutation is likely to clarify the nature and process of development. Finally, we have sampled from a diverse array of areas in developmental psychology—not simply the traditional areas of social and cognitive development. In this and in future volumes, we include chapters concerned with atypical development, comparative developmental psychology, psychobiology, communicative and linguistic development as well as the more traditional areas. Likewise the contributors have been chosen because their work is relevant to the central concerns of developmental psychologists, even though the authors themselves may be clinical, experimental or social psychologists, psychiatrists, behavioral pediatricians, and the like.

Volumes in this series will appear roughly every 18 months. We expect them to provide valuable heuristic syntheses for professionals and graduate students wishing to keep abreast of conceptually important advances in developmental psychology and ancilliary fields.

Michael E. Lamb
Ann L. Brown

1 Sex Role and Sex-Related Attributions: Constancy and Change Across the Family Life Cycle

Sharon Churnin Nash
S. Shirley Feldman
Stanford University

Despite the burgeoning interest in sex-role research evident in the past two decades, the field is still plagued by unclear terminology and controversy over what, in fact, is being studied. The term *sex role* itself remains frustratingly ambiguous: According to Angrist (1969), "Sex role singularly suffers from absence of specific definition—its meaning is connotative instead of denotative [p. 218]." This confusion has arisen in part from the very distinct foci emphasized by the three major disciplines that most commonly employ the term. Anthropologists have stressed the normative expectations that members of a given culture hold about the *position* men and women should occupy—the term *position* implying the division of labor between the sexes and the societal tasks assigned to each sex within structured social settings. For sociologists, sex role grows out of self-development during the socialization process. Individuals learn their own and others' roles through social interaction. The emphasis here is on *relationships,* or the process of role taking within dyads or larger groups of varying structure. In contrast, psychologists have focused on distinguishing characteristics of women and men (with social context being less relevant). The stress here is on behavior, as measured by object preferences, school achievement, and occupational choices, and on behavior-related attributes of the individual, such as personality, adjustment, need achievement, and aspirations (see Maccoby & Jacklin, 1974; Nash, 1979, for summaries of relevant research). The sex-related dichotomies emphasized by this approach seem to reinforce the trait theory notion (Angrist, 1969) that "women are women and men are men wherever they may live, eat, play, work, or interact [p. 217]." Such a position implies consistency across diverse behaviors, situations, and time.

1

In particular, then, the approach to sex roles promulgated by psychologists has caused considerable ambiguity in the literature. Has the psychological definition of sex role strayed from the traditional meaning of the role concept? The word role is derived from the old French word *rôle*—that is, the "roll" of paper used in the theater for the actors' scripts. A role is most frequently viewed as the set of expectations that arise from the position one holds in society—a position (sometimes called a status) being a collectively recognized category for classifying people. Despite their prescriptive–proscriptive nature, most social roles specify few exact behaviors; more often, they consist of clear but general guidelines as to how to conduct oneself. There is a range of acceptable performances, just as a stage role may be interpreted differently by different actors. To a certain extent, social roles are interdependent—that is, they establish their boundaries, and derive their meaning in partnership with complementary roles.

The notion of role involves an integration of activity and relation in terms of cultural expectations. According to Bronfenbrenner (1979), "it is the embeddedness of roles in this larger context that gives them their special power to influence—and even to compel—how a person behaves in a given situation, the activities she engages in, and the relations that become established between that person and other persons present in the setting [p. 86]." The work of Zimbardo and his colleagues, using a simulated prison situation, dramatically demonstrated the powerful impact of roles: Placing comparable, normal individuals in different roles (even in the same physical setting) radically influenced their behavior and interpersonal dynamics (Haney, Banks, & Zimbardo, 1973). In fact, the considerable body of research generated by self-perception (D. J. Bem, 1967) and attribution theories (Jones & Davis, 1965) has repeatedly emphasized the human tendency to overestimate the degree to which behavior is influenced by enduring personality traits of the individual, and underestimate the degree to which it is caused by external factors. In other words, we presume more cross-situational consistency than actually exists. Thus, the evidence of social-learning theory challenges our intuitive bias towards dispositional explanations and demonstrates the importance of situation, location, and context—so vital to the sociological and anthropological definitions of role—in determining our behavior. To the extent that sex-role behaviors represent a category of social role, they should be sensitive to changes in social context.

The question remains, however, whether sex roles are really "roles" or whether the term *role* is a misnomer. At best, sex role is an unusual use of the role concept. Unlike other roles, sex roles are ascribed at birth on the basis of gender, and are not achieved or acquired by choice. Other ascribed characteristics (such as age, race, and class) are seldom discussed in terms of role prescriptions. Most roles are focused within a "situated activity system," activity that occurs entirely within the walls of a single social establishment (Goffman, 1961). In contrast, sex roles are unfocused or diffuse in the larger society; they intrude upon other key roles, introducing considerable modulations in their performance.

From a somewhat different point of view, Bates (1956) described sex roles as "dominant," superceding or influencing other latent roles. Being a male or a female is dominant in the sense that it affects most other role interpretations (e.g., parent, spouse, worker, etc.). Despite some disagreement as to which roles are most appropriately viewed as focal, both these positions touch upon what is unique about sex roles—namely, their pervasiveness: According to Angrist (1969), "To delineate the exact context for sex role is to encompass the whole set of roles an actor is heir to [p. 219]." Thus, sex role involves not one, but a multitude of roles and role combinations that vary across social settings (Spence & Helmreich, 1978).

It would seem, then, that sex roles may be considered roles, albeit unique in nature. Yet, psychologists persist in using sex role as an "all-purpose" label for all the ways males and females are presumed to differ [Spence & Helmreich, 1978], "... not merely to identify observable behavior but also to identify (hypothetical) internal properties, such as personality characteristics differentiating the sexes [p. 14]." The roles we play have many consequences: They define the behaviors expected of us by others, they are a major source of our feelings about ourselves, and they expose us to experiences that can affect later attitudes, feelings, and behaviors (Sales, 1978). Important roles leave a residue in the personality. It has been proposed that the personality is an integration (rather than a simple sum) of all the roles that have been played (Brown, 1965). Turner (1978) has been more specific in his speculations as to when the role and the person are most likely to "merge"—that is, why sex roles are (by their nature) so readily linked to the traits of the individual. Based on the dimensions of the role in question, Turner derived a set of propositions that indicate the probability that a person will be conceived of by others in terms of the characteristics of the role. For example, roles lodged in broader settings are more widely and frequently visible, and as such they are more likely to be used as clues to the person's nature. Turner (1978) writes: "Sex roles do seem to afford confirmation for such an inference. Probably no assumption has been more generally and uncritically made than men and women are different—that they are not merely playing roles [p. 9]." Another such proposition is that the more conspicuous and widely recognizable the role cues, the greater the tendency for others to conceive the person as revealed by the role. In the case of sex roles, few role cues are as blatant or unmistakable as gender. Finally, the greater the extent to which a role in one setting determines allocation and performance of roles in other settings, the greater the tendency for others to view the role as an index of the person. Because, as mentioned earlier, sex roles are "intrusive," they commonly determine the individual's "eligibility" for and interpretations of many other roles.

Thus, from this subset of principles, it appears that sex roles, by their unique nature, strongly influence the attributions of others regarding the individual. Attribution theorists have studied external versus internal attributions of causation, which can be translated into the question of whether an actor is merely playing a role (external) or whether the behavior and the sentiments expressed through the role are those of the person (internal). In the case of sex roles, the internal attribution seems more probable.

Another factor that has helped to perpetuate the notion that sex roles are linked to stable behavioral sex differences is methodological—that is, the fragmented, age-limited nature of the data typically reported. Most attention has been devoted to sex differences during childhood and adolescence, and to a lesser extent, among the aged. There is a conspicuous lack of information about how the sexes compare during the active adult years—that is, during the 40+ years between the ages of 21 and the early 60's. Perhaps this disparity between the study of sex-related differences in the early years and their fate during adulthood reflects the assumption of stability of individual differences once formed, at least until they are altered by biological deterioration in old age. Although social-learning theorists (e.g., Bandura, 1977; Mischel, 1973) no longer presume the constancy of traits across situations and time, their conceptual contributions have not significantly touched the psychology of sex differences and of sex role.

Given the special nature of sex roles, it is easy to understand why a trait-like psychological definition evolved. However, a critical assessment of the psychological approach raises the serious issue of how valid sex-role measures are if no attention is paid to the delineation of other impinging characteristics or to the pertinent social location. Furthermore, it would be of considerable value to clarify the ambiguous relationship between sex roles and sex differences. The psychological position implies that they are synonymous—that is, that sex roles include the full set of differences between males and females. However, there are subsets of sex-related differences that may not be accurately subsumed under the heading of sex roles—for example, biological and cognitive differences, as well as, according to Spence and Helmreich (1978) "properties of the behaving organism [p. 14]."

One type of information that would be helpful in clarifying some of the aforementioned issues is developmental data, or more specifically, a life-cycle view of sex roles and their relation to sex differences. Are sex-role prescriptions stable across situation and time or do they vary over the life cycle? Are time-tied fluctuations in sex roles reflected in the sex differences manifested? Theories that contend that socialization continues throughout adulthood might predict changes in sex-role–related differences over the life cycle (Emmerich, 1973). Each stage of life is defined by distinctive and specific situational demands that may or may not require differential behavior and attitudes from males and females. At certain points in the life cycle, role prescriptions are quite similar for males and females; for instance, a training role such as that of a college student requires comparable attitudes from each sex. At other times, very distinctive behaviors are called for, as in the case of certain familial roles: mother versus father of an infant (Feldman & Nash, 1978). Accordingly, when the social demands of a role diverge for males and females, sex differences should emerge.

LIFE-CYCLE ASPECTS OF SEX ROLES

In trying to understand the nature and impact of sex roles across the adult years, a not-so-trivial issue is how to conceptualize the life span to be studied. Developmentalists interested in childhood have frequently used chronological age as an index of change, despite the fact that age is not a psychological variable—it simply refers to the amount of time that has elapsed since birth. It is true that for the very young (under 5 years) and the very old (over 70 years), many biological milestones seem reasonably well linked to age. However, chronological age is a less useful marker of development for the middle adult years when there are a minimum of biological changes with discernible sequelae and few age-graded compulsory, environmental encounters. To the extent that every society has a system of social expectations regarding age-appropriate behavior, many life events are correlated with age (Neugarten & Datan, 1973). However, methodologically, age is a problematic variable to study. Differentiating each year would present an overwhelming sampling problem across the life cycle. On the other hand, if (for the sake of expediency) blocks of years are studied, an equally troublesome problem arises. How can these somewhat arbitrary time units be chosen to assure that the findings obtained do not obscure the real distribution of the variable? Chronological age may have some value when a new variable is being investigated in that it may highlight periods when closer scrutiny of many age-correlated variables will be profitable. Because our own interest has been to identify some of the direct causal antecedents to sex-role change across the adult years, age was, in and of itself, set aside as an explanatory variable.

Besides age, there are two general modes of viewing change over the life course: the *organismic* and the *mechanistic/environmental*. These models differ on many dimensions (Looft, 1973), including the locus for developmental change. Organismic theories place the developmental dynamic internal to the organism, whereas mechanistic theories place it in external environmental forces. The notion of the developmental dynamic is particularly useful for structuring alternate ways of conceptualizing change during the life course.

Organismic or internally generated stage theories such as those of Piaget (1950) and Kohlberg (1969) carve the life cycle (or portions of it) into qualitatively different stages, each of which has internal coherence described as psychological structure. A hierarchical organization of the stages ensures that they occur in an invariant order. Impetus to progress from one stage to another comes from within the individual as he or she acts upon the environment. Such strong stage positions are crucially dependent on elaborated theories to account for well-documented, universal developmental phenomena. As a result, the application of these theories to date has been limited to childhood and adolescence. In contrast, weak stage theories provide descriptive accounts of sequences in development (Erikson, 1950; Levinson, Darrow, Klein, Levinson, & McKee, 1978), and are more frequently applied to adulthood. Weak stage theories give the environment a larger role in fostering change, although the force for development still remains within the organism. Universal environmental encounters precipitate conflict or crises that must be resolved. To date, weak stage theories rest on more narrow, culture-bound data bases, and lend themselves better to postdictive explanations than to hypothesis generation.

In contrast to the previous approaches, which focus on changes emanating primarily from within the individual, sociologists and, to a certain extent, social psychologists have tried to understand the contribution of major life events in creating personality and behavioral change.From birth, children are socialized for participation in society: they learn the roles appropriate to their age/stage of life, their sex, their ethnic group, and so on. Simultaneously, they incorporate those attributes and traits that are consistent with the roles they are enacting. As the children encounter new situations and new roles in the succession of life tasks or life events, they learn the appropriate social prescriptions. This learning is an on-going process; in adulthood, many new roles are assumed that require change in the person, making socialization a lifelong process (Brim, 1966). To the extent that these role expectations are cognitive, this approach is not purely mechanistic.

The life-events perspective assumes that across a diversity of people there is some commonality in the definition and experience of major life situations. Most frequently, objective events in the life cycle that can be readily identified by the researcher rather than subjective experiences or idiosyncratic events are studied. Among the more frequently used categories of observable events are *family-status* changes (such as marriage, parenthood, grandparenthood, etc.), *occupational occurrences* (such as onset of wage-earning status, major promotion, retirement, etc.), and *health and biological functioning* (such as puberty, menopause, major illness, etc.). To date, this perspective has been displayed most clearly and effectively in the works of Duvall (1977), Hill (1965), Neugarten (Neugarten & Datan, 1973), and Lowenthal (Lowenthal, Thurnher & Chiriboga, 1975), to name a few. More recently, Hultsch and Plemons (1979) have provided a thoughtful review of life events and life-span development in which they argue that the concept of life events needs to be refined if we hope to understand its impact on behavior and personality. Distinctions might be made between events individuals can control versus those they cannot, events involving gain versus those involving loss (Lowenthal et al., 1975), single versus multiple role changes, the centrality of the life event (Holmes & Rahe, 1967), and the timing and sequence of events (Neugarten & Datan, 1973).

Given the inappropriateness of age and stage theories to an exploratory study of sex roles across the life cycle, it is fortuitous that a life-events approach is as suitable for our purposes as it is. As Flavell (1970) has argued, "Adulthood is the nearest thing we have to a pure experiment in nature for assessing the change-making power of experience alone, that is, relatively unconfounded by significant and directional biological change [p. 250]." Among these powerful and almost universal experiences are common markers in the family life cycle: adolescence, single adulthood, marriage, expectancy, the various phases of parenthood, postparenthood (the launching of children), and grandparenthood (Neugarten, 1966). Such milestones may be viewed as ''crucial turning points'' (rather than independent variables), which impose new role demands and confer a certain commonality of experience (Bolton, 1961; Kirkpatrick, 1967; Magrabi & Marshall, 1965). If sex roles are in fact roles, we should expect to see some variation in their manifestation across life events. Ahammer (1973) has proposed that symbolic processes in the form of role prescriptions and expectations exert a powerful influence to change when one moves into a social situation (or role) that is distinctly different from previous situations. This is particularly compelling when the behaviors appropriate for the new situation differ from those previously appropriate, and are clearly specified, as in life events such as marriage and parenthood. These larger, more enduring life situations require behavioral changes in all participants as a function of interaction of spouses and of parents and children, respectively. In addition, they necessitate modifications in role prescriptions that redefine the consequences of role-related behavior. By focusing on family life events, one resolves the difficult problem of ''location'' in studying sex roles—that is, the social location becomes the nuclear family. Although this represents only one of many areas in which sex roles are operative (e.g., school, career, and so on), it is not a trivial one: In the context of the family life cycle, female means wife and mother; male means husband and father. Sex modifies, sometimes strongly and sometimes weakly, most of the family life events one engages in.

RESEARCH ISSUES

Many psychologists have convincingly theorized that development continues throughout adulthood (Erikson, 1950; Havighurst, 1973; Levinson et al., 1978; Neugarten, 1968). Yet, remarkably little empirical evidence exists to verify the nature of such change. Research involving sex-role behaviors is conspicuously lacking in such data. Moreover, little in the way of theoretical guidelines has been offered to generate the necessary research. In one of the few overviews of the area, Emmerich (1973) proposed that sex differences could be thought of as serving important social functions at the points in development at which they appear. Accordingly, Emmerich (1973) wrote, ''somewhat different patterns of sex differences would be expected to occur during each period in the life cycle [p. 126].'' Despite this provocative thesis, the life-span perspective has rarely been applied to the observation of sex-role–related behavior. For the most part, life-span developmental psychologists have tended to concentrate on methodological issues, model building, and research geared towards teasing apart age-related from other effects. According to Neugarten (1977), ''They have been more successful, then, at telling us *how* to study the life span than at helping us decide *what* to study [p. 633]."

Finding a sex-role–related behavior that is consistent and meaningful across wide spans of life is a considerable challenge. Sex-role behaviors that are quite satisfactory for investigations of childhood (such as doll play, rough-and-tumble play, etc.) rarely persist in comparable form at later stages of life. Studying transformations of such behaviors over time presumes a clear understanding of precisely what is being converted into what (across individuals). If transformed behaviors are studied in the search for continuities, problems arise when developmental differences occur: Are the differences real or are they a function of changing what we measure?

Responsiveness to Babies Across the Family Life Cycle

One classical sex-role–related behavior that has only recently begun to receive some attention in the literature is *responsiveness to babies*. It is appealing as a dependent variable for a number of reasons. It is not narrowly age-bound and thus can be observed in subjects of all ages and at all stages of life. Secondly, it is an important behavior, one of evolutionary significance: To be viable, a society has to have enough interest in babies to nurture them to adulthood. The infant's innate physical and behavioral characteristics are optimally designed to encourage such interest and responsivity (Lorenz, 1943). Because responsiveness to babies is seen as stereotypically feminine, linked to childbearing and nurturing roles, it has been commonly accepted that females more than males are attracted to infants. This presumption makes responsivity to babies a particularly inviting variable to study; as with most other sex-role–related behaviors, a constant, continuous sex difference has been assumed to exist with very little question. After all, primary responsibility for the care and nurturance of the young is generally assumed by females in our society and only rarely by males. Thus, there must exist a quality of "motherliness" that predisposes females (more than males) to be interested in babies. Responsiveness to children in males is seen as a socially delegated characteristic, generally adopted in conjunction with fatherhood, rather than a state providing intrinsic psychological satisfaction.

Our research has been designed to test these "truths." Does this feminine sex-role behavior represent a stable sex difference, or, as with other roles, does situational context result in fluctuations in its salience across the life span according to defining life events?

In a series of cross-sectional studies, we have observed peoples' interest in and responsiveness to babies—both actual babies and pictures of babies. Detailed reports of these studies appear elsewhere (Feldman & Nash, 1978, 1979a, 1979b; Feldman, Nash, & Cutrona, 1977; Nash & Feldman, 1980). For this chapter, we have combined the data from these studies together with some unpublished data to yield a picture of changes across the family life cycle.

A total of 500 middle-class, American-born subjects were studied. They belonged to different stages of life, with males and females approximately equally represented in each stage. The groups included children aged 4–9 years, adolescents aged 14–19 years, childless adults (single, cohabiting, and married) aged 20–32 years, people expecting their first child, first-time parents of an infant, parents whose youngest child was 8–14 years old, empty nesters (i.e., parents whose grown children no longer lived at home), and grandparents who had at least one grandchild younger than 18 months of age. All of the couples in our married and parenting groups (through grandparenthood) were members of *intact* first marriages. As Nock (1979) has indicated, "relationships which exist between many family life variables and stages in the family life cycle disappear when length of marriage is removed from the relationship [p. 15]."

While waiting to take part in a picture-preference task, subjects were observed for 12 minutes from behind a one-way mirror. In the waiting room, a mother and her 6-month-old baby, who were seated apart and equidistant from the subject, were also apparently waiting to participate in the study. In fact, these were research confederates. The subjects' reactions to the baby and the mother were recorded every 6 seconds from behind one-way mirrors. Two scores were derived from this waiting-room situation: (1) *responsiveness to baby,* a standardized composite score involving both proximal bids such as touching and approaching baby, and distal bids, such as looking or smiling at baby; and (2) *ignores baby,* the sum of the 6-second intervals in which the subject did not respond to the baby's vocalization or to the onset of noise from the child's toy. In another room, subjects were shown 30 pictures of everyday objects, including four pictures of babies, and were asked to choose their favorite five. The number of baby pictures chosen constituted the measure of *preference for baby pictures.*

Table 1.1 is a summary of our data for the different stages of life.[1] Overall, there were sex differences on each of the measures: Women were more responsive to the infant ($p < .001$), they ignored the infant less ($p < .01$), and they chose more baby pictures among their favorites ($p < .01$). Given our hypothesis that sex differences fluctuate over the life span, we were more interested in sex differences within each stage of life. As predicted, there was a pattern of waxing and waning sex differences.

Study 1: Childhood to Adulthood.   Despite a very early awareness among children that females are more likely to be care-givers than males (Kuhn, Nash, & Brucken, 1978), our first study showed that boys and girls under the age of 10

---

[1]In the interest of economy, we have combined certain stages previously reported separately: "Children" refers to nursery schoolers and 8–9 year olds; "mature parents" includes parents of both elementary school children and adolescents. Furthermore, the variable "responsiveness to baby" has been standardized for the total sample. Consequently, the values reported in Table 1.1 may differ in detail from those published previously.

TABLE 1.1
Means and Sex Differences[1] for Measures of Interest
in Babies Across the Family Life Cycle

	Responsiveness to Baby		Ignores Baby		Picture Preference	
Study 1	Males	Females	Males	Females	Males	Females
Children (N = 32)	43.6	44.5	29.6	24.8	.7	.8
Young adolescents (N = 32)	42.8	45.3	30.7 [a]	21.0	.3 [c]	.9
Single adults (N = 30)	46.7	49.1	41.2	41.5	.7	.7
Study 2						
Midadolescents (N = 32)	44.5	43.7	49.9	49.9	.5	.6
Late adolescents (N = 32)	44.8	48.1	38.6	53.4	.8	.6
Study 3						
Cohabiting adults (N = 30)	47.9	50.1	39.6	31.5	.7	.6
Married childless (N = 30)	49.4	52.1	17.5	26.7	.9	.8
Expectants (N = 30)	47.8	47.8	34.3	41.9	1.0	1.0
Parents of infants (N = 30)	50.1 [c]	58.8	45.0 [b]	26.2	1.0	1.1
Study 4						
Mature parents (N = 30)	48.1 [a]	51.9	40.8	32.4	.5 [b]	1.0
Empty nesters (N = 28)	48.4	54.0	38.1	32.3	.8	.8
Grandparents (N = 26)	51.9 [b]	58.4	38.1 [c]	13.3	1.1	1.4

[1]All tests of sex differences are one-tailed tests.
[a]$p < .10$
[b]$p < .05$
[c]$p < .01$

were remarkably similar in their responsiveness to an unfamiliar baby. In contrast, early adolescence (14–15 years) was marked by a considerable divergence between the sexes: Young adolescent girls showed more interest in babies and were less able to ignore a baby's bids for attention. By young adulthood (20–30 years), childless men and women were again more similar than different in their reaction to babies.

Thus, at least at these earlier stages of life, no stable, enduring sex difference existed in nurturance and sensitivity. Females did not display heightened interest in infants early in the course of normal development, nor did they maintain this "predisposition" into adulthood. Adolescence is noteworthy from a social-role perspective because it is a transitional period, marked by considerable uncertainty in the variability that can be tolerated in role expression. Faced with this uncertainty, the young adolescent retreats to the safety of stereotypic attitudes and behaviors learned as a child. Sex-related roles are particularly important to the young adolescent undergoing sexual maturation and beginning heterosexual relations. Deviation from sex-appropriate behavior brings sanctions somewhat stronger for males than for females (Maccoby & Jacklin, 1974). In fear of social condemnation and uncertain as to the limits of acceptable masculine behavior, the adolescent male behaves in accordance with the masculine stereotype, avoiding conspicuously feminine behaviors.

Study 2: Adolescence Transition.   Given the feminine sex-typed nature of responsivity to babies, we would expect early and midadolescent boys to be reluctant to demonstrate male-inappropriate interest in babies. In contrast, girls may comfortably exhibit overt interest, thereby creating a role-related sex difference in behavior. Later in adolescence, when sex-role identity is secure, more leeway is allowed for the expression of opposite-sex–typed interests and few, if any, differences between males and females in responsiveness to babies are predicted.

Attempts to trace the fate of this sex-role–related difference from early adolescence to its disappearance in early adulthood have been scattered and the outcome highly dependent on the measure. Relatively passive components of interest in babies have been assessed, including ratings of pictures (Berman, Goodman, Sloan, & Fernander, 1978; Fullard & Reiling, 1976; Goldberg & Kriger, 1980; Sternglanz, Grey & Murakami, 1977), physiological reactivity to videotapes (Frodi & Lamb, 1978), and incidental reactions to a baby in the presence of its mother (Feldman et. al., 1977; Frodi, Murray, Lamb, & Steinberg, 1980). Such situations may underestimate behavioral sex differences because they require less active or instrumental interest to register an effect, thereby overvaluing casual interest, while leaving largely untapped more interactional forms of responsivity. To clarify this situation, we assessed adolescents in a number of situations that varied in the opportunity for expressing active-instrumental versus passive reactions to infants, thus allowing for a more systematic understanding of the nature and extent of any sex-related differences found. Perceptual measures assessed the more passive forms of interest, because they elicited noninstrumental reactions to inanimate stimuli—namely, photographs of babies. Allowing for more active reactions was the waiting-room situation with an actual baby and mother. Finally, responsivity to a baby without the security of a responsible care-giver in the room represented the opportunity for the most instrumental interaction with the infant.

By studying the extent to which comparable adolescents at two different stages were interested in babies, we sought to trace the fate of sex differences found among younger adolescents in the studies previously cited. By examining differing intensities of interest in babies, we hoped to clarify the extent and strength of this phenomenon for each sex.

In this second study, we observed two matched age groups of subjects equally divided by sex: 16–17-year-old college-bound high school juniors and seniors (midadolescents), and 18–19-year-old college freshman (late adolescents). As previously described, we assessed subjects' incidental interest in a baby in a waiting-room situation, and their preference for baby pictures over other pictures. As the subjects were preparing to depart, they were casually asked to "help out" the researcher by returning to the waiting room so babies' reactions to previously seen strangers could be assessed. In this situation, the baby was lying alone on the floor and the mother was absent. Subjects were instructed to "act naturally" and were left alone with the infant for 6 minutes. Their only instruction, that the baby could not sit unaided, was designed to heighten their sense of responsibility for the infant. Based on detailed time sampling of 18 behaviors, we derived three measures: distal interaction, physical contact, and disinterest. These measures are described in detail elsewhere (Feldman & Nash, 1979a).

As shown in Table 1.1, no sex differences were found for either the picture measures or waiting-room measures of interest in babies. However, when the subject was given the responsibility for the infant, there were marked sex differences among high schoolers on all of the measures; girls interacted more (proximally and distally) with the baby ($p < .05$ or beyond), whereas boys were more disinterested ($p < .05$). In contrast, there were no sex differences among college students in the same situation. Thus, the clear sex differences evident among 14–15-year-olds in the previous study gradually disappeared, earlier with more passive measures, and later with more instrumentally active ones. By 18–19 years of age, at least for college students, males and females were equally interested in babies.

These findings of sex differences present among high schoolers but absent among college students are at variance with the only other developmental study of interest in babies across the adolescent years. Fullard and Reiling (1976) assessed ratings of attractiveness of animal and human baby pictures and found sex differences emerging in sixth grade that were maintained until young adulthood. In their study, however, picture attractiveness was evaluated in classrooms in mixed-sex groups, a situation known to depress ratings given by college males, and to slightly elevate those given by college females (Berman, Abplanalp, Cooper, Mansfield, & Shields, 1975). Thus, mixed-sex groupings overestimate sex differences, at least for older adolescents.

Our results based on the more commonly employed measures of interest suggest that the previously documented sex differences in interest in babies evident among 14–15 year olds (Berman et al., 1978; Feldman et al., 1977; Frodi & Lamb, 1978; Fullard & Reiling, 1976) are brief and nonenduring. Based on perceptual measures of interest as well as on behavioral reactions in the protected environment of the mother-present condition, it appears that by 16–17 years of age, adolescents of both sexes were remarkably similar in their more passive expressions of interest. Quite striking, however, were the sex-differentiated behaviors exhibited by these same high school students when left alone with a baby. The girls assumed a more active, instrumental role in this feminine domain. The boys, in contrast, were unmoved by the brief opportunity for nurturant responsibility. They were noticeably unaffected by the baby's bids for attention and even seemed somewhat indifferent to the baby's gaze.

The sex-related differences found among high school students were not evident among college students of comparable intelligence and background. The disappearing role differentiation was largely attributable to the greater comfort with babies demonstrated by older adolescent males in contrast to the younger ones. Apparently, by college age, males were more willing to express feminine-typed behaviors if they were situationally appropriate, as was evident from their responsive behavior with the baby. Concomitantly, they described themselves in more expressive, feminine-typed terms on the Bem Sex Role Inventory; 56% of college males were classified as androgynous (high on both expressive and instrumental traits) in contrast to only 21% of the high school males.

This pattern of results makes sense in terms of viewing adolescence as a period of transition, marked by distinctive phases during which the tasks of sex-role identity undergo recognizable changes. During early and midadolescence, the need for clarity and reduction of ambiguity concerning appropriate sex-role behavior results in a reliance upon stereotypes. Even among college youth, those who are sex-stereotyped in their self description are more likely to behave in classically sex-typed ways (Bem, Martyna, & Watson, 1976). By late adolescence, sex-role identity is more firmly established and generally consolidated; sex-role prescriptions may no longer be a major determinant of behavioral choices. As a result, the individual differences are not sex-related, as demonstrated by the remarkably similar levels of interest in babies exhibited by college males and females in this well-educated Californian sample.

Study 3: Young Adulthood. This decreasing sex difference persisted throughout young adulthood prior to the advent of children. In our third study of young adults with cohort held constant, life situation was varied to establish its impact on this sex-role–related behavior (Feldman & Nash, 1978). Men and women between the ages of 20 and 32 years who were either cohabiting, married and childless, expecting their first child, or were parents of an infant were observed with an unfamiliar baby. Distinctive sex differences were expected to occur only during those periods when role demands concerning infants differ for men and women. For example, because cohabitation and marriage serve needs for intimacy and sexual relations, but do not require men and women to behave differently towards children, sex differences in interest were not expected. In contrast, parenthood, and to a lesser extent pregnancy, typically elicit distinguishable sex-specific role activities from men and women, at least in our society. For the man, parenthood usually involves the role responsibility for providing financial and physical security for his now-expanded family—a role (in many cases) previously shared with his wife. In addition, the role of husband often undergoes considerable redefinition in accord with his wife's exacting new roles. The woman, on the other hand, is typically the primary care giver to the child, and remains responsible for the quality of that care regardless of whether she administers it or delegates it to others. What makes this transition "profound" (Bernard, 1974) is that it represents a complete change in life approach, particularly for the woman. She typically relinquishes her role as paid worker towards the end of her pregnancy. Her experience with shared or communal responsibility at work and at home is replaced for many by the stark reality of sole responsibility for the care and nurturance of the child. The former balance between work and leisure time is now upset by the full-time "on-call" role of mother, with relatively little compensatory time off. Even the woman's problem-solving strategies may be altered with the onset of motherhood. The direct goal-oriented attack on problems, found so successful during the childless years, may be dysfunctional for the mother who must give priority to her baby's physical and emotional needs before achieving closure on other role-related tasks (e.g., homemaking). Some old, familiar roles are maintained, but they require extensive redefinition (e.g., that of daughter, wife, etc.). Clearly, the role changes explicit and implicit during the transition to parenthood are of considerable magnitude and breadth (especially for women). Thus, it was expected that parenthood would elicit the most prominent sex differences in responsiveness to babies.

In fact, among young childless adults, whether single, cohabiting, or married, men and women did not differ in responsivity to babies. Even expectancy did not precipitate sex differences in our laboratory measures of interest in infants. Both parents-to-be were equally interested in babies, whether it was an actual infant or pictures of babies. With the birth of their first child, new mothers were markedly more responsive to the unfamiliar baby than new fathers. For men, stage of life did not influence responsiveness to baby, ignores baby, or the number of baby pictures chosen. Fatherhood may have had more of an effect on men than our results indicate, but the effect may have been limited to interest in their own infant. Questionnaire data confirmed that fathers in this study were involved with their own infants. Learning theory suggests that a wide generalization gradient exists when there is overlearning (e.g., extensive contact, reinforcement), as in motherhood, and a narrow generalization gradient exists when there has been less exposure, as in fatherhood. Thus, because men typically have limited experience with infants, their responsivity may be more narrowly focused on their own child. Motherhood provides more extensive opportunities for contact, and so the interest of women may generalize to other infants.

The aforementioned research was based on a "traditional" sample of middle-class subjects: The childless women were gainfully employed, the expectant women resigned (or were planning to resign) from their jobs during their third trimester, and new mothers were devoted to their roles as parent, spouse, and homemaker, with the new father assuming the position as sole breadwinner. In contrast to this traditional sample, recent (unpublished) research in our laboratory confirmed that men with more extensive contact and involvement with their infants showed generalized interest to unfamiliar babies. We carried out a short-term longitudinal study of 31 highly educated expectant couples who were seen twice: once in the third trimester of the wife's pregnancy, and again when their infant was approximately 6 months old. Among numerous other measures, we observed interest in unfamiliar infants at both visits. In this sample, the men were very involved in expectancy and parenthood: They attended prenatal exercise classes with their wives and were informed via books, movies, and filmstrips on childbirth and childrearing. They all attended the birth of their child, where they frequently served as coach for the wife during labor and delivery, and typically held their infants within the first few minutes of life. As fathers, these men were quite psychologically invested in their offspring, despite their traditional assumption of the breadwinner role. They played with their babies nightly, looked after them in their wives' absence, carried out many care-taking routines, either on a regular or "as needed" basis, and described fathering in glowing terms. For these men, the advent of fatherhood was associated with marked increases in responsiveness to baby ($p < .01$). In fact, these highly involved fathers changed on our laboratory measures to the same extent as their wives did. Thus, it appears that under certain conditions, the narrow generalization gradient for men's interest in infants may be broadened.

Study 4: Middle and Mature Adulthood. The full impact of a broader generalization gradient for women becomes more obvious when the duration of this sex-related difference across the life span is revealed (see Table 1.1). Throughout the active parenting years, women continued to demonstrate more interest than men by making more spontaneous bids to unfamiliar babies. This role-related difference persisted until the empty-nest years, when the difference began to subside and showed up in our data only as a trend. According to Turner's (1978) principles, referred to earlier, the power of the sex-related role of motherhood/nurturance is impressive. Because of this, the role has high probability of enduring or being "merged" with the woman's personality. Among its compelling qualities are: (1) the intensity and consistency with which significant others identify her on the basis of this role; (2) the wide range of settings in which this role behavior is meaningful; (3) its appeal as a highly positively valued role; (4) the great amount of time and effort invested in this role; (5) the extensive sacrifices made in the course of gaining and maintaining this role; and (6) the very public and visible nature of this role.

Like the early phase of parenthood, grandparenthood was marked by significant stage-of-life effects across sexes. As a group, grandmothers and grandfathers initiated more responses to an actual baby, and publicly proclaimed more baby pictures to be among their favorites. However, grandmothers were more reactive than grandfathers to the baby and ignored the baby less.

Cross-sectional studies such as those just described contain a potential confounding between cohort effects and stage of family life cycle. Perhaps the stage-of-life effects apparent for the grandparent group were not due to systematic role changes as their families matured, but reflected cohort differences in exposure to sociohistorical movements. Phenomena such as women's liberation may affect attitudes regarding family relationships and assumption of child-care responsibilities or interests. If this were the case, we might expect the oldest group, the grandparents who demonstrated the most "traditional" interest in infants, to express more traditional sex-related self-concepts; that is, men would be more likely to describe themselves in masculine (not feminine) terms, and conversely, women would be inclined towards feminine (not masculine) self-descriptions. Self-report measures on the Bem Sex Role Inventory revealed just the opposite pattern for this sample: An increase in feminine self-description for grandfathers and an increase in masculine-typed ratings for grandmothers suggests that this group's sex-related self-concepts were not more stereotyped than those of the younger groups. Because the average age difference between grandparents and empty nesters was only 5 years, and because we selected only those couples whose first marriage had remained intact, these subjects were probably less heterogeneous regarding familial issues than the general population. Thus, although cohort differences are always a consideration in a cross-sectional design, they may not have had a major impact on this study.

One theorist who has attempted to specify why sex-related differences appear across the life cycle is Gutmann (1975). He speculates that sex specialization takes place during parenthood as a result of the uncompromising needs of the offspring for physical and emotional security. The new mother inhibits her more aggressive and competitive urges, which might hamper her nurturant caring for the child. In a complementary fashion, the new father limits dependency needs or expressivity, which might compromise his obligations as protector–provider. As the child matures and takes on more of the responsibility for his or her own security, both parents are freer to express the potentials they had previously foregone in the service of parental obligation. Mature men can exhibit more nurturance, and women, more independence and assertiveness with less role conflict. Thus, Gutmann suggests that so-called masculine and feminine traits are not merely sex specific, but also a function of the role demands of each stage of life.

Certainly during the active parenting years, we saw the sort of sex-role specialization in nurturant responsivity Gutmann refers to. Gutmann does not specify, however, precisely when the *chronic sense of parental emergency* ceases.

If we assume it ends when a generation of children become parents themselves, then our findings support Gutmann's theory, at least regarding men. Grandfathers were more willing to publicly express their nurturant interests and to allow expressive behavior to surface. Similarly, on another overt measure, the Bem Sex Role Inventory, there was a significant increase in the extent to which men considered feminine characteristics typical of themselves. Interestingly, men's masculinity scores did not show a significant change in the later stages of life. Thus, to amend Gutmann's proposal, men manifested more feminine expressive traits in later years, but not at the expense of their well-established masculinity. It is not possible to ascertain from this study whether females behave in a more masculine manner in the later stages of life, because a feminine-typed behavior was investigated. Clearly, females did not abdicate their feminine nurturant role, especially when it was primed by the birth of a grandchild. Based on their Bem Sex Role self-ratings, it seemed rather that women mirrored men's response pattern. They tended to show an increase in their masculinity scores without a decline in femininity.

By examining the family life cycle, it becomes evident that, like other roles, responsiveness to babies fluctuates according to the appropriateness of life situation and even social context (Berman, 1980). An alternative explanation for this behavioral sex difference is provided by sociobiology. According to this position, sex-related differences (especially in reactivity to babies) are in large part mediated by the contrasting hormonal changes of the developing female and male. Thus, starting in puberty the females' heightened estrogen level translates into more nurturant behavior towards babies, reaching a peak during pregnancy and the first year of parenthood, maintaining a plateau during the childbearing years, and dropping notably after menopause. The life course of responsiveness to babies for males is predicted to be level and low—that is, significantly lower than for females during the childbearing years. In fact, sociobiology provides us with an approximation of some of the fluctuations that occurred over the life span. The sexes did not diverge until early adolescence, as sociobiology would predict. However, the sex difference was due less to the increasing interest in babies of adolescent girls than to declining male interest. Recent work suggests that postpubescent girls may even decrease in responsiveness to babies (Frodi et al., 1980). Sociobiology does not easily accommodate these results nor the findings of convergence of the sexes from later adolescence until the onset of parenthood. Similarly, it is simply not the case that females' interest in babies atrophies at menopause; if anything, grandmothers showed a heightening of contingent responsiveness during this stage of life. Nor did men's responsivity follow the low flat curve suggested by sociobiology. Fathers of infants and grandfathers were more behaviorally responsive to babies than were males at any other point in the family life cycle. Like all theoretical perspectives, sociobiology readily admits additional factors to explain discrepant results. For example, the heightened interest in babies exhibited by grandparents might be attributed to genetic investment reactivated by the stimulus of a grandchild. However, this would not adequately explain the sex difference apparent among grandparents; grandmothers did not have more of a "genetic investment" in their grandchildren than grandfathers did.

The sociobiological position has greater value when more emphasis is put on the "socio" factors. Each stage of life may be characterized by distinctive and specific situational demands that require different behaviors and attitudes from males and females. With regard to interest in babies, it is possible that certain periods in the family life cycle necessitate different reactions from each sex for the optimal functioning of the family, whereas at other stages males and females may respond quite similarly without affecting the family adversely. For example, in contrast to childless young adulthood, the requirements of early parenthood precipitated heightened sex-role differentiation and specialization. As offspring approach self-sufficiency and leave home, the necessity for sex-differentiated responsivity to infants diminished. The advent of grandchildren once again primed interest in babies for both sexes, with women showing more reactivity commensurate with their history of well-developed nurturing skills and the newly granted cultural permission to once again involve themselves in their adult child's life.

Life-Cycle Fluctuations in Sex-Related Self-Attributions

It appears, then, that sex-role behaviors may be modified in response to changing life circumstances. Do individuals perceive these sex-role–related changes taking place? Or, do their self-attributions remain fairly stable across life events? Even if an individual's behavior varies across situations, there is a human bias to disregard or reinterpret such fluctuations, thereby keeping intact the belief in a consistent personality (Mischel, 1973). Self-descriptions, once applied, have a certain resistance to change because it is easier to reclassify behavior than to alter one's self-concept. Furthermore, trait descriptions are so broad that many diverse behaviors can be subsumed under each label.

Surprisingly, the life-span perspective has rarely been applied to the examination of sex-related self-attributes.[2] Accordingly, we designed a study to systematically assess the development of sex-related self-concepts from adolescence through grandparenthood. We sampled subjects at varying stages in the *family* life cycle for two reasons. The first is based on Gutmann's hypothesis that certain aspects of family formation are conducive to sex-role differentiation; thus, stages that mark the development of the family unit throughout adulthood might provide

---

[2]Sections of this study are reprinted from Feldman, S. S., Biringen, Z. C., & Nash, S. C. Fluctuations of sex-related self-attributions as a function of stage of family life cycle. *Developmental Psychology*, in press. Copyright (1981) by the American Psychological Association. Reprinted by permission.

valuable information about the emergence and ultimate dissipation of such sex-related differences. Secondly, as was indicated earlier, chronological age, per se, is not always a meaningful predictor of life experiences, given the disparate rates at which individuals develop. In contrast, a stage of life represents a larger, more enduring social situation, which requires the performance of a distinctive set of adaptive tasks (Brim, 1966; Duvall, 1977) and the reevaluation of attitudes and behaviors (Parsons & Bales, 1955). Because it has been demonstrated that behavior is modified in response to transitory, experimentally induced situational changes, it is possible that more salient and extended life situations will effect comparable (or greater) changes. Many important life experiences can be characterized as requiring varying degrees of so-called masculine and/or feminine qualities for their effective performance. For example, caring for a young child or developing a relationship with a significant other may be enhanced by the feminine qualities of tenderness and compassionate understanding. Success in business, on the other hand, may be related to the more masculine assets of competition and self-sufficiency. Accordingly, the present study explored the hypothesis that changes in the demand characteristics of family-related life circumstances are related to fluctuations in sex-related self-perceptions during adulthood.

The Bem Sex Role Inventory (BSRI) (Bem, 1974) was used to assess sex-related personality attributes in 804 subjects who were classified according to stage in the family life cycle. Eight groups were assessed, including one of adolescents, three of preparenting adults (singles, married–childless, and expectants), two active parenting groups (parents whose youngest child was less than 10 years old, hereafter called young parents, and those whose youngest child was 14–17 years old, hereafter called mature parents), and two postparenting groups (empty nesters, whose grown children no longer lived at home, and grandparents). All subjects were White, American-born, well-educated, and relatively homogeneous in terms of their middle- to upper middle-class status.

The 20 ''masculine'' and 20 ''feminine'' adjectives on the BSRI were factor analyzed and the results subjected to an oblique rotation. Nine readily interpretable factors emerged and are described elsewhere (Feldman, Biringen, & Nash, in press). For the purpose of this chapter, we present only four of the factors: two instrumental and two expressive. These factors, and the items that load on them with weights ± .30 are as follows: (1) *leadership* (leadership, acts as leader, dominant, competitive, ambitious); (2) *autonomy* (self-reliant, self-sufficient, independent, individualistic, ambitious); (3) *compassion* (understanding, sensitive, sympathetic, compassionate, eager to soothe hurt feelings); and (4) *tenderness* (tender, affectionate, warm, gentle, cheerful, loves children).

Because we predicted waxing and waning sex differences across the family life cycle, we examined sex effects separately for each stage of life. The results are shown in Table 1.2. Men and women were similar in instrumental qualities in young adult years when, typically, both sexes are involved in salaried work. In

TABLE 1.2
Mean Factors Scores and Sex Differences on
Instrumental and Expressive Factors, by Sex and Stage of Life

	Leadership		Autonomy		Compassion		Tenderness	
	Men	Women	Men	Women	Men	Women	Men	Women
Adolescents (N = 195)	51.3	50.1	47.5	49.8	47.0	*c* 52.1	48.4	*c* 52.2
Single adults (N = 123)	48.5	49.6	49.2	40.1	44.5	*c* 51.6	45.6	*b* 49.5
Married–childless (N = 60)	53.2	*a* 45.2	50.8	48.2	48.2	52.7	52.5	53.6
Expectants (N = 100)	55.4	*c* 44.9	53.1	*b* 47.0	47.1	*a* 52.1	48.0	*a* 52.8
Young parents (N = 121)	55.7	*c* 49.1	52.5	*a* 49.9	47.1	*c* 55.0	48.1	*c* 53.6
Mature parents (N = 67)	57.7	*b* 48.6	53.7	50.1	50.2	*b* 56.0	49.8	*a* 54.4
Empty nesters (N = 56)	53.8	*a* 48.0	51.2	49.9	50.4	53.2	47.7	*b* 55.5
Grandparents (N = 82)	51.0	49.0	52.7	53.0	51.8	*b* 56.0	54.4	54.7

$^a p < .05.$
$^b p < .01.$
$^c p < .001.$

contrast, expectancy and the early years of parenthood were marked by sex differences in both autonomy and leadership. By the height of the mature parenting years, only the sex difference in leadership remained, perhaps because the roles of both father and mother require a considerable amount of autonomy, albeit in different domains: Men make career-related choices, and women resolve family-oriented issues. Because the woman's sphere of influence is frequently focused on the home, it may be that leadership of other adults is less relevant to her than to her husband, whose locus of control includes the business world. Thus, the sex difference in leadership continued throughout the active parenting years. The difference in autonomy was ephemeral, emerging only during expectancy and young parenthood, periods of time marked by the woman's withdrawal from the role of wage earner and the presence of dependent offspring.

On the expressive factors, compassion and tenderness, women surpassed men at most stages of life. Sex differences in tenderness were absent at two stages as a result of men's elevated scores. The first was among married–childless adults, whose developmental task is to establish intimacy (Duvall, 1977; Erikson, 1950). The second was among grandparents. Without the responsibility and demands of daily interactions with children (e.g., establishing authority, presenting a masculine role model, etc.), and with the reduction of both work pressures and the need to provide for an expanding family, grandfathers seemed more comfortable than younger men in being emotionally demonstrative or tender.

Because we predicted stage-of-life effects to be sex specific, we analyzed our data separately for males and females. For those scores showing a significant stage-of-life effect, we compared each group to the remaining same-sex subjects in the sample by means of planned comparisons. The results are shown in Table 1.3.

The masculine factors varied across the family life cycle for men, but not for women. This may be because we divided the life cycle into family-related markers, which makes differentiations in nurturance and expressivity more salient to the primary care-giving woman than instrumentality is to her. Perhaps if one were to examine the career life cycle, the more masculine factors would vary for women as well. In any case, these factors fluctuated for men in revealing ways. Leadership increased during the active parenting years when men perceive themselves as the head of a family. Concomitantly, career involvement reaches a peak, and one is called upon to be a leader vis-a-vis other adults in order to succeed. Later in life, the demands of the work world subside, and leadership becomes less relevant, as it had been in earlier years, before the push to provide. The departure of children from the home marks the diminishing functionality of the empty-nest father's leadership position in the family. In contrast, the other masculine factor, autonomy, was elevated during expectancy, and remained heightened throughout adulthood. In light of the fact that autonomy implies having the right or power of self-government, it is interesting that men did not perceive themselves as becoming truly self-reliant until the anticipation of parenthood. At this time, the wife often withdraws from her paid job, and the husband is struck with the realization that he is the sole provider for the family. In traversing the threshold of fatherhood, the man graduates from the first to the second generation. Just as he himself was once provided for, now he must provide for his offspring; there is no one to respectably rely upon except himself for the rest of his life. Note, however, that the finding of increased autonomy among grandfathers should be interpreted with caution. Our sample of grandfathers may have been a somewhat more select (or ''self-selected'') group. Unlike any other stage of life, there was a high refusal rate among grandfathers (almost 50%). Although they declined to fill out the questionnaires themselves, these men graciously volunteered their (usually willing) wives for the task. Thus, the men who did participate may have been somewhat more autonomous and outgoing than their less adventurous peers.

The feminine factors varied for men and women across the stages of the family life cycle. Women were clearly more comfortable than men in the expressive domain, especially prior to marriage, and again throughout parenthood. However, the experience of grandparenthood was marked by a heightening of expressiveness for both sexes in distinctive ways. Women rated themselves

TABLE 1.3

Effects of Stage of Life (Using *t* Tests Between Each Group and the Remaining Same-Sex Sample), Separately by Sex

	Leadership		Autonomy		Compassion		Tenderness	
	Men	*Women*	*Men*	*Women*	*Men*	*Women*	*Men*	*Women*
Adolescents vs. others	-2.02^b	2.48^c	-3.75^d					
Single adults vs. others	-2.58^c				-2.98^c		-2.84^c	-3.69^c
Married–childless vs. others		-2.09^b					1.99^b	
Expectants vs. others	1.66^a			-1.82^a				
Young parents vs. others	2.46^c		1.76^a					1.96^b
Mature parents vs. others	2.29^b		2.17^b					
Empty nesters vs. others								
Grandparents vs. others			1.73^b	3.03^c	2.24^b		3.03^c	1.69^b

[a] $p < .10$.
[b] $p < .05$.
[c] $p < .01$.
[d] $p < .001$.

higher in compassionate understanding than at any other point in their lives (significantly more than they had prior to parenthood). The more distant stimulus of a grandchild seemed to elicit as strong a compassionate response as a child of one's own. For men, the increase in expressiveness was evidenced in tenderness. Women may have had less role conflict over exhibiting tender, loving feelings throughout their lives, so few stage-of-life effects were manifested.

In contrast to our findings, a recent study of four stage-of-life groups reported by Spence and Helmreich (1979) found only a single stage effect (and a stage × sex interaction) in instrumentality for males, and an absence of stage-of-life effects for expressiveness for either males or females. At first glance, these results appear to contradict the numerous stage-of-life effects that we found. To better understand the apparent discrepancy, we analyzed data from three of our groups that correspond to theirs (i.e., adolescents, young parents, and mature parents) and completely replicated their findings. These results suggest that caution is necessary in interpreting stage-of-life effects based on a limited or widely spaced sampling of groups. The fewer stages in the life cycle studied, the greater the likelihood that potential effects will be overlooked or obscured. For example, our data indicated that the expressive factor compassion increased in a near-linear manner for men from single adulthood to grandfatherhood; when the postparenting groups (empty nesters and grandparents) were not sampled, the stage-of-life effect was not manifested. Similarly, among women, we found the instrumental factor autonomy was highest for grandmothers and lowest for expectant mothers, two groups not studied by Spence and Helmreich. Clearly, an accurate mapping of life-cycle effects is enhanced by the systematic study of numerous, neighboring stages of life.

Gutmann's (1975) speculation that instrumental and expressive attributes are better understood as specific to stage of life rather than as traits affixed to one sex or the other, was supported by our data. Our factor analysis allowed us to refine Gutmann's portrait by specifying the aspects of instrumentality and expressivity involved and clarifying the periods of their ascension and descension. For example, men surpassed women in instrumentality in the adult years, but more so in leadership than in feelings of autonomy. The difference emerged somewhat earlier than had been thought, during expectancy in *anticipation* of the "chronic sense of parental emergency." The difference became less prominent prior to grandparenthood, when the children leave home. The sexes also differed in both expressive factors, but here the difference became notable early in parenthood when it is needed for effective primary child care. The sexes described themselves very similarly by the time they were grandparents. In line with Gutmann's predictions, the grandfathers rated themselves as more compassionate and tender than did young fathers, yet their self-assessed instrumentality remained comparable to that of younger men. Conversely, grandmothers expressed a heightened sense of autonomy, but realistically, not of leadership. However, their self-descriptions remained very high in both expressive qualities. Thus, with the alleviation of the role constraints of active parenting, both sexes perceived themselves as having more cross-sex–typed assets, yet did not feel they were any less masculine as men or feminine as women.

As previously mentioned, in any cross-sectional life-course study, there is a potential for confounding between stage of life and age. Short of studying highly deviant groups (such as 30-year-old grandparents or 50-year-old parents of an infant), it is impossible to disentangle age and stage completely. However, by utilizing the normally occurring variations in timing of major family life events, we were able to compare the relative plausibilities of age versus stage-of-life hypotheses. First, we held age constant and studied stage-of-life effects; then, we reversed the procedure and held stage constant and checked for age effects. Internal analyses were performed only when we had three comparison groups of 18 or more subjects, approximately equally divided by sex. Age was held constant for the 20–29 year olds (where we had adequate samples of singles, married–childless, and expectants), and for the 50–59 year olds (which included mature parents, empty nesters, and grandparents). For both age cohorts, we essentially replicated the stage-of-life effects (see Feldman et al., in press, for details). To assess age effects, stage of life was held constant for young parents, and 20 year olds, 30 year olds, and 40 year olds were compared: No age effects emerged for the instrumental or expressive factors. It may be that age will turn out to be more important for the young (adolescents) and the old (65+ years), but this is speculation that remains to be tested. It is the case, however, that during the adult years (20–50 years), stage of family life influences self-attributions, regardless of age.

It appears, then, that the sexes do perceive themselves as changing (sometimes in complex ways) across the family life cycle. The waxing and waning of sex differences highlight the continuing developmental changes occurring with stage-of-life–related role shifts. These findings suggest that the results of studies in which only one age or stage-of-life group is assessed should not be extrapolated across adulthood.

A number of research questions were generated by these findings. For one thing, is the differential impact of life situations great enough to affect the sex-role attitudes of a single cohort of subjects who find themselves in very different life circumstances? A second issue is: Do these cross-sectionally derived findings hold when one group of subjects is followed longitudinally from one stage of life to another? We have completed studies that elucidate both of these points and lend further evidence to the proposition that sex-role–related beliefs and attitudes, like sex-role behaviors, are sensitive to changes in larger situational contexts. The first study, which we summarize shortly, compared the sex-role attitudes of young adults who varied according to marital or parental status. In the second study, which we also describe, we followed a group of expectant couples through the birth of their child and traced both changes and stabilities in their sex-role ideation during this transition.

Sex-Role Attitudes During Young Adulthood

In the first study (reported in detail elsewhere—see Abrahams, Feldman, & Nash, 1978), matched samples of young adults between the ages of 22 and 34 years who were either single–cohabiting, married–childless, expecting their first child, or parents of an infant filled out a battery of questionnaires including the Miller Masculine and Feminine Interest Questionnaires, which assessed sex-role attitudes on a modern–traditional dimension. For women, a traditional role orientation emphasizes family roles (e.g., there is nothing more fulfilling to a woman than the raising of her children; a woman must get married to feel completely fulfilled). In contrast, the modern role orientation emphasizes career and self-fulfillment apart from family roles, and the sharing of child care and domestic duties by both spouses (e.g., a husband and a wife should spend equal time raising the children; having a challenging job is as important to me as being a wife and mother). For men, a traditional role orientation emphasizes sex differences, sex-linked divisions of labor, and the man's role as protector/provider in the family (e.g., men are a lot better than women at things like business, logic, and politics; a man's most important role is as the breadwinner). The modern role for men gives equal emphasis to family involvement and career (e.g., having children and raising a family are as important to a man as his work and career; a husband and wife should spend equal time in raising the children). Twelve statements were selected from each of the questionnaires on the basis of their conceptual relationship to the purpose of the present study.

Because this study was designed to test a particular set of hypotheses, the method of planned comparisons was used to determine if the data points from the four groups fit the curve predicted on the basis of the characterization of each life situation. The results for men and women on the measure of sex-role attitudes are presented in Table 1.4. A high score indicates a modern, nonsex-typed attitude towards the roles of men and women, whereas a low score indicates a more traditional, sex-typed attitude. The two predictions tested on the measure of

TABLE 1.4
Sex-Role Attitudes (on a Modern–Traditional Dimension)
Among Males and Females in Four Life Situations

Subjects	Cohabiting	Married	Expectant	Parents	Planned Contrasts
Females	(N = 15)	(N = 15)	(N = 15)	(N = 15)	(N = 60)
X̄	41.29	39.27	39.39	34.40	2.32[a]
SD	10.05	6.51	4.68	6.56	
Males	(N = 15)	(N = 15)	(N = 15)	(N = 15)	(N = 60)
X̄	33.93	31.20	31.07	30.40	2.08[a]
SD	4.60	4.84	3.83	5.10	

[a]$p < .025$.

sex-role attitudes were the same for men and women: that the attitudes of the parents would be most traditional, those of the singles group would be least so, and those of married and expectant persons would be intermediate between the singles and the parents, with the married group endorsing slightly more traditional attitudes than those expecting their first child. Planned comparisons on the sex-role scores were significant for women and for men, showing the anticipated shift towards more traditional attitudes across the four situations. As predicted, the greatest changes for both men and women occurred between the single and married groups and between the expectant and parent groups. The difference between the married and expectant groups was minimal, as the similarity of role distributions within the two situations led us to anticipate. No direct comparison was possible between the performance of men and women, because the questionnaire items for the two sexes were not identical.

The data support the hypothesis that sex-role attitudes reflect attributions from behavior in specific life situations. This suggests that it is possible to identify discrete life situations that call for more or less stereotypically masculine or feminine behaviors and to predict with some accuracy the direction of attributions that people involved in those situations will make about their own sex-role attitudes.

Although it could be argued that the cross-sectional design of the study left open the possibility of self-selection into the four situations on the basis of prior sex-role attitudes, there was no empirical or logical evidence to support this conclusion. Empirically, the subjects were comparable to one another on the factors of socioeconomic status and educational and cultural background, so that no difference between them in exposure to or endorsement of traditional sex-role standards would be expected on those bases. Logically, it seems implausible that the women who had a child did so because they were initially more sex typed than the expectant women who were soon to have a child, or that the expectant women decided to have a child because they were originally more sex typed than the married, childless women in the sample (all but two of whom indicated on a background questionnaire that they definitely planned to have children). Finally, it seems unlikely that the married women chose marriage in preference to cohabitation because they were initially more sex typed than the cohabiting women, when, in fact, many of the married women in the sample reported cohabiting prior to marriage.

Expectancy to Parenthood: A Longitudinal Study of the Impact on Sex-Role Behavior and Sex Typing

In all the aforementioned studies of sex-role behavior, sex-related attitudes, and self-attributions, the onset of parenthood stands out as a stage of life marked by considerable sex differentiation. The traditionalizing effect of parenthood on sex roles has been noted by others, including Blood and Wolfe (1960) in their study of family decision making, and in theory by Gutmann (1975). Nonetheless, the evidence has been indirect at best. Therefore, we undertook a short-term longitudinal study from pregnancy to parenthood, with sex roles and sex typing as its foci (this study is reported in detail elsewhere—see Feldman & Aschenbrenner, under review).

We distinguished between sex roles (those identifiable behaviors that result from differentiated positions men and women occupy in society) and sex-typed identity (the extent to which men and women rate themselves as being masculine and feminine). Even though Pedhazur and Tetenbaum (1979) and Feldman et al. (in press) have shown that sex-typed identity measures are independent of expressive and instrumental personality traits, and highly correlated with gender, we do not know either their relationship to sex roles, or whether such basic self-descriptions are responsive to life events.

We studied 31 upper middle-class, highly educated, American-born Caucasian couples who were expecting their first child. The mean age of the women was 27.9 years (SD = 3.5) and of the men 31.0 years (SD = 4.3). More than half the women were working in professional or semiprofessional occupations at the time they were first seen in the last trimester of the pregnancy, and the remainder had stopped work during the previous 3 months. The men were in professional (35%), managerial (32%), or technical and sales positions (32%). The men as well as the women were immersed in the pregnancy experience: They attended prenatal exercise classes together, read books on childbirth and childcare, and subsequently the husband attended the delivery.

Couples were seen twice: once in the last trimester of the woman's pregnancy, and again 7–8 months later when their infant was approximately 6 months old. At each visit, interest in an unfamiliar infant was assessed, questionnaires and rating scales filled out, and subjects interviewed (individually and at length during pregnancy; jointly and more briefly during parenthood). During pregnancy and again at parenthood each individual received both a masculinity and femininity score in each of two domains: sex roles and sex-typed identity. The masculine and feminine *sex-role scores* were derived from behavioral observations and self-ratings as described in Table 1.5. Using the scores from men and women at both stages of life, the distribution of each of the measures entering into the sex-role composite was divided into quartiles and scores were assigned ranging from 1 (lowest quartile) to 4 (highest quartile). The mean of the quartile scores served as the sex-role measure. *Sex-typed identity* was assessed from the items "masculine" and "feminine," which appear on the BSRI. Subjects rated themselves on these items on a 7-point scale.

On the role and identity scores, we carried out two-way ANOVAS on femininity, masculinity, the absolute difference between femininity and masculinity, sex-appropriate scores (i.e., femininity for women, masculinity for men), and cross-sex scores (masculinity for women and femininity for men). The results appear in Table 1.6.

TABLE 1.5
Sex-Role Measures Used in a Longitudinal Study from Pregnancy
to Parenthood, for Both Men and Women

Measure	Description/Sample Items
Feminine Sex Role	
Interest in unfamiliar infant (observation)	6 sec. time sampling of proximal and distal bids to baby in waiting room.
Nurturance (self-ratings, two items)	(Rate the extent to which . . .) —you feel loving and giving; —you will arrange your life around the infant.
Satisfaction with expressiveness (self-ratings, six items)	(Rate the satisfaction you feel in . . .) —the emotional support you give your spouse; —the warmth that you show your friends.
Feminine household tasks (self-ratings, three items)	(Rate the extent to which you are responsible for . . .) —daily housework, marketing, cooking or baking (during pregnancy); —child care, time devoted to infant, getting up at night (during parenthood).
Masculine Sex Role	
Ignores unfamiliar baby (observation)	6 sec. time sampling in waiting room of the frequency baby's vocalizations were ignored.
Satisfaction with instrumentality (self ratings, six items)	(Rate the satisfaction you feel in . . .) —your ability to make decisions; —the sense of accomplishment you feel.
Masculine household/ wage earning tasks (self-ratings)	(Ratings of . . .) —amount of time working outside home; —proportion of family income brought in.

As expected, significant sex differences were found on the masculinity and femininity scores. Men surpassed women on masculinity, and women surpassed men on femininity. Of greater interest, however, is that sex typing is more marked among men (especially expectant men) than among women. On the identity measures, men rated themselves higher on sex-appropriate identity and showed a larger difference between their self-ratings of "masculinity" and "femininity" than did women. Men also showed fewer cross-sex role behaviors than women. Three significant stage × sex interactions revealed men as more sex typed than women at expectancy, but not at parenthood. Expectant men showed more sex-appropriate role behavior, less cross-sex role behavior, and more differentiation between masculine and feminine role behavior than women ($p < .01$ or better). These findings fit with other reports that childless men are more traditional than women in many domains, including family and domestic roles (Osmond & Martin, 1975; Roper & Labeff, 1977). In our sample, pregnant women enacted equally both the more culturally valued masculine role and the sex-appropriate feminine role.

Parenthood brought marked changes for men and women: Between expectancy and parenthood, feminine role behavior and identity increased, whereas masculine role behavior decreased. The absence of significant interaction terms indicates that the birth of the first child affected the behavior and identity of both men and women. Our sample, however, was not representative of all couples undergoing a first pregnancy. They were a self-selected, older, highly educated, and financially secure group that was suburban in life style and contemporary in outlook. The men were involved in the expectancy experience and parenthood.

TABLE 1.6
Means, Standard Deviations, and Results of ANOVAS on
Masculinity and Femininity Scores of Males and Females
in Two Domains

	Role Behavior		Identity	
	Femininity	*Masculinity*	*Femininity*	*Masculinity*
Expectancy				
Women	2.5	2.4	5.3	2.2
($N = 31$)	(.7)	(.6)	(1.1)	(1.2)
Men	1.6	3.1	1.8	5.9
($N = 27$)	(.8)	(.5)	(.9)	(.9)
Parenthood				
Women	3.0	2.1	5.6	2.5
($N = 31$)	(.8)	(.7)	(1.0)	(1.2)
Men	2.0	2.9	2.1	6.0
($N = 27$)	(.9)	(.6)	(1.3)	(.9)
ANOVAS (F scores)				
Masculinity and Femininity Scores				
Sex	42.7[d]	37.5[d]	154.3[d]	179.3[d]
Stage	22.0[d]	8.6[c]	5.5[b]	ns
Interaction	ns	ns	ns	ns
Sex Appropriate Scores				
Sex		ns	5.7[b]	
Stage		ns	ns	
Interaction		20.0[d]	ns	
Cross-Sex Scores				
Sex		3.7[a]	ns	
Stage		ns	4.8[b]	
Interaction		10.5	ns	
Difference between Masculinity and Femininity				
Sex		5.4[b]	4.6[b]	
Stage		ns	ns	
Interaction		26.0[d]	ns	

[a]$p<.10$.
[b]$p<.05$.
[c]$p<.01$.
[d]$p<.001$.

These couples are representative of a class of individuals who, according to Gladieux (1978) "are likely to be in the forefront of creating and experiencing the impact of changing social and sexual norms, as well as family relationships and patterns [p. 280]." Although the results are thus timely and of relevance, they are not necessarily generalizable to all couples expecting a baby. In particular, the question remains for further research whether the birth of a child influences the sex typing of more traditional men who are less involved in the parenting experience.

Not only feminine and masculine role behaviors were responsive to major life events such as the birth of a first child, but even basic components of self-concept, such as one's identity as "masculine" or "feminine," were affected by changing life situations. Feminine identity, but not masculine identity, increased over the transition from expectancy to parenthood. To the extent that fatherhood is sometimes viewed as an affirmation of men's masculinity (Humphrey, 1977), changes in masculine identity may occur earlier, around the time of the verification of conception, or when knowledge of the pregnancy becomes public.

Although the changes in masculinity and femininity were similar for both sexes across this important transition, the net outcome was quite different for men and women. The increasing feminine and decreasing masculine role behavior found between expectancy and parenthood resulted in more traditionally sex-typed women but somewhat less stereotypically sex-typed men. The change in sex typing is clearly revealed by the analyses of sex-appropriate, cross-sex, and difference between masculinity and femininity role scores (see Table 1.6) where there were significant stage $\times$ sex interactions. Among men, sex-appropriate role behavior decreased, cross-sex role behavior increased, and the difference between masculinity and femininity decreased (all at $p < .05$). Conversely, women showed large increases in sex-appropriate behavior ($p < .001$), a decrease in cross-sex role behavior, and an increase in the (absolute) difference score between masculinity and femininity ($p < .05$).

Thus, men who were involved in expectancy and parenthood showed decreasing traditionalism in sex roles between expectancy and parenthood, whereas women showed increasing traditionalism. For these highly educated women, many of whom had postponed childbearing for career development, motherhood elevated feminine role over masculine role behaviors. These findings correspond to the type of change that occurred in the lives of men and women with the advent of parenthood. Men's involvement with their infants did not supplant occupational concerns, but became an additional focus and arena of emotional investment in their lives. For most women in our study, the birth of the child involved a major role change that entailed drastic reorientation of daily activities and reordering of priorities. Most women gave up work and devoted the majority of hours to child and home.

Thus, the longitudinal design enables us to draw a conclusion that our previous cross-sectional work suggested: Changing life situations, particularly the birth of the first child, have a clear impact on sex roles and sex-related self-descriptions of both men and women.

CONCLUSIONS

Our position has evolved from a consideration of data gathered from males and females across the family life cycle. There appears to be a subset of sex differences that are role related. These differences are not fixed in time, but rather undergo a series of changes throughout adulthood. It has been proposed that the adoption of new roles is one major source of behavioral and attitudinal change, and specifically that variations in sex-role requirements contribute, in part, to the fluctuating pattern of sex differences evident across the family life cycle.

We have tried to maintain a neutral position in the *trait* versus *role/situational specificity* debate with regard to sex typing. The modern trait position does not require that an absolute level of behavior be maintained across situations: It suffices that rank ordering among people shows some stability. Similarly, the role theory position neither assumes the total absence of a transcendant self nor that the self recreate itself instantly in each and every situation. An interaction between sex-role situational demands and the qualities or traits of the individual will most likely provide the best model of sex typing. Clearly, there is a need for more multimeasure longitudinal studies to allow for the assessment of correlations between measures and across time, as well as mean change over time. Such comparisons are crucial for clarifying whether or not these different measures are related to each other in a coherent and consistent way and thus for tapping underlying sex-differentiated traits. Regardless of whether the measures we used are correlated, we have shown that all of them—sex-role behavior, sex-related self-concepts, sexual identity, and sex-role attitudes—fluctuate across changing family situations, sometimes in similar and sometimes in different ways for men and women.

By studying sex-role behaviors and related self-attributions across the life span, it becomes clear that sex roles do not merely define a catalogue of traits that "consistently" differentiate males and females. The psychological study of sex roles must include a consideration of social context, from the subtle to the more pervasive situational constraints. In particular, the performance of sex-role behaviors is affected by the presence of other people, and may vary as a function of the age or sex or role status of these people (Berman, Sloan, & Goodman, 1979; Feldman & Nash, 1979a; Fullard & Reiling, 1976). Further work is needed to map the distinctive situational factors that may modify the definition of sex-role appropriateness for each sex as a function of age or stage of life.

Our own work has focused on changes across stages in the family life cycle in one particular feminine sex-role behavior, responsiveness to babies. Similar explorations of other feminine, and especially analogous masculine sex-role behaviors (e.g., competitiveness, assertiveness, etc.) would be of considerable value in establishing comparable situational specificity for these behaviors. It would be of special interest to clarify the relationship between various masculine sex-role behaviors and the male-typed self-attributions reported in this chapter. Given the fact that we studied family life-cycle markers, which are commonly described as more significant to female development (Angrist, 1969), it is noteworthy that we found as many stage-related behavioral and self-perceived fluctuations among men as we did. Although a substantial effect of career life cycle has been speculated for men, our data suggest that the impact of family formation on males has remained largely underestimated. Our samples were chosen from a largely homogeneous middle- to upper middle-class educated population. It is probable that the nature and extent of the effects of the family life cycle we found would be somewhat different for other socioeconomic or ethnic groups, depending on how the salient features of the masculine and feminine roles are defined. For example, among groups that equate fatherhood with manhood and the protector role, we would not expect the rise in feminine role behavior with the onset of parenthood noted among our middle-class sample. Similarly, among women who view motherhood as an affirmation of their adult status, we might expect a rise in feelings of independence and autonomy with the birth of the first child. Thus, like other roles, the notion of sex role is embedded in the larger context of cultural expectations (Bronfenbrenner, 1979).

Because it was our premise that sex-role appropriateness varies according to life circumstances, it would be important for future research to document sex-role fluctuations as a function of other life situational markers, such as atypical family events (e.g., voluntary childlessness, single parenthood, middle-aged onset of parenthood, etc.) or less traditional family roles (e.g., househusband, full-time employed mothers with live-in help, etc.). In addition, somewhat overlapping though independent life-cycle timelines should be explored—for example, those defined by school or occupational development. To the extent that these life situations (rather than people) can be characterized in terms of how stereotypically masculine or feminine they are, it will be of great value to observe the relationship of these situations to sex-role behavior and sex-related self-attributions.

REFERENCES

Abrahams, B., Feldman, S. S., & Nash, S. C. Sex-role self-concept and sex-role attitudes: Enduring personality characteristics or adaptations to changing life situations? *Developmental Psychology,* 1978, *14,* 393–400.

Ahammer, I. M. Social-learning theory as a framework for the study of adult personality development. In P. B. Baltes & K. W. Schaie (Eds.), *Life-span developmental psychology: Personality and socialization.* New York: Academic Press, 1973.

Angrist, S. S. The study of sex roles. *Journal of Social Issues,* 1969, *25,* 215–232.

Bandura, A. *Social learning theory*. Englewood Cliffs, N.J.: Prentice-Hall, 1977.

Bates, L. Position, role, and status: A reformulation of concepts. *Social Forces*, 1956, *34*, 313–321.

Bem, D. J. Self-perception: An alternative interpretation of cognitive dissonance phenomena. *Psychological Review*, 1967, *74*, 183–200.

Bem, S. L. The measurement of psychological androgyny. *Journal of Consulting and Clinical Psychology*, 1974, *42*, 155–162.

Bem, S. L., Martyna, W., & Watson, C. Sex typing and androgyny: Further explorations of the expressive domain. *Journal of Personality and Social Psychology*, 1976, *34*, 1016–1023.

Berman, P. W. Are women more responsive than men to the young? A review of developmental and situational variables. *Psychological Bulletin*, 1980, *88*, 668–695.

Berman, P. W., Abplanalp, J., Cooper, P., Mansfield, P., & Shields, S. Sex differences in attraction to infants: When do they occur? *Sex Roles*, 1975, *1*, 311–318.

Berman, P. W., Goodman, V., Sloan, V. L., & Fernander, F. Preference for infants among black and white children: Sex and age differences. *Child Development*, 1978, *49*, 917–919.

Berman, P. W., Sloan, V. L., & Goodman, V. Development of sex differences in preschool children's interactions with an infant: Spontaneous behavior and response to a caretaking assignment. Paper presented at the Society for Research in Child Development, San Francisco, March, 1979.

Bernard, J. *The future of motherhood*. New York: Penguin Books, 1974.

Blood, R. O., & Wolfe, D. M. *Husbands and wives: The dynamics of married living*. New York: Free Press, 1960.

Bolton, C. Mate selection as a development of a relationship. *Journal of Marriage and the Family*, 1961, *23*, 234–240.

Brim, O. G., Jr. Socialization through the life cycle. In O. G. Brim, Jr. & S. Wheeler (Eds.), *Socialization after childhood: Two essays*. New York: Wiley, 1966.

Bronfenbrenner, U. *The ecology of human development*. Cambridge, Mass.: Harvard University Press, 1979.

Brown, R. *Social psychology*. New York: Free Press, 1965.

Duvall, E. M. *Family development* (5th ed.). Philadelphia: Lippincott, 1977.

Emmerich, W. Socialization and sex-role development. In P. B. Baltes & K. W. Schaie (Eds.), *Life-span developmental psychology: Personality and socialization*. New York: Academic Press, 1973.

Erikson, E. *Childhood and society*. New York: Norton, 1950.

Feldman, S. S., & Aschenbrenner, B. *The effect of the first born child on sex roles and sex-related differences*. Manuscript under review.

Feldman, S. S., Biringen, Z. C., & Nash, S. C. Fluctuations of sex-related self-attributions as a function of stage of family life cycle. *Developmental Psychology*, in press.

Feldman, S. S., & Nash, S. C. Interest in babies during young adulthood. *Child Development*, 1978, *49*, 617–622.

Feldman, S. S., & Nash, S. C. Changes in responsiveness to babies during adolescence. *Child Development*, 1979, *50*, 942–949. (a)

Feldman, S. S., & Nash, S. C. Sex differences in responsiveness to babies among mature adults. *Developmental Psychology*, 1979, *15*, 430–436. (b)

Feldman, S. S., Nash, S. C., & Cutrona, C. The influence of age and sex on responsiveness to babies. *Developmental Psychology*, 1977, *13*, 675–676.

Flavell, J. H. Cognitive changes in adulthood. In L. R. Goulet & P. B. Baltes (Eds.), *Life-span developmental psychology: Research and theory*. New York: Academic Press, 1970.

Frodi, A. M., & Lamb, M. E. Sex differences in responsiveness to infants: A developmental study of psychophysiological and behavioral responses. *Child Development*, 1978, *49*, 1182–1188.

Frodi, A. M., Murray, A. D., Lamb, M. E., & Steinberg, J. Biological and social determinants of responsiveness to infants in 10- to 15-year-old girls. Unpublished manuscript, 1980.

Fullard, W., & Reiling, A. M. An investigation of Lorenz's "babyness." *Child Development,* 1976, *47,* 1191-1193.

Gladieux, J. D. Pregnancy—the transition to parenthood: Satisfaction with the pregnancy experience as a function of sex-role self conceptions, marital relationship and social network. In W. B. Miller & L. F. Newman (Eds.), *The first child and family formation.* Chapel Hill, N.C.: Carolina Population Center, 1978.

Goffman, E. *Encounters: Two studies in the sociology of interaction.* Indianapolis: Bobbs-Merrill, 1961.

Goldberg, S., & Kriger, A. *Preference for pictures of infants in pre- and post-menarchal girls: Evidence for biological influences.* Paper presented at the Southeastern Conference on Human Development, Minneapolis, March 1980.

Gutmann, D. Parenthood: Key to the comparative psychology of the life cycle. In N. Datan & L. Ginsberg (Eds.), *Life-span developmental psychology: Normative life crisis.* New York: Academic Press, 1975.

Haney, C., Banks, C., & Zimbardo, P. Interpersonal dynamics in a simulated prison. *International Journal of Criminology and Penology,* 1973, *1,* 69-97.

Havighurst, R. J. History of developmental psychology: Socialization and personality development through the life span. In P. B. Baltes & K. W. Schaie (Eds.), *Life-span developmental psychology: Personality and socialization.* New York: Academic Press, 1973.

Hill, R. Decision making and the family life cycle. In E. Shanas & G. F. Streib (Eds.), *Social structure and the family.* Englewood Cliffs, N.J.: Prentice-Hall, 1965.

Holmes, T. H., & Rahe, R. H. The social readjustment rating scale. *Journal of Psychosomatic Research,* 1967, *11,* 213-218.

Hultsch, D. F., & Plemons, J. K. Life-events and life-span development. In P. B. Baltes & O. G. Brim (Eds.), *Life-span development and behavior* (Vol. 2). New York: Academic Press, 1979.

Humphrey, M. Sex differences in attitude to parenthood. *Human Relations,* 1977, *30,* 737-749.

Jones, E. E., & Davis, K. E. From acts to dispositions: The attribution process in person perception. In L. Berkowitz (Ed.), *Advances in experimental social psychology* (Vol. 2). New York: Academic Press, 1965.

Kirkpatrick, C. Familial development, selective needs, and predictive theory. *Journal of Marriage and the Family,* 1967, *29,* 229-236.

Kohlberg, L. *Stages in the development of moral thought and action.* New York: Holt, Rinehart, & Winston, 1969.

Kuhn, D., Nash, S. C., & Brucken, L. Sex role concepts of two- and three-year olds. *Child Development,* 1978, *49,* 445-451.

Levinson, D. J., Darrow, C. M., Klein, E. B., Levinson, M. H., & McKee, B. *The seasons of a man's life.* New York: Ballantine, 1978.

Looft, W. R. Socialization and personality throughout the life span: An examination of contemporary psychological approaches. In P. B. Baltes & K. W. Schaie (Eds.), *Life-span developmental psychology: Personality and socialization.* New York: Academic Press, 1973.

Lorenz, K. Die angebornen formen möglicher erfahrung. *Zeitschrift fur Tierpsychologie,* 1943, *5,* 235-409.

Lowenthal, M. F., Thurnher, M., & Chiriboga, D. *Four stages of life.* San Francisco: Jossey-Bass, 1975.

Maccoby, E. E., & Jacklin, C. N. *The psychology of sex differences.* Stanford, Calif.: Stanford University Press, 1974.

Magrabi, F. M., & Marshall, W. H. Family development tasks: A research model. *Journal of Marriage and the Family,* 1965, *27,* 454-461.

Mischel, W. Toward a cognitive social learning reconceptualization of personality. *Psychological Review,* 1973, *80,* 252-283.

Nash, S. C. Sex role as a mediator of intellectual functioning. In M. A. Wittig & A. C. Petersen (Eds.), *Sex-related differences in cognitive functioning.* New York: Academic Press, 1979.

Nash, S. C., & Feldman, S. S. Responsiveness to babies: Life situation specific sex differences in adulthood. *Sex Roles*, 1980, *6*, 751–758.

Neugarten, B. L. Adult personality: A developmental view. *Human Development*, 1966, *9*, 61–73.

Neugarten, B. L. Adult personality: Toward a psychology of the life cycle. In B. L. Neugarten (Ed.), *Middle age and aging*. Chicago: University of Chicago Press, 1968.

Neugarten, B. L. Personality and aging. In J. E. Birren & K. W. Schaie (Eds.), *Handbook of the psychology of aging*. New York: Van Nostrand Reinhold, 1977.

Neugarten, B. L., & Datan, N. Sociological perspectives on the life cycle. In P. B. Baltes & K. W. Schaie (Eds.), *Life-span developmental psychology: Personality and socialization*. New York: Academic Press, 1973.

Nock, S. L. The family life cycle: Empirical or conceptual tool? *Journal of Marriage and the Family*, 1979, *41*, 15–26.

Osmond, M. W., & Martin, P. Y. Sex and sexism: A comparison of male and female sex-role attitudes. *Journal of Marriage and the Family*, 1975, *37*, 744–758.

Parsons, T., & Bales, R. F. *Family, socialization and interaction process*. New York: Free Press, 1955.

Pedhazur, E. J., & Tetenbaum, T. J. Bem sex role inventory: A theoretical and methodological critique. *Journal of Personality and Social Psychology*, 1979, *37*, 996–1016.

Piaget, J. *The psychology of intelligence*. London: Routledge & Kegan Paul, 1950.

Roper, B., & Labeff, E. Sex roles and feminism revisited: An intergenerational attitude comparison. *Journal of Marriage and the Family*, 1977, *39*, 113–119.

Sales, E. Women's adult development. In I. H. Frieze, J. E. Parsons, P. B. Johnson, D. N. Ruble, & G. L. Zellman (Eds.), *Women and sex roles: A social psychological perspective*. New York: Norton, 1978.

Spence, J. T., & Helmreich, R. L. *Masculinity and femininity*. Austin: University of Texas Press, 1978.

Spence, J. T., & Helmreich, R. L. Comparison of masculine and feminine personality attributes and sex-role attitudes across age groups. *Developmental Psychology*, 1979, *15*, 583–584.

Sternglanz, S M., Grey, J. H., & Murakami, M. Adult preferences for infant facial features: An ethological approach. *Animal Behavior*, 1977, *25*, 108–115.

Turner, R. H. The role and the person. *American Journal of Sociology*, 1978, *84*, 1–23.

ACKNOWLEDGMENTS

Preparation of this chapter was supported in part by funds from the Boys Town Center for the Study of Youth Development at Stanford University. Thanks to Barbara Aschenbrenner for her able assistance in carrying out the research reported herein, and to P. Berman, A. Frodi, C. Holahan, C. N. Jacklin, M. Lamb, and especially to J. T. Spence and P. Cowan for critical readings of an earlier draft.

2

Development of Individual Differences in Temperament

Mary Klevjord Rothbart
Douglas Derryberry
University of Oregon

Temperament is an ancient concept. Since the time of Vindician (Diamond, 1974), it has been used to establish conceptual links between behavior and the constitution of the individual. Temperament also has much to offer the modern student of development. It gives us a place to begin thinking about the origins of cognitive and affective structures, and a framework for relating these structures to underlying physiological systems of reaction and regulation. It gives us a place to begin tracing the developing patterns of experience that constitute the lives of individuals.

In this chapter we will define temperament as constitutional differences in reactivity and self-regulation, with "constitutional" seen as the relatively enduring biological makeup of the organism influenced over time by heredity, maturation, and experience. By "reactivity" we refer to the characteristics of the individual's reaction to changes in the environment, as reflected in somatic, endocrine, and autonomic nervous systems. By "self-regulation" we mean the processes functioning to modulate this reactivity, e.g., attentional and behavioral patterns of approach and avoidance.

In our view, temperament may be differentiated to some extent from the more inclusive concept of personality by its emphasis on the dynamic or energetic characteristics of responsivity. These characteristics include the temporal and intensive functioning of response systems: response threshold, latency, amplitude, rise time to peak intensity, and recovery time. Personality extends beyond temperament to include informational and conceptual structures, for example, the self concept and other belief systems, which interact in a regulatory manner with temperament. This distinction provides a perspective from which we can consider the mutual interaction between the conceptual and energetic aspects of personality.

The study of temperament poses both possibilities and problems for the student of development. Since it is concerned with biological structures underlying affect and motivation, the study of temperament provides a new perspective from which to view emotional development. Affective responses vary greatly across individuals, and the occurrence of developmental "landmarks," such as stranger and separation anxiety, should therefore not be taken for granted for each individual (Rheingold & Eckerman, 1973). Instead, a temperament approach encourages appreciation of the affective capacities and limitations of the individual, and at the same time, brings to light the individual's developing capacity for control over self and environment.

Temperament also offers new perspectives from which to view cognitive development. It focuses upon variability in the cognitive systems themselves, including variability in the time course and intensity of the alerting, orienting, and detecting components of attention (Posner & Rothbart, in press). Temperament provides a basis for the study of the continuing development of these attentional systems, including their interaction with emergent capacities for memory, imagery, and propositional thought. In addition, a temperament perspective emphasizes the individual's use of selective attention in the service of affective-motivational systems. It also provides insight about the development and elaboration of important cognitive structures. Central cognitive organizations, including the child's self concept and the child's view of the caregiver, are seen as influenced from the earliest days by temperament variables.

Consideration of temperament also offers a new approach to understanding social development. The rationale for this approach has existed for some time. Developmental psychologists no longer see infants as uniform in their basic reactions, with differences in child behavior the result of environmental shaping by social reinforcement (Bell, 1968, 1971). We have come instead to appreciate both infant and caregiver as an interacting "couple," with the pre-existing structures of each member exerting influence on the other (Schaffer, 1977). We are now aware of some of the infant characteristics that influence and are influenced by caregiver behavior; these correspond closely to constitutionally based responsivity, including distress and smiling, attentional activity, soothability, and activity level (Clarke-Stewart, 1973; Korner, 1973; Robson & Moss, 1970).

A temperament approach places affective motivational systems at the center of the developing personality. In this way, it provides a framework within which the emotional, cognitive, and social domains can be integrated. It allows a view of the individual as an integrated system, consisting of a range of affective-motivational capabilities and limitations, together with a set of cognitive, behavioral, and social "strategies" for fulfilling these requirements. In cognition, for example, emotion can be seen to initiate and direct information processing in order to enhance or attenuate the individual's inherent affective capacities or limitations. In the social domain, biological structures underlying emotion influence both the direct impact of social stimulation and the child's cognitions of social events. Temperament can thus be seen to provide a constraint upon the ways in which the individual is influenced by and influences the physical and social worlds.

Temperament is a psychobiological concept; it has been used in connection with the study of individual differences in other animal species (Diamond, 1957), in research on behavior genetics (Goldsmith & Gottesman, in press), and in research on human infants (Thomas & Chess, 1977; Thomas, Chess, Birch, Hertzig, & Korn, 1963). Temperament offers an important opportunity for establishing links between the nervous system and behavior, and the possibility for studying the temporal organization of behavioral and physiological processes across time and development. Although we expect that the constitutional aspects of personality may change as a function of maturation and experience, a certain amount of continuity is nevertheless expected. For example, biologically determined "sensitivities" to certain forms of stimulation may themselves be stable, or stability may be reflected in consistent use of particular strategies for dealing with stimulation. At the same time, temperament allows for a view of the tremendous diversity and individual integrity of functioning existing even from the earliest months of life.

This chapter proposes a tentative framework for organizing developmental research on temperament, relating the framework to important concepts from theory on adult temperament and to the study of social development. In addition, recent work on the assessment of temperament via caregiver reports and home observation are critically reviewed.

Our conceptual framework for organizing temperament research is described in the section *Conceptual Issues*. In the next section, we raise developmental questions related to temperament and consider developmental stability. We relate temperament to social behavior in the third section. We review the empirical assessment of temperament by caregiver reports and home observation in the fourth section. Finally, we summarize and present our conclusions in the last section.

In the first section, we attempt to derive a set of promising temperament variables from a review of developmental and adult research and theory in temperament and attention. In addition, we consider the developmental course of these variables, and describe possible psychobiological bases for some of the temperament dimensions.

CONCEPTUAL ISSUES

Defining Temperament

When Thomas, Chess, and their colleagues (Thomas, Chess, & Birch, 1968; Thomas et al., 1963) began to report their important work on individual differences in infancy, they did not use the term *temperament,* but referred instead to their study of "primary reaction pattern" and "initial reactivity." By 1977, however, Thomas and Chess identified their variables as assessing temperament as that term had been defined by Cattell (1950) and Guilford (1959). Thomas and Chess (1977) propose that:

> Temperament may best be viewed as a general term referring to the *how* of behavior. It differs from ability, which is concerned with the *what* and *how well* of behaving, and from motivation, which accounts for *why* a person does what he is doing . . . Temperament can be equated to the term *behavioral style* [p. 9].

Buss and Plomin (1975) have also stated that temperament deals chiefly with stylistic aspects of behavior: "*how* the response is made: fast or slow, mild or intense, sparse and unelaborated or adorned and elaborated, etc. [p. 5]." In addition, they require that a characteristic be genetically inherited and developmentally stable throughout the life span in order to qualify as a "temperament."

One difficulty with the "style" definition is that it may be taken to imply that a temperamental characteristic is so pervasive as to be evident in all behaviors of the child. Sroufe and Waters (1977), for example, state that a temperament characteristic is "a set of behaviors that are constantly and uniformly operative . . . [p. 1185]." In this view, a withdrawing child would be seen as continually moving away from objects and people, even when s/he is at home with familiar objects and people. Temperament researchers such as Escalona (1968), however, make it clear that temperamental characteristics must be studied in the context of stimuli appropriate to eliciting them. This view does not imply that a highly withdrawing infant will show withdrawal in all situations, but that the infant will show a high probability of withdrawal within the presentation of a relatively broad range of novel or intense stimuli.

A "style" definition also suggests that a given response characteristic applies to all modalities of expression, so that a child showing intense distress would also be expected to show intense positive affect and intense motor activity. We will suggest that evidence for generalization of the response characteristic of intensity is not strong, and that one of the interesting aspects of temperament may be the child's most frequently used response system—for example, vocalization, motor activity, or emotional expression.

Because of the confusions associated with the "style" definition, and in view of the limitations of models based on behavior alone, we have chosen to approach temperament through a framework more closely tied to the constitution of the individual. In our model, temperament refers to individual differences in reactivity and self-regulation assumed to have a constitutional basis. *Constitutional* is defined here as the relatively enduring biological makeup of the organism influenced over time by heredity, maturation, and experience. *Reactivity* refers to the excitability, responsivity, or arousability of the behavioral and physiological systems of the organism, whereas *self-regulation* refers to neural and behavioral processes functioning to modulate this underlying reactivity (Rothbart & Derryberry, in press).

Although the constructs of reactivity and self-regulation are extensively interrelated, they provide a valuable perspective from which to view temperament and development. One major advantage is their flexibility and generality—that is, they can be utilized to describe temperament at the neural level, at the level of interacting physiological systems, and at the behavioral level. In this way, the concepts of reactivity and self-regulation allow us an integrative view of the biological and behavioral aspects of temperament. At the same time, they can be applied with varying degrees of specificity, so that a model of sufficient complexity for delineating individual differences can be generated. In addition, these two concepts are central to contemporary models of adult temperament, and they thus provide us with an important link between infant and adult approaches to temperament. Finally, the concepts of reactivity and self-regulation are especially relevant to a consideration of the development of temperament, for development may be seen as involving changes over time in the balance between reactive and regulatory processes.

We will begin with a discussion of the response systems through which reactivity can be approached. In the process we will focus on five response characteristics which provide a conceptual and empirical framework for viewing the functioning of reactivity in different response systems. We will then consider self-regulatory mechanisms functioning to modulate the reactive processes.

In describing the model, we will use some examples of individual differences from our current laboratory study of infants seen longitudinally at 3, 6½, 10, and 13½ months of age. In this work, infants are presented with visual, auditory and tactile stimuli designed to elicit emotional, vocal, motor, and autonomic reactions. The stimuli presented vary in their degree of intensity, complexity, novelty, and incongruity. In addition, we assess distractibility through infants' reactions to peripheral probe lights presented with a central auditory–visual stimulus, their tendency to startle through presentation of a rapidly opening parasol, their frustration tolerance by varying the accessibility of attractive toys, and their soothability through several calming presentations. These data are now being collected and have not yet been fully analyzed, but our laboratory observations provide good examples of temperamental variability, and we describe them anecdotally in the next section for purposes of illustration only.

We also report some relevant results from a recently completed longitudinal study (Rothbart, 1980). In this research, parents filled out a caregiver–report temperament instrument, the Infant Behavior Questionnaire, and independent home observations of infant temperament were made for a longitudinal sample of 46 infants at 3, 6, and 9 months of age. Three home observations 30–45 minutes in length were made for each subject at each age, and temperament-related behaviors were coded sequentially using a 46-item code.

Temperament Response Characteristics

Before considering the response systems reflecting reactivity, we would like to propose a set of measures that may be used to characterize the dynamics of an individual response. Some of these characteristics have been studied as temperament dimensions by previous researchers, who, in their definition of temperament as "style," have proposed that a given quality of response generalizes across response systems.

The dynamic characteristics of responsivity may be seen as including both intensive and temporal qualities. The intensive characteristics we consider are response threshold and intensity. The temporal characteristics are response latency, rise time, and recovery time.

Threshold

The dimension of threshold, which reflects the infant's sensitivity to low intensities of stimulation, has been studied by a number of researchers (Escalona, 1968; Korner, 1973; Thomas & Chess, 1977; Thomas et al., 1963, 1968). For Thomas and Chess (1977), threshold was the only parent interview measure providing significant correlations between 1 and 5 years of age. Korner (1973) reports evidence of individual variability in sensory thresholds as early as the newborn period, and emphasizes the importance of sensory sensitivity for the developing infant. She suggests that early sensitivity and regulation may provide the predispositional core that later influences the development of cognitive control styles and defense mechanisms. Escalona (1968) also stresses the importance of the infant's sensory thresholds. In an earlier study, she found evidence of a link between unusual sensitivity and later psychosis (Bergman & Escalona, 1949).

An important issue to consider in connection with threshold is not specific to threshold alone, but involves other characteristics of reactivity as well. This question concerns whether there exists a general, common threshold that is stable across the different sensory modalities and responses, or whether thresholds (and reactivity in general) vary according to the sensory channel of stimulation and/or the response system through which they are expressed. Birns (1965) found that most newborn infants could be characterized as being slightly, moderately, or highly responsive to stimulation, regardless of whether the stimulation was presented through auditory or tactile channels. Korner (1970) also provides evidence for general, cross-modal reactivity; newborns were found to have consistent thresholds across both the auditory and visual modalities. Escalona (1968), on the other hand, suggests that some children may be particularly sensitive to stimulation in a specific modality. Some infants may be especially responsive to tactile stimulation, others to auditory stimulation, and others to visual stimulation. In a significant extension of the construct of sensitivity, Escalona goes on to propose that infants may also differ in their thresholds for interoceptive stimulation and suggests that some babies are more reactive than others to internal physiological signals. This issue of the general versus the modality-specific nature of reactivity can best be resolved through assessment and comparison of thresholds and response intensities along a number of different sensory channels.

Intensity

The peak of responsivity has been extensively studied as a temperament variable within the dimension of *intensity*. This temperamental dimension has been proposed by Thomas et al. (1963) and has been measured by Carey (Carey, 1970; Carey & McDevitt, 1978). Thomas and Chess (1977) define intensity as "the energy level of response, irrespective of its quality or direction [p. 21]." Given this definition, measures of intensity of smiling, laughter, and distress would be expected to be part of the intensity dimension.

In caregiver–report measures, Carey and McDevitt (1978) measure intensity with items that do not allow us to determine whether high-intensity responses in laughter and distress are correlated. For example, parents are asked to indicate whether "The infant reacts strongly to foods, whether positively (smacks lips, laughs, squeals) or negatively (cries)" and whether "The infant greets a new toy with a loud voice and much expression of feeling (whether positive or negative)." Before combining these two sets of responses in a single item, we must determine empirically whether they are positively correlated, since the characteristics of reactivity may be specific to the modality being assessed. Pederson, Anderson, and Cain (1976) and Rothbart (in press) were not able to develop caregiver–report scales with adequate internal reliability for intensity because intense reactions in one response system (e.g., activity) were not correlated with intense reactions in other systems (e.g., distress).

Laboratory studies have also examined intensity of the infants' motor, vocal, and autonomic reactivity. Birns (1965) found newborns to differ in the intensity of their behavioral responses to auditory, tactile, and oral stimulation. These differences were stable across four sessions between the 2nd and 5th days of life. In a follow-up study, Birns, Barten, and Bridger (1969) examined a number of temperament dimensions across the first 4 months of life. Vigor of response was not found to be stable, although the conceptually related dimensions of sensitivity, irritability, and tension showed stability across the 4 months. In a study of cardiac reactivity, Lipton, Steinschneider, and Richmond (1961) examined a group of infants during the newborn period and again at 2½ and 5 months of age. Individual differences in peak magnitude of the infants' heart-rate responses were found to be stable from 2½ months to 5 months of age.

As with the threshold dimension of temperament, the child's intensity of reaction will greatly affect the nature of the infant–caregiver relationship. For example, caregivers who appreciate intense displays of positive affect are likely to find their interactions with an ebullient infant particularly rewarding. As a result, the infant may experience greater contact with the mother (Clarke-Stewart, 1973), as well as contact of a more playful and positive nature than would a more sober infant. Greater contact can also be a result of infants' high intensities of negative affect, but here the interaction is of a distinctly different nature. Rather than facilitating engagement and excitement, the caregiver's role in instances of distress is often one of promoting distraction and soothing.

As with the threshold dimension, the issue of general versus system-specific reactivity arises in relation to response intensity. Although early activation theorists spoke of a unitary dimension of general arousal, it now appears that response magnitude varies not only across individuals, but across response systems as well (Lacey, 1967). The idea of a general, overall "level" of arousal has thus been replaced with models describing the patterning of intensity within and across different response systems. Given this multidimensional approach to reactivity, it makes little sense to infer "overall intensity" from the measurement of a single response channel such as motor or cardiac activity. We instead suggest that assessment be made across a number of response systems, and that attention be paid to the patterning as well as the level of reactivity.

Temporal Response Characteristics

In addition to intensive aspects of response, the functioning of response systems may also be approached in terms of temporal response characteristics, such as response latency, rise time, and recovery time. Individuality in *latency of response* can be seen in even the most simple reactions. For example, in our research, when a bell is rung in a 3-month-old's periphery, some infants turn toward it almost instantaneously, others orient after several seconds, and still others, even though they show evidence of having heard it (e.g., heart-rate deceleration), do not turn toward it at all. Such differences may reflect an important aspect of temperament: the rapidity with which orienting responses are programmed and elicited. In behavioral terms, these response latencies represent one aspect of a more general temperament dimension, namely "alertness." Brazelton (1973), for example, assesses neonatal alertness through measures of the latency and duration of responsivity, as well as through the brightness and wideness of the infant's eyes.

The rise time of a response, that is, the time required for a response to build to its peak intensity, is another source of variability. When confronted with a stimulus, young infants often respond with varying degrees of diffuse motor excitation (Tennes, Emde, Kisley, & Metcalf, 1972). In some babies, this agitation increases rapidly, and they may become overwhelmed and distressed at the same time. Other infants, however, may build to the same peak of excitation over a longer time period, allowing them the possibility of processing more information before they become distressed. In general, a more gradual rising phase of reactivity should allow the infant or caregiver greater opportunity to facilitate or alleviate reactivity prior to its peak. Except for Brazelton's (1973) neonatal "rapidity of build-up" scale, the rising aspects of reactivity have received little attention in infant research.

Finally, individuality is evident in the temporal course of an infant's *recovery* from a peak of excitation. Infants differ greatly in how quickly they recover from their peak of response, and this resiliency will have profound effects on their interaction with the world. For example, the falling phase of distress has received attention under the dimension of *soothability*. Birns, Barton, and Bridger (1969) observed some consistency of soothability across the first 4 months of life as assessed with laboratory procedures. Korner (1973) has suggested that soothability and the capacity for self-comforting are major infant differences that may be related later to seeking of others for comfort, and Escalona (1968) stressed the importance of bodily self-stimulation in the infant's self-regulation of state. In addition to its relevance under conditions of distress, recovery may also prevent reactivity from building to unpleasant levels. In other words, infants whose somatic and autonomic reactions are fairly resilient may escape the prolonged levels of excitation that often result in distress.

When considering these temporal aspects, we must again keep in mind the multidimensional nature of reactivity. It is important to note that the expression of reactivity follows differing time courses along different response systems. In soothability, for example, we must consider a sequential recovery along facial, vocal, autonomic, and hormonal channels. Two infants, both of whom demonstrate similar facial and vocal recovery, may in fact differ in their soothability along autonomic and endocrine channels, and such differences may influence the reoccurrence of visible distress.

Summary and Discussion

The five response characteristics just outlined describe the phasic nature of responsivity: Responses are initiated, rise in intensity, peak, and subside across time. Phasic responses are not, however, the result of a single excitatory component, but are instead the net result of the interplay between excitation and inhibition, or in more general terms, between reactive and regulatory processes. By measuring the intensive and temporal aspects of response, we should be better able to assess the relative contributions of both reactive and regulatory components.

Although we have discussed the response characteristics primarily in relation to stimulus intensity, reactivity can arise from other sources as well. Berlyne (1971) has provided a convenient description of the stimulus properties related to arousal: "Psychophysical" properties include stimulus intensity, size, rate, and duration; "collative" properties, involving the comparison of the stimulus with a model stored in memory, include novelty, incongruity, and surprisingness; and "ecological" properties include the associated biological significance and affective meaning of the stimulus. In addition to these stimulus properties, however, reactivity is a function of the particular nervous system through which the stimulus is processed.

Temperament Response Systems

If we now consider component response systems separately, they may also be seen to correspond to several of the dimensions identified by previous temperament researchers. Although we mention some behavior genetics research in connection with these systems, we are not able to discuss heritability issues in detail. The reader is referred to Goldsmith and Gottesman (in press) and Bates (in press); both articles provide discussions of the behavior genetics of temperamental characteristics.

The response systems through which reactivity and self-regulation are expressed include the somatic, endocrine, and autonomic nervous systems, each of which consists of a number of component subsystems. Responses are also combined into more complex patterns of behavior by means of higher-order emotional and motivational systems. This coordination is accomplished by means of interacting reactive and regulatory systems within the central nervous system.

Somatic Activity

The somatic nervous system includes structures responsible for the patterning of gross motor activity, such as crawling and walking, and also fine motor activity, such as that involved in vocal articulation, manipulation, and facial expression.

Motor Activity. The child's motor activity or activity level has probably been the most frequently studied dimension of temperament (e.g., Buss & Plomin, 1975; Escalona, 1968; Fries, 1944; Schaffer, 1966; Thomas et al., 1963). Escalona (1968) considered activity level to be an important dimension of individuality in the infant and related activity level to perceptual and social development. Animal studies suggest that high activity level can be transmitted genetically (Fuller & Thompson, 1960; Gray, 1971), and both Willerman (1973) and Buss and Plomin (1975) have reported higher intraclass correlations for mother-rated activity levels in identical than in fraternal twins. Studies by Goldsmith and Gottesman (in press) and Torgersen and Kringlen (1978) have also found evidence for heritability of activity level.

The age at which activity level may be identified as a stable individual characteristic is in some dispute. Buss and Plomin (1975) reviewed longitudinal studies, concluding that activity level shows stability as an individual characteristic only after the period of infancy. In the early months, however, Birns, Barton and Bridger (1969) found consistency of activity for infants in the laboratory between the ages of 1 to 4 months. In our own research (Rothbart, 1980), we found significant stability in activity level via both parent report and home observation of infants across the 3-, 6-, and 9-month periods. Additional longitudinal research bridging the period from infancy to the preschool years will be necessary to clarify the stability question.

One possible resolution of this question may be that motor activity as measured during the early months remains stable over a short-term period, but that activity measured later than the first year of life reflects a somewhat different temperamental characteristic. Much infant activity occurs in reaction to exogenous stimulation (e.g., the squirming connected with being confined or restricted, or the limb movement occurring when an object is presented). After children are able to move about, they become able to engage in movement in the relative absence of directly instigating stimuli. Activity after 1 year of age may thus reflect stimulation-seeking, a characteristic related to the temperamental concept of extraversion (Eysenck, 1963). To the extent that activity level measured in infancy reflects the sensitivity of the child to external stimulation, we need not predict that a sensitive child would later seek added stimulation through activity. Indeed, we might predict that individuals who are highly reactive to normal levels of external stimulation may be *less* likely to seek additional sources of stimulation. Bell, Weller, and Waldrop's (1971) findings of a reversal in intensity of motoric reaction between removal of the nipple in the newborn and preschool activity in response to the presence of a barrier may support this position.

Vocal Activity. In addition to variability in motor activity, infants appear to differ in the quantity and quality of their early vocal reactions. Vocal activity has rarely been studied as an aspect of temperament, although it is often part of the infant's response to stimulation. Early work by Kagan (1971) found greater stability of vocalization in girls than boys, but this sex difference was not replicated in a later sample (Kagan, Kearsley, & Zelazo, 1978). Such results point to a difficulty facing much research in this area: Caregivers may also differentially stimulate a given response system, with girls, for example, being exposed to greater stimulation of the auditory/vocal channels and boys, greater stimulation in motor channels (Moss, Robson, & Pedersen, 1969). Nevertheless, we have found stabilities across 3, 6, and 9 months of age in vocal expression in parent reports and from 3–9 months in home observations in our own research, and individual differences in the expression of excitement through the vocal channel would seem important to development. They may, for example, influence the caregiver to communicate with the child at primarily a verbal rather than a physical level, which might in turn facilitate the development of the child's auditory and linguistic capacities. In contrast, the child whose excitement is expressed primarily through motor channels may encourage an interactional style that enhances the development of visual–motor and motor skills.

Facial Expression. Another somatic response system closely related to communication is that involved in facial expression. Apart from structural differences in their faces, infants differ dramatically in the expressive and communicative features of their usual facial expression. Variability exists in such tonic features as the brightness and openness of the eyes, characteristic tension in the brow, and expressiveness of the mouth. Phasic changes in facial expression, such as smiling and frowning, are of particular interest in connection with temperament because these facial responses are so closely tied to the infant's affective state. They are discussed later, in connection with integrated emotional activity.

Autonomic and Endocrine Activity.   Also important in the development of temperament are differences in the autonomic and endocrine systems. Both of these systems are comprised of a number of interacting subsystems forming complex, differential patterning across individuals (Lacey, 1967; Mason, 1975). Within the autonomic nervous system, for example, some individuals may show their maximum reactivity through the cardiovascular system, whereas others may be more reactive in the electrodermal system. The cardiovascular system has received a good deal of attention during infancy, and evidence has accumulated in support of the existence of individuality in the tonic and phasic aspects of cardiac reactivity (Lewis, Wilson, Ban, & Baumel, 1970; Lipton et al., 1961). In research on the endocrine system, Tennes and her coworkers (Tennes, Downey, & Vernadakis, 1977; Tennes & Vernadakis, 1979) have found individual differences in adrenocortical reactivity from the age of 4 weeks. One-year-old infants possessing relatively high levels of cortisol showed greater distress to separation from the mother, and stability of cortisol production from 1 to 3 years of age was suggested in a follow-up study. Further research, particularly involving concurrent measurement of several subsystems, is required before we can adequately assess and make predictions from an infant's autonomic and hormonal profiles. Nevertheless, these areas have much to contribute to our understanding of temperament.

Emotional Activity

The four response systems just discussed (i.e., the motor, vocal, endocrine, and autonomic nervous systems) differ in their temporal and intensive coordination across individuals. In addition to these structural and temporal aspects, however, the qualitative nature of the overall patterning is extremely important. The functioning of response systems is embedded within higher order emotional–motivational patterning from the earliest days. It is at this level of emotionality that the basic functioning of temperament is most clearly revealed.

Emotional reactions have been a frequent focus of temperament study, as in Thomas et al.'s (1963, 1968) *mood* dimension, Buss and Plomin's (1975) *emotionality* dimension, and Birns et al.'s (1969) *irritability* dimension. Buss and Plomin consider only negative affect in their discussion of emotionality. Both positive and negative emotions are included by Thomas et al. (1963) in their Quality of Mood Variable, which scales smiling and laughter in a reverse direction to fussing and distress. Noting that some children may show little smiling and laughter *or* fussing and crying (Washburn, 1929), we (Rothbart, 1980) have measured smiling and laughter on a separate scale from distress to stimulation. We found significant stability of smiling and laughter from 3–12 months in the caregiver's report and from 3–6 and 6–9 months in home observations.

During the first months of life, individuality in negative emotionality may be approached in terms of the duration or intensity of stimulation that can be endured before a distress threshold is reached. For example, some infants will become quite upset following a vigorous startle reaction, whereas others remain placid, even though they show similar motor and cardiac responses. Some infants may also cry following a loud noise, whereas others may remain calm after a louder noise, even though they show a startle reaction and a more intense cardiac acceleration. Even when their motor and autonomic indices of arousal are similar, infants thus appear to differ in the levels of stimulation or arousal that they can experience before distress is elicited. Once such a threshold is attained, infants also differ in the peak to which their distress reactions rise: Some infants seldom move beyond moderate fussiness, whereas others build all the way to hard, harsh wailing. It is obvious that such differences in the threshold and intensity of distress reactions will greatly affect the nature of the caregiver's, as well as the infant's, experience and development. Korner (1973), for example, has pointed out the extent to which the infant's cry is a predictable initiator of interactions with the mother during the first months of life. With these initial differences in crying, an irritable infant might be expected to initiate interaction with the caregiver more frequently than a more placid infant.

Differences in the temporal course of negative affect are also evident during the early months of life, and these differences are at least as important as the intensive aspects. For example, two infants may have similar thresholds and potential peaks of distress. However, one child may rise gradually toward this peak, perhaps by moving through successively more intense steps of fussiness and crying, whereas another child may move rapidly to the level of intense crying. The first infant's gradual buildup may allow him or her greater opportunity to contain or diminish the rising distress through self-regulatory behaviors than the second infant. At the same time, a caregiver would have more opportunity to provide soothing ministrations to the first infant, and such an infant may not be as likely to experience intense distress and disruption. Before concluding that rise time is all important, however, we must also consider recovery aspects of the distress reactions, for the resiliency of the baby's reactivity will influence the efficacy of any self-soothing or caregiver interventions. For example, an infant's slow-rising distress may carry with it a considerable amount of momentum that is difficult to deflect through self-regulation. The converse may also be evident in certain infants—that is, rapidly rising distress may be coupled with a potential for fast recovery so as to facilitate self-regulatory behavior. At this stage of our research, we are holding open the possibility that the rising and falling aspects of reactivity are functionally independent, which would generate four types of distress response: slow rise–slow recovery; slow rise–fast recovery; fast rise–fast recovery; and fast rise–slow recovery.

Infants also differ in the extent of their positive emotionality, as expressed through smiling and laughter. For example, some children smile during our parasol episode, and the smiles differ in their latencies, intensities, and overall durations. In this episode, the child is led to fixate a twirling parasol located 2 feet away. When the parasol is subsequently closed and then opened rapidly, startle reactions varying from slight blink reflexes to vigorous body flexions are elicited. Smiling under these conditions is somewhat surprising, for the fast, looming nature of the stimulation more often gives rise to negative affect. Smiling and positive affect may also be measured under conditions of social stimulation, and here, too, the infants differ greatly. Some show small fleeting smiles interspersed with gaze aversions, others respond with broad, long-duration smiles, and still others do not smile at all. As with negative affect, response thresholds for smiling appear to be especially variable. Some infants smile easily and often, following low intensities or short exposure to pleasant stimulation, whereas others seem to require a greater amount of stimulation before positive affect is elicited.

These differences, in addition to their direct effects upon the infant's experience, will be very important in his or her interaction with the social world. Robson and Moss (1970) have reported that mothers describe their infants' smiling, eye contact, and visual responsiveness to have been instrumental in leading to the mothers' perceptions that their child recognized them as a special person, the mothers' recognition of the child as an individual, and the mothers' feelings of love for the infant. We might further speculate that the infant's positive emotionality will also influence the quality of social interactions, often giving rise to exchanges of a playful and stimulating nature. Finally, the infant who easily expresses positive affect may provide the caregiver with valuable cues concerning his or her preferred modes of interaction and levels of stimulation (Rothbart, 1973).

Summary and Discussion.   In this section, we have utilized the construct of reactivity as a framework within which to view previously studied dimensions of temperament. In so doing, we have delineated both intensive and temporal characteristics of reactivity, and we have discussed some of the response systems and emotional organization through which reactivity is expressed. The value of this approach lies in integrating dimensions of temperament within a framework tied to the functioning of the nervous system, while providing for a more precise view of the diversity of such functioning; we elaborate on this point in later sections of this chapter. By identifying the intensive and temporal sources of individuality, we are also better able to consider the quality of the infant's experience, the nature of the infant–caregiver interaction, and most important, the characteristics of the regulatory processes functioning to shape this reactivity. We now consider temperamental mechanisms involved in self-regulation.

Self-Regulation

In this section, we are concerned with the mechanisms through which levels or patterns of reactivity are regulated. Self-regulation refers to the functioning of multilevel processes serving to increase, decrease, maintain, and restructure the patterning of reactivity in either an anticipatory or correctional manner. As in the case of reactive processes, regulatory processes can be assessed in terms of their intensive and temporal characteristics. Although self-regulation may occur at multiple levels, here we focus upon behavioral processes, discussing individual differences in the capacity for self-regulation through approach and avoidance behavior, attentional behavior, and "self-stimulatory" and "self-soothing" behaviors.

Approach and Avoidance Behaviors. The older infant's ultimate means of self-regulation is through approach and avoidance. By leaning toward, reaching, grasping, and manipulating, the child is able to enhance his or her reactivity to a novel or familiar stimulus. By inhibiting approach tendencies, leaning away, or turning away, the child is potentially able to contain increasing activation and reduce the impact of novel or intense stimulation. Approach and avoidance behaviors thus serve to regulate the amount and quality of stimulation with which the child makes contact.

Thomas et al. (1963, 1968) have identified a temperament variable, *Approach-Withdrawal;* their measure of this dimension includes affective as well as motor reactions to new stimuli. Smiling and vocalization are scaled at the approach pole of the dimension and crying and fussing at the withdrawal pole. Our own (Rothbart, 1980) measure of fear is also an approach–withdrawal measure. Fear has been proposed as a temperament dimension by Diamond (1957) and is incorporated by Buss and Plomin (1975) with aggressiveness in their emotionality variable. Evidence for heritability has been reported in anxiety ratings for both child and adult twin pairs (Gottesman, 1963; Scarr, 1966) and on the age of development of fear of strangers in infancy (Freedman, 1965). Animal studies suggest that inherited individual differences in fear exist in rats, dogs, and chimpanzees (Fuller & Thompson, 1960; Hall, 1951; Yerkes & Yerkes, 1936).

Infants demonstrate great variability in their avoidance responses. When faced with an unpleasant stimulus, differences range from inhibited approach to cautious leaning away to immediate and vigorous turning away. In addition to these differences in the intensity of response, variability is also evident in the thresholds at which avoidance is initiated. Some infants begin to demonstrate behavioral avoidance at relatively low levels of stimulation, whereas others endure greater intensities or durations of stimulation before beginning to regulate their reactivity.

Individuality can also be found in infants' approach response. Even before they have mastered grasping, babies differ greatly in their response to an attractive toy. Some struggle vigorously and extensively in their attempt to obtain it, others approach the object with moderate intensity and duration, and other infants merely look at the toy, showing no approach tendencies at all. The durations of these early approaches may be related to later appearing behavioral persistence in the face of an obstructed object or blocked goal. Individual differences in infants' reactions to frustrating conditions are also readily apparent. For example, Kramer and Rosenblum (1970) studied the reactions of one year olds when a glass barrier was placed between the child and an attractive toy. They observed three kinds of responses to the barrier: some infants were persistent and managed to obtain the toy; others gradually shifted their interest to some other environmental focus without securing the toy; and a third group became distressed and abruptly lost interest in the toy. Evidence for heritability of persistence or goal orientation has been put forward by Torgersen and Kringler (1978) and Goldsmith and Gottesman (in press).

Another important aspect of a child's approach behavior involves the latency of the response. Apart from the intensity of the approach, infants differ in how quickly they will approach a novel stimulus. Some immediately reach for the toy upon its presentation, while others examine it for a while before beginning their approach. Latency of approach has previously been utilized as an index of "wariness" in the face of novelty (Schaffer, Greenwood, and Parry, 1972), which in many instances may be a reasonable interpretation of a child's hesitant behavior. However, given theories emphasizing the interaction between simultaneously-activated approach and avoidance systems (e.g., Montgomery, 1955), a long approach latency might also result from a relatively less intense or slower rising approach tendency.

Attention.   The on-going nature of self-regulation may also be observed in an infant's deployment of attention to selectively regulate incoming information. For example, an infant can direct his or her attention toward or away from a source of stimulation so that reactivity is initiated (by directing attention towards), enhanced (by attending intently), maintained (by extended attention), reduced (through momentary redirection of attention), or terminated (by redirecting attention). In this respect, attentional mechanisms provide the infant with a major means of self-regulation (Rothbart & Derryberry, in press).

Posner and Rothbart (in press) have described a framework for considering individual differences in attentional processes. In this view, individuals may differ in tonic levels of alertness, in the relative alerting effects of stimulation, and in the orienting of sensory receptors and of the central mechanism of attention toward the source of stimulation. As the infant develops, the temporal and intensive reactivity of these systems increasingly becomes a function of what is known and what is expected, and the activation of memory pathways influences the direction of the infant's attention. For example, highly familiar stimuli will lead to less orienting than more novel stimuli (Cohen, 1975), whereas misexpected or surprising events lead to an orienting reaction (Charlesworth, 1969).

Thomas et al. (1963) have suggested that important differences exist among infants in attention, and they have proposed the temperamental categories of distractibility, attention span, and persistence. The first of the attentional categories we consider is *distractibility*. Although some infants are capable of sustained orienting when subjected to peripheral stimulation, others tend to orient to even slight environmental changes. In our laboratory investigations, we assess distractibility by flashing peripheral lights while infants are fixating a central audio–visual display. Not only do the infants differ in terms of whether or not they are distracted by these lights, but they also differ in how quickly and for how long they turn toward the distracting stimulus.

Orienting of the central mechanism of attention is of special interest. Keele, Neill and deLemos (1978) have recently provided evidence that the speed of orienting to internal and external events is correlated over a variety of tasks in adults. To the extent that realignment of attention serves to regulate the arousing nature of stimulation, distractible infants should be at an advantage in controlling their reactivity. Apart from the rate and frequency with which attention is shifted, distractible infants may also benefit through caregiver-regulation. Infants are often soothed through distraction, for example, by directing their attention to an object, the sound of the caregiver's voice, and so on. Children who are more distractible may thus be more readily soothed. On the other hand, infants who have difficulty sustaining their attention on one area for any length of time may be at a disadvantage in that their assimilative processes are curtailed. Moreover, their information processing might be subject to greater interference and disruption from environmental changes, which as a result may subject them to greater arousal.

The dimension of *attention span* or duration of orienting may also be of importance to the infant's self-regulation. In older infants, duration of orienting may reflect speed of schema formation, and several researchers have noted that infants reliably differ in their rate of habituation—that is, in decrements of fixation time toward a stimulus over successive repetitions of that stimulus. McCall (1971) and Cohen (1975) have identified "slow" and "rapid habituators" and Horowitz (1974) has described a subgroup of "short lookers." Beyond reflecting differences in formation of cognitive structures, however, these differences in fixation rate may reflect variability in infants' ability to disengage themselves from a stimulus.

Also of interest in this respect are individual differences in patterns of visual orienting. Some infants stare raptly at a stimulus for an extended period, whereas others intersperse their fixations with subtle gaze aversions. By deflecting their attention briefly away from the stimulus, these latter infants may be initiating a recovery process that allows them to continue processing the information without becoming overaroused (cf. Stern, 1974; Tennes et al., 1972).

Thomas et al.'s (1963) third attentional variable is that of *persistence*, combining pursuit of obstructed activity with attention span. Additional empirical work is required to determine whether these dimensions may be appropriately combined.

Self-Stimulation and Self-Soothing. In addition to the primarily attentional mechanisms, infants also utilize a number of different body behaviors which often appear to regulate the impact of incoming information. The most familiar of these behaviors is thumb or finger sucking, which often ensues following an initial indication of distress, and which frequently allows the child to continue processing the stimulus. Bruner (1973) has suggested that an infant's use of a pacifier may serve to "buffer" the effects of an arousing visual stimulus, and this may also be the case when the infant engages in hand-to-mouth activity.

Other rhythmical activities, such as rocking and banging, may also serve regulatory functions. For example, when a child is presented with a toy that is slightly out of reach, s/he will often resort to pounding on the table. Of special interest here would be whether such a behavior serves to "discharge" the frustration-induced tension, or whether it serves to increase activation by providing additional kinesthetic and auditory stimulation for the infant. On the basis of other research, it seems likely that the same behavior may come to serve both functions, depending on the child's "level" of arousal and the on-going behavioral context. In this regard, Sroufe, Stuecher, and Stutzer (1973) examined the stereotypic finger flicking of an autistic child, finding that it served multiple functions including both cardiac acceleration and deceleration.

Regardless of the functional meaning of these behaviors, infants differ greatly in their utilization of them. Some infants become quite distressed without showing evidence of these techniques. Other infants appear to utilize them effectively and economically, engaging in them primarily under conditions of arousal or distress. Of those utilizing these behaviors, differences appear in the arousal levels at which regulatory behaviors are initiated. These differences range from apparently calm, alert states to states of extreme motor, autonomic, and vocal agitation. Variability also appears in the effectiveness of the self-regulation; some infants calm immediately, whereas others require more time to bring their reactivity under control.

Summary and Conclusions. In discussing self-regulation, we have emphasized the attentional and behavioral means through which the impact of stimulation is dampened, maintained, and/or enhanced. It should be apparent that the infant is by no means a helpless, reactive organism, but is instead equipped from a very early age with developing techniques for actively controlling both self and environment. These self-regulatory processes provide structure for the underlying reactivity—that is, they influence the intensive and temporal aspects of response. At the same time, however, the regulatory processes are in turn a function of the underlying reactivity, for their own intensive and temporal nature depends on the characteristics of responsivity. In an approach emphasizing the on-going, simultaneously interacting nature of reactive and self-regulatory processes, the two are virtually inseparable. Self-regulatory systems come into play at the earliest phases of the processing sequence, influencing the resultant reactivity at every level. Reactivity is shaped through self-regulation, and from such a perspective, behavior is very much an active process.

The significance of the interaction between reactive and regulatory processes can perhaps be clarified within the context provided by adult models of temperament. In their utilization of affective and motivational constructs, these models provide important conceptual links between reactivity and self-regulation. Furthermore, they offer valuable neurophysiological frameworks within which the two processes are described. These theories of adult temperament are truly integrative in nature, combining data from such diverse areas as behavior genetics, neurophysiology, psychopharmacology, learning theory, and personality theory. In this respect, we expect that substantial progress will be made in the years to come, and we view this progress as directly applicable to the infant.

Adult Models of Temperament

Conceptualizations of adult temperament have gone through several transitions in their views of arousal and self-regulation. Early theories, such as that of Pavlov (1935/1955), were primarily interested in arousal in terms of stimulus intensity rather than motivation, whereas later theories, Eysenck's (1967) in particular, provided a powerful motivational framework in the construct of an "optimal level" of arousal. The most recent theories (e.g., Gray, 1971, 1973, 1979; Zuckerman, 1979) appear to be shifting away from the idea of an "optimal level" of arousal, toward one emphasizing the balance between different regulatory systems.

Pavlov (1935–1955), Teplov (1964), and Nebylitsyn (1972) have developed a typology framed around what might be called "basic properties" of the nervous system. The most important of these properties is the "strength" of the nervous system. This property was originally measured through the experimental phenomenon of "transmarginal inhibition"—that is, a response decrement occurring when a certain level of increasing stimulus intensity is reached. Pavlov proposed that subjects who were able to endure high levels of or prolonged exposure to stimulation before such inhibition set in possessed "strong" nervous systems, whereas subjects demonstrating lower inhibitory thresholds were seen as having "weak" nervous systems. Subsequent research (Nebylitsyn, 1972) revealed that these inhibitory thresholds are complemented by corresponding excitatory thresholds; that is, individuals with "weak" nervous systems possess lower threshold levels than do individuals with "strong" nervous systems. The "strength" dimension thus describes two populations of individuals represented by overlapping inverted-U functions. Individuals with relatively weak nervous systems demonstrate their initial response, peak response, and subsequent response decrement at lower stimulus intensities than do individuals with relatively strong nervous systems, whose curve is shifted toward the right. In other words, the weak end of the dimension represents individuals who are more reactive or sensitive to stimulation, and the dimension itself might better be considered as one reflecting reactivity or sensitivity rather than "strength," as Strelau (1975) has also suggested.

In addition to the "strength" dimension, Soviet researchers have proposed several properties involving the temporal aspects of reactivity. These include mobility (the speed with which the signal value of a conditioned stimulus can be altered), lability (the speed with which neural processes are set off and arrested), and dynamism (the speed with which the potential intensity of a process is generated). Although there appear to be some similarities between these temporal properties and the response characteristics we have discussed, it would be difficult to equate these concepts with any degree of certainty.

Nevertheless, the "strength" of the nervous system has much to offer the areas of infant and adult temperament. In research on infants, we are led to focus upon the differences in stimulus intensity required for infants to demonstrate response thresholds and peak reactions, and these individual differences can be most revealing. The general approach can also be extended to assess thresholds and intensities of orienting and defensive reactions in relation to other kinds of reactivity, including those related to novelty and meaning. In its emphasis on stimulus properties and reactivity, however, Pavlov's model provides us with little insight into motivational processes.

The model of temperament developed by H. J. Eysenck (1967) is quite similar to Pavlov's, but it is more detailed in its use of neurophysiological and motivational constructs. According to Eysenck's theory, introverts possess a higher level of activity in the ascending reticular activating system (ARAS), which results in their being subject to higher levels of cortical arousal than are extraverts. His treatment of individual differences in arousability directly parallels the Pavlovian "strength" dimension, with introverts representing the "weak" or reactive type of nervous system, and extraverts the "strong" or unreactive type.

Eysenck's theorizing extends beyond that of the Soviets' in its utilization of affective-motivational constructs. The most central of these is the notion of an "optimal level" of arousal. According to this model, stimulation of moderate arousal potential is experienced as pleasurable and is therefore approached, whereas stimulation of relatively low or high arousal potential elicits negative affect and is avoided. For example, because introverts' reticular activating systems are seen as being more reactive than those of extraverts, they would be expected to reach an optimal level of arousal at lower levels of stimulation. Their behavioral preferences for less intense and novel forms of stimulation function to contain their reactivity around such lower optimal levels. The less-reactive extraverts, on the other hand, tend to seek out novel and intense stimulation, as if greater stimulation is required for them to attain or maintain an optimal level of arousal. In other words, introverts appear to be motivated to correct for their "overarousal," whereas extraverts must compensate for their relative "under-arousal."

Models such as Eysenck's are particularly relevant to research in infant temperament, for they allow us to consider differences in infants' optimal levels or ranges of arousal. This is a convenient approach, for infants are often quite demonstrative concerning their location along a hedonic dimension. Thus, we may be able to assess infants' optimal levels through their expressions of positive and negative affect, as well as through the utilization of approach and avoidance behaviors. Such an analysis in turn allows us to appreciate the great variability in the use and effectiveness of these regulatory strategies, almost to the point where they seem to overshadow the reactive elements.

J. A. Gray (1971, 1972, 1973) has offered a revision of Eysenck's (1967) model that moves away from the emphasis on general reactivity, the reticular activating system, and optimal levels of stimulation. Instead, Gray focuses on the reactivity and interaction of three specific neural systems, including an approach system, a behavioral inhibition system, and an arousal system. Extraverts are hypothesized to be more reactive in terms of the approach system, involving the median forebrain bundle and lateral hypothalamus. Extraverts are also seen as more sensitive to signals of reward or nonpunishment, and the primary characteristic of their behavior is impulsivity. In contrast, introverts are thought to have more sensitive behavioral inhibition systems, whose circuits include the orbital frontal cortex, the medial septal area, and the hippocampus. Introverts are considered more susceptible to threats of punishment or nonreward, their behavior is correspondingly inhibited, and they are characterized by anxiety. In addition to influencing the directionality of behavior, the approach and behavioral inhibition systems both have a positive input into the arousal system, which functions to increase behavioral intensity or vigor via the reticular activating system.

By shifting emphasis from stimulus properties and the reticular activating system to the interaction between three neural systems, Gray's theory moves beyond contemporary optimal-level-of-arousal models. A very similar approach has been provided by Zuckerman (1979) to account for individual differences in "sensation seeking." Arousal is no longer seen to possess intrinsic affective or motivational value at low, medium, or high levels. The occurrence of approach or avoidance depends instead on the balance between co-occurring positive and negative emotional states associated with underlying approach and avoidance systems. Such an approach allows for a more flexible consideration of the behaviors demonstrated during infancy. Differences are not reduced to a single dimension of arousability, but instead, the relative sensitivities of two opposing regulatory circuits are emphasized. An infant may be highly arousable in the sense of having low reticular thresholds, and may still possess strong approach tendencies. In contrast, another child may function at a relatively low tonic level of arousal, but may still demonstrate an inclination for behavioral inhibition or avoidance. Furthermore, the greater structural specificity involved in Gray's model provides a much broader framework within which to relate the maturational and experiential aspects of temperament. Thus, we can view individual differences in the development of particular systems concerned with the regulation of reactivity.

The models of temperament proposed by Pavlov, Eysenck, and Gray demonstrate an increasing importance attributed to the regulatory functions. Pavlov's model features a primarily reactive organism, Eysenck emphasizes both the

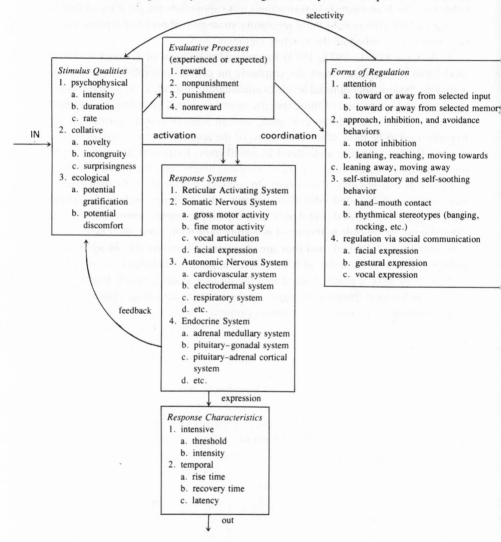

FIG. 2.1.   A framework for the study of temperament.

reactive and regulatory aspects of temperament, and Gray places more importance on self-regulatory mechanisms in delineating individual differences. In many ways, the process of development itself reflects a similar kind of transition. The newborn infant is primarily a reactive organism, responding to state and environmental changes in a relatively passive manner. Soon, however, the capacity for voluntary self-regulatory behavior emerges, and the infant begins to actively assume control over various aspects of self and environment. The progressive extension of such regulatory capacities, coupled with a progressive elaboration of reactive functioning, forms the basis of development.

Figure 2.1 represents a general, simplified summary of the framework we have presented. We suspect that constitutional variability may be encountered at each point in the diagram. In addition, the individual differences will be a function of the maturational status of the component functions. More specifically, it is assumed that the regulatory, coordinating functions mature subsequent to the reactive, activating components, and thus differences in the length of time between these sequential maturational events will be very important. We turn now to this developmental process.

TEMPERAMENT AND DEVELOPMENT

Development in the First Year

In this section, we would like to examine the reactive and self-regulatory aspects of temperament as they relate to the maturation of the nervous system. We argue that new and more complex forms of reactivity and self-regulation become functional throughout development. These changes are discussed loosely within the context of Hughlings Jackson's (1884, 1931) classic theory of brain development.

According to Jackson's model, a given function is represented hierarchically at different levels of the nervous system. The brain is postulated to mature rostrally from the caudal portion progressively to the cortex, with lower excitatory centers maturing earlier than forebrain inhibitory centers. As the higher levels mature, they mediate the functioning of lower levels through inhibitory control. This regulation is accomplished in an increasingly finely tuned fashion as maturation proceeds.

Given this idea of increasing modulation through forebrain structures, we might first look at a few of the lower-level excitatory influences relevant to temperament. Three of these ascending influences, in caudal to rostral sequence, include the norepinephrine, dopamine, and serotonin projections arising from the brain stem. The norepinephrine pathways have usually been associated with drive-reducing consummatory types of reward (Crow, 1973; Mogenson & Phillips, 1976), whereas dopamine appears related to drive-increasing incentive rewards (Crow, 1973; Olds, 1976). In contrast, serotonin has been found to be involved in punishment and the suppression of behavior (Stein, 1974; Wise, Berger & Stein, 1973).

It is not difficult to see the importance of the relative strengths and maturational status of these three chemical systems to early temperament. For example, maturation of the dopamine network may facilitate the reward value of goal-oriented behavior such as visually directed reaching. A perhaps more obvious example would involve the differential maturation of chemical networks mediating punishment and avoidance. Infants whose inhibitory systems are late in maturing may experience more positive interaction with objects before their approach behavior comes under the influence of increasing modulation.

Although additional research is required to clarify the structural and functional relationships of these transmitter systems (see Routtenberg & Santos-Anderson, 1977, and Gray, 1979, concerning the questionable rewarding effects of norepinephrine), we suspect they will prove highly significant in the development of temperament. It is unfortunate that the maturational status and relative levels of these chemical systems cannot yet be directly assessed in humans. However, peripheral measurements may help us to reflect back upon the central neurotransmitters. Porges (1976), for example, has proposed that peripheral assessment of sympathetic–parasympathetic balance within the autonomic nervous system may be useful as an index of catecholaminergic–cholinergic balance within the central nervous system. He provides evidence that sympathetic dominance is related to the disorder of hyperactivity, parasympathetic dominance to psychopathy, and high levels of plasma serotonin to autism. Rapoport, Pandoni, Renfield, Lake, and Ziegler (1977) have found low significant correlations between plasma levels of dopamine–beta–hydroxylase (DBH) measured during the newborn period and measures of fussiness and irritability at 5 and 12 months of age. Since DBH is the enzyme which converts dopamine into norepinephrine, these results suggest that differences in the relative balance between the catecholamine transmitters may be related to the infants' emotionality.

Studies with adults (Murphy, Belmaker, Buchsbaum, Martin, Ciaranello, & Wyatt, 1977; Schooler, Zahn, Murphy, & Buchsbaum, 1978) have found significant negative correlations between the trait of "sensation seeking" and platelet monoamine oxidase (MAO), an enzyme that degrades norepinephrine. Sostek, Sostek, Murphy, Martin, and Born (1980) have recently examined the relationship between platelet MAO and newborn characteristics as assessed by Brazelton's Neonatal Behavioral Assessment Scale. Infants with lower platelet MAO were found to be more highly aroused and more difficult to soothe than those with higher MAO activity. For a model of temperament attempting to integrate Gray's (1973) neural systems with the neurotransmitter systems (including neuroregulators such as MAO and the gonadal hormones), we refer the reader to Zuckerman's (1979) discussion of sensation seeking.

More concrete forms of early excitatory response can be seen in the young infant's motor, electro–cortical, and autonomic response systems. For example, a variety of brain-stem reflexes, such as the Moro, Babinski, and palmar grasp are readily activated during the early months, but become progressively inhibited as the infant grows older. Such inhibition has been seen as reflecting increasing forebrain control over lower motor centers (Parmelee & Michaelis, 1971; Peiper, 1963). There is also an increasing organization of the infant's state with maturation. For example, behavioral activity accompanying sleep decreases across the first 2 months of life (Emde, Gaensbauer, & Harmon, 1976), undifferentiated REM states diminish (Emde & Metcalf, 1970), quiet sleep increases greatly (Dittrichova & Lapackova, 1969; Parmelee, Wenner, Akiyama, Schultz, & Stern, 1967), and the infant becomes able to sustain longer periods of sleep (Emde et al., 1976). Another change occurring around 2 months of age involves the easier elicitation of a deceleratory heart-rate response. Graham and Jackson (1970) suggest this change may reflect the maturation of limbic and cortical areas presumed to control the cardiovascular system.

These examples of progressive inhibitory control over already existing excitatory processes have been considered by theorists of infant development to reflect a major biobehavioral transition occurring between 2 and 3 months of age. Emde (1977) characterizes this transition as a shift from endogenous to exogenous control—that is, behavior becomes less a function of internal state and endogenous rhythms and more a function of external stimulation and environmental conditions. Individual differences in the occurrence of this shift or in the maturation of the specific neural structures involved can have important effects on the young infant's experience. For example, the shift is accompanied by a decrease in nonhunger fussiness (Emde et al., 1976; Tennes et al., 1972). According to Benjamin (1965), maturation of subcortical input pathways at about the age of 3–4 weeks leaves the child especially vulnerable to arousing effects of stimulation, as evidenced in bouts of paroxysmal crying and general fussiness. By the age of 8–10 weeks, however, a "stimulus barrier" becomes functional and the forebrain acquires increased inhibitory control over subcortical excitation. Benjamin hypothesizes that individual differences in the impact and duration of the vulnerable period might have predictive value for the predisposition to anxiety. Tennes et al. (1972) have explored Benjamin's model empirically, suggesting that an active stimulus barrier does not become well established until the fourth month of life.

Benjamin's model is important in that it emphasizes the sequential emergence of both reactive and regulatory processes; the child becomes vulnerable to new forms of arousal only later to acquire appropriate regulatory capacity. The maturation of the cortex is particularly important in the emergence of new kinds of reactivity and control. For example, increasing maturation of the primary sensory areas allows for finer resolution of "psychophysical" stimulus properties such as complexity and rate. This development appears to be related to fixation time for complex visual patterns (Karmel & Maisel, 1975), and perception of higher levels of complexity represents an increasing source of arousal for the infant.

The "arousal potential" of the environment is also elaborated through maturation of the cortical processes involved in the storage of information. These include the "collative" forms of arousal associated with misexpectation. As the cortex matures and memory capacities increase, incoming information is matched against stored schemes or models. If a mismatch occurs, orienting and related arousal processes are elicited, the intensity of which may depend on the degree of mismatch. Thus, infants with more mature memory capacities will be more sensitive to environmental properties such as novelty, surprisingness, and incongruity, and are likely to experience more of the associated forms of arousal than less mature infants. They may become aroused and possibly distressed if the discrepancy is unassimilable (Kagan, 1974). On the other hand, the more mature infant's arousal may result in positive affect, as in instances of "effortful assimilation" (Kagan, 1971; Oster, 1978).

A related form of cortically mediated reactivity involves the meaning of a stimulus or event. As the infant becomes able to relate present events to stored associates and to form anticipations, new sources of emotional arousal become available. For example, at a relatively early age positive affect will come to be associated with the preparation of food, with the infant becoming excited in anticipation of the pleasurable event. This would be an example of Berlyne's "ecological" stimulus properties, through which stimuli associated with biologically important occurrences elicit arousal. At a later age, the infant who can infer the caregiver's approaching departure may activate negative affect related to the caregiver's past absence and thereby become distressed.

These examples of maturing forms of reactivity appear to be related to a second developmental transition appearing between 7 and 9 months of age (Emde, 1977; Kagan, Kearsley, & Zelazo, 1978; McCall, Eichorn & Hogarty, 1977). This increase in reactivity has been observed in connection with the appearance of such behaviors as fear of strangers, separation distress, wariness, and latency of approach to novel objects. If there is variability in the timing of this transition (Wilson, 1978), we might expect that individual differences in the time of occurrence of these shifts may result in major differences in temperamental behavior and experience at any given point. Though slower maturers might develop the maturationally advanced behavior patterns at a later point, we might expect that the quality of experience of early- and late-maturing infants would vary in the intervening period. For example, the later-maturing infants might be expected to experience greater interaction with and habituation to novel objects during this period than the earlier-maturing infants. The earlier-maturing infants, on the other hand, might be expected to develop enhanced self-regulatory capacities for coping with their greater reactivity.

The self-regulatory capacities facilitated through forebrain maturation are extremely important to the infant's developing temperament. We have already considered some of these, such as the increasing organization of infant state. Others, including finer control of motor, vocal, and attentional mechanisms, play more crucial roles in the child's regulation of self and environment. For example, cortical contributions to motor coordination facilitate the approach and avoidance reactions involved in grasping, manipulating, and locomotion. The child with early-maturing locomotor skills will have greater resources for exploring or avoiding environmental stimuli.

Although we have thus far emphasized the development of finer sensory discrimination and motor control involved in forebrain maturation, the concept of self-regulation becomes most powerful when the infant's developing attentional capacities are taken into consideration. During the early months of life, infants' visual attention is often "captured" by exogenous stimulation, a phenomenon that appears to result in increased arousal and distress (Stechler & Latz, 1966; Tennes et al., 1972). Development during infancy in many ways reflects the infant's bringing various peripheral mechanisms, such as the eyes, the head, and the hands under the endogenous control of developing cortical attentional mechanisms (Bruner, 1968; Posner & Rothbart, in press).

Variability in the age at which endogenous attentional mechanisms assume volitional control over the oculomotor system, thereby allowing for more selective visual attention, will profoundly affect the reactivity and experience of the infant. In addition to determining what to attend to, self-regulation may also come to involve how much attention is allocated to particular sensory channels. During later infancy, as the child becomes able to orient attention to the semantic memory system, further and more flexible modes of self-regulation become available. The child can then selectively attend to positively toned structures so as to offset the impact of less-than-optimal environmental conditions. For example, the distressed child may be able to orient to the image of the absent caregiver or to think about the caregiver's return, thereby attaining some degree of comfort and relief. One source of possible stability in self-regulatory processes may be found in the relationship between early individual differences in attentional strategies and later cognitive controls or cognitive "styles." Early differences in the sensitivity and intensity of attentional systems, along with the child's practice in selective deployment of attention under arousing circumstances, may establish strategies for future selection of information (Santostefano, 1978). These strategies are extremely important, not only in extracting information from the environment, but also in dealing with information related to self-evaluation.

The picture we have presented of maturation is one involving the development of higher and higher levels of control over basically reactive processes. As we have seen, however, the process is not only one of increasing regulation, for new and more complex forms of reactivity emerge with development. Nor is maturational process by any means complete after the first year of life; the nervous system continues to mature for several decades (Yakovlev & Lecours, 1967), and capacities emerging during infancy continue to develop, particularly during the early years. Issues of self-control remain of central importance in individual differences reflected during the preschool and early school years (Block & Block, 1979). Essential to the continuing development of temperament-related behavior is the balance between maturing reactive processes and capacities for self-regulation.

Although we have stressed maturational change in our description of the first year of life, developmental changes must always be seen as occurring within the context of experience. For example, a highly reactive child in an extremely stimulating environment might be expected to develop more self-regulatory controls than either a highly reactive child in a quiet environment or a less reactive child under high levels of stimulation.

The child's systems of reactivity and self-regulation must also be seen to operate within a larger social system involving the caregiver. From the outset, the caregiver serves as a source of both stimulation and regulation for the infant. In fact, the infant's reactions of distress and smiling and laughter have direct effects on the caregiver's regulative acts—in the case of distress, eliciting soothing ministrations, and in the case of smiling and laughter, the continued presentation of stimulation (Rothbart, 1973). The emotional responses of the child may thus be seen as conveying information about the infant's condition to the caregiver. The caregiver then provides regulations based on this information. In the context of the larger social system, we might expect a child whose caregivers provide regulatory soothing whenever the infant is upset to be less likely to practice means of self-soothing and more likely to look to others for comfort when distressed. The child who is rarely soothed will either develop effective self-soothing techniques, or experience extended periods of distress.

Temperamental Stability

The framework for temperament we have proposed and the developmental context in which it is placed suggest the great importance of undertaking multivariate longitudinal studies in this area. The child's temperament develops over time and is influenced by maturation in the context of experience. In order to understand temperament, we need to be able to identify both developmental changes in reactivity and self-regulation and the sources of those changes. This view conflicts with Buss and Plomin's (1975) decision to make lifespan stability a requisite for temperament. However, at the same time it suggests that during periods when there are no major maturational shifts or changes in environmental conditions, stabilities in temperament will be found.

We also expect that, even with maturational or experiential transitions in temperament, a child's previous temperamental characteristics will constrain the changes in behavior that can occur over time. Viewed in this way, temperament at time 1 will delimit the range of possible changes by time 2. As yet, we do not know the rules for these changes, but their identification should be a primary focus of future longitudinal study.

Our view also implies that our understanding of instabilities in temperament through longitudinal research will greatly enhance our knowledge of temperament. To insist on lifetime stability as a criterion for temperament is to insist that differences in early temperament remain unperturbed by either maturational development or by the quality of the infant's experience, and we do not believe this to be the case.

TEMPERAMENT AND SOCIAL BEHAVIOR

In each of our descriptions of response characteristics and response modalities of temperament, we have proposed illustrations of the ways in which infant temperament may influence infant-caregiver interaction. We have also argued in the last section that the infant's developing reactivity and self-regulation must be viewed within the larger caregiver-infant social system, with the caregiver serving to both stimulate and regulate the infant.

We now suggest a major way in which a view of individual differences in temperament must affect our thinking about the child's social environment. We then use the concept of temperament in order to reconsider one of the classic problems in social development—that is, the question of the development of attachment.

Temperament and the Effective Social Environment

In Escalona's important book on infant development, *The Roots of Individuality* (1968), she proposes that objective coding of the parents' behaviors fails to record the most important aspect of the social interaction for the child—namely, the child's subjective experience in social interaction. Thus, objectively identical environments may have quite different effects on the experience of two children who differ in reactivity and self-regulation, and two objectively different environments may have quite similar effects on the experience of two children who differ from each other. Escalona (1968) describes two children who might be seen to live in quite different social environments:

One mother holds him often, speaks to him frequently, and in general maintains direct contact with him during most of his waking hours. She also tends to touch him vigorously, to speak or sing to him fairly loudly, and to be generally energetic in her dealings with him. The other mother holds and touches her infant only when it is necessary, leaves him alone unless he appears to be in bodily discomfort, and also happens to be very gentle in her approach. She is a mother who speaks softly, touches the baby gingerly, and so forth. The environments of these two infants differ in that one exposes the baby to frequent and fairly intense maternal ministrations, whereas the other offers the same type of stimulation only rarely, and then at a lower level of intensity. In terms of an objective description of what is provided by the milieu, they are at opposite extremes [p. 64].

Escalona further notes that these two children differ from each other, with one infant being more sensitive to perceptual stimulation than the other. If their experience can be assessed by describing their reactions to the situations, both infants may be observed to kick, wave their arms, vocalize, and chuckle. The experience of the two children is thus similar—that is, the *effective* social environment is the same, even though both the children's temperamental characteristics and their environments are different.

Over time, the affective and cognitive experiences of children in the effective social environment will influence their future reactions in similar situations. For example, to return to a consideration of simplified individual cases, we may consider the development of a withdrawal reaction to strangers in connection with individual temperament and experience. Child A is highly reactive and becomes distressed easily; he has had an experience with a stranger in which the stranger treated him gently, but he nevertheless became distressed. Child B is less reactive and not easily distressed, but she has had an experience with a stranger who treated her roughly and upset her. Both children now develop a similar pattern of withdrawal with strangers that does not allow them to experience the positive aspects of interaction with others. Child C is not highly reactive and has had an experience with the same stranger as Child A; the result was a positive interaction, with approach and smiling, which led to an extended satisfying interaction with the stranger, and did not detract from the child's future approach to strangers. In this example, similar patterns of experience have resulted from objectively different conditions of stimulation (Children A and B), and different patterns of experience have resulted from objectively similar conditions of stimulation (Children A and C). The intervening variable in both instances is the temperamental characteristics of the child.

The negative extreme of the continuum of caretaking casualty (Sameroff & Chandler, 1975) may be seen as providing an extended sequence of interactions resulting in repeated unfavorable experiences for the more vulnerable infant. In this view, patterns of experience for a given infant may be understood, to some extent, on the basis of characteristics of the child and of the caregiving environment, but they may also be seen as highly flexible, since the caregiver and/or the child may act to change the patterns of experience. If children are not highly effective in structuring their own social experience, as in the case of vulnerable infants, the caregiver's role becomes more important.

Temperament and Attachment

We now view some implications of individual differences in temperament for the development of attachment. We argue that the infant's temperament plays an important role in attachment. When attachment behaviors are viewed as maintaining or regaining "felt security" (Sroufe & Waters, 1977), their regulatory function becomes readily apparent. Unfortunately, many theorists in the area of attachment have neglected the child's temperamental capacities and limitations (e.g., Sroufe & Waters, 1977), and have thus overemphasized the role of the mother in the formation of the "attachment bond" (e.g., Ainsworth, 1973). Ainsworth (1973) has argued that whether a child becomes attached to another person depends on the sheer amount of time the two have spent together, but that the *quality* of attachment depends on the sensitivity of the mother to the infant's signals and the extent of separation experienced between mother and child. She suggests that either lack of maternal sensitivity or the experience of separation will lead to insecure attachment in the child; these are evident either as an apparent lack of involvement with the mother in the "strange situation" (Group A infants), or as insecurity during preseparation and as mixed anger and approach during reunion (Group C infants). Securely attached infants (Group B infants), on the other hand, show interest in the mother before her departure and positive greeting upon her return. In this traditional view of attachment, constitutional individual differences in the infants' reactivity under potentially stressful conditions have been neglected, as have been differences in infants' capacities for effective forms of self-regulation other than those we might refer to as "attachment behavior."

The nature of the mother–infant attachment process can differ in many ways in light of our discussion of temperament and social behavior. The role of the mother as a source of security or comfort depends not only on her sensitivity to the infant's signals, but also on the infant's requirements for such security. For example, some infants, with low or quickly recovering reactivity, may not require much maternal intervention and may not experience the felt insecurity that initiates regulatory or attachment behaviors. Other infants may be relatively reactive, but may require little intervention because of the efficacy of their own self-regulatory processes. Other relatively reactive infants may achieve security through attachment behaviors, and it is these infants who would be most likely to develop concepts of the mother as a source of comfort. Still other infants, due to high or poorly modulated reactivity, may find that even the mother's presence is not enough to overcome their feelings of distress. These 4 groups of infants would not demonstrate the same quality of attachment behavior, for they differ in both their reactive and regulatory predispositions under conditions of potential insecurity, and they differ in their construction of the mother as a source of comfort as well. Temperament thus plays an important part in the attachment process.

In addition to the infant's temperament, the mother's role (indeed, her own temperament) must also be taken into consideration in the developing attachment relationship. Caregivers do differ in their sensitivity to the infant's signals, and also in their potential for flexibly adjusting their ministrations to the child's needs.. These qualities will naturally affect the infant's perception of the caregiver as a source of comfort or stimulation. Also, mothers differ in their own characteristic reactivity and regulatory strategies, and thus they differ in the extent to which the infant becomes a source of comfort and stimulation to the mother. Finally, caregivers differ in the channels through which they prefer to attenuate or augment the child's reactivity. For example, some caregivers may favor the use of visual or auditory modalities in soothing the infant, while others may prefer utilizing tactile or kinesthetic channels of stimulation.

The developing attachment relationship must therefore be viewed from both the infant's and the caregiver's perspective. As important as the mother's sensitivity and flexibility may be, the role of the child's constitutional capacities and limitations in shaping her behavior should not be underestimated. Nor should the sensitivity and flexibility of the infant be neglected, for infants vary greatly in their capacity to augment or reduce their own reactivity, and to bring distress or pleasure to their caregivers. It seems essential that the mother–infant interaction and the resulting attachment process be viewed as a function of two intricate and flexible interactional systems, which can achieve a "balance" in a number of different ways.

This resultant balance involving contributions of both the infant and caregiver may demonstrate considerable stability over time. Such stability has been reported in Waters' (1978) finding of stable attachment patterns in the strange situation from 12–18 months, and in Matas, Arend, and Sroufe's (1978) findings of a relation between security of attachment at 18 months and reactions of children in a stressful problem-solving situation at 2 years of age. In the latter case, Matas et al. argue that the continuity is not the result of stability of "negative temperament"; however, the 2-year measures showing differences between children designated as secure and insecure at 18 months include crying and whining, positive affect, negative affect, frustration reactions, and aggression toward the mother, as well as enthusiasm for the task. For both the 18-month and the 2-year assessments, the child was accompanied by the mother in the laboratory situation, which may thus reflect characteristics of both the mother and the child under stressful circumstances.

Given the importance of temperament to social development, measures assessing the infant's temperament in the home have been much sought after for use in socialization research. In the next section, we review available measures in this area, suggesting some major cautions for researchers who wish to employ them.

HOME ASSESSMENT OF TEMPERAMENT

Problems in Home Assessment of Temperament

Although it has been the hope of researchers developing parent-report measures and observing temperament-related behavior in the home to tap the temperamental characteristics of the child, it is clear that a report of the infant's behavior in the home will reflect much more than this. At the least, the infant's behavior represents the child's own balance of reaction and self-regulation set within the regulating and arousing social context of the family. Caregiver behavior in this system is in turn affected by stressful or benign circumstances such as unemployment, moving, divorce, or financial status, impinging from the larger social order on the family unit.

Aside from possible response biases in the parent (discussed by Bates, in press), either the caregiver report or observation of temperament-related behavior in the home assesses the results of a complex of social and constitutional factors. Temperament as assessed in the home thus cannot represent an *independent* contribution of the child to family interaction.

We might expect, for example, that parents who engage in more highly arousing and stimulating games when bathing their children might have infants who either laugh or become distressed in the bath more often than parents who rub their infants with a wet cloth before putting them into the bath water, and then bathe them without talking or playing with them. If we were to ask two different caregivers who interacted with a child on different occasions about the child's behavior, we should expect some lack of agreement about the child's behavior due not only to differences between the 2 adult–child systems of interaction, but also to differences between the adults as observers.

These considerations concerning home assessment of temperament suggest that we cannot assess a child's temperament in the home separately from the interactive system of which the infant is a part, and that scales of infant temperament derived from the home observation may therefore not be used as independent predictions of the infant's contribution to caregiver–infant interaction. To the extent that such temperament measures are validated, they may be used for comparisons of group similarities and/or differences (e.g., sex differences [Carey & McDevitt, 1978; Rothbart et al., 1977], or differences between Down's syndrome and normal infants [Hanson, 1979]). In these cases, however, interpretations of results should bear in mind that the scales measure the infant's behavior as seen in a particular social system involving caregivers and siblings. Studies of longitudinal stability and instability of such measures are also of interest (Rothbart, 1980).

Keeping these cautions in mind, we now review some of the parent-report and home-observation measures of infant temperament presently available. This review does not include teacher report measures of child temperament.

Caregiver Report and Home Observation of Infant Temperament

Traditional measures of infant temperament beyond the neonatal period (see St. Clair, 1978, for a review of neonatal measures) have used parent report to assess the temperamental characteristics of the child. The first attempt at large-scale longitudinal assessment of infant temperament was the study of Thomas et al. (1963, 1968). Their study is described in detail here, because it has been most influential in later research in this area. Thomas et al.'s research sample was drawn from middle- and upper middle-class families, predominantly Jewish, living in New York City. One hundred-forty one children from 85 families were involved in the study. Parent interviews were the major source of data on children in the first 2 years; detailed accounts of the infants' reactivity to everyday situations were elicited through extensive probing. After a content analysis of the first 22 children's protocols, Thomas et al. (1963) extracted categories meeting their criteria of being scorable for all protocols and allowing sufficiently wide distribution of scores to permit comparison of infants on the dimensions. They thereby identified the following nine characteristics for further analysis: (1) activity level; (2) rhythmicity of body functions (e.g., eating, elimination, and sleep); (3) approach versus withdrawal from new objects or persons; (4) adaptability to changes in the environment; (5) threshold for response; (6) intensity of response; (7) general mood; (8) distractibility; and (9) attention span and persistence. A three-point scale was devised for each of these variables, and a child's protocol (i.e., a complete written transcript of the interview) was scored for all possible behavior items that might be assessed for a particular category. Thus, a mother might respond to the question, "What does your child do when his nails are being cut?" with the answer, "He kicks and whimpers." This statement was scored as high activity, negative mood, and mild intensity. Since any given statement was frequently scored in two, three, or more categories, some intercorrelation of measures would be expected as a result of the method. After a protocol had been scored nine times, once for each variable, a preponderance score was determined for each scale by tallying the frequencies of high, medium, and low responses for the child.

Thomas and Chess (1977) computed correlations on pooled temperament scores for years 1 to 5. They reported low to moderately significant correlations from one year to the next for all variables except approach/withdrawal, distractibility and persistence. As the time span of their predictions increased, the number of significant correlations decreased, until only threshold showed a significant correlation from year 1 to year 5. Both activity level and adaptability showed patterns of significant stability correlations from one year to the next.

Thomas et al. (1968) also identified approximately 40% of their sample as "easy" children, whom they stated were characterized by positive mood, regular body functions, low to moderate intensity of reaction, adaptability, and approach to new situations. A second group, approximately 10% of their sample, were described as "difficult" children: Irregular in body function, intense in reactions, slow to adapt, tending to withdraw from new stimuli, and generally negative in mood. A third type of child was also identified, labeled "slow to warm up," with low activity level, a tendency to withdraw from new situations, negative mood, and low-intensity response. The origins of these designations is not altogether clear; for example, we do not know whether the method used to assign children to these categories was a clinical procedure or whether it was based on temperament scores (Bates, in press). Although it is generally believed that "difficult" infants had a greater chance of developing behavior problems, neither individual temperament scales indicating difficulty nor their factor A (including approach, adaptability, intensity, and mood as measured in infancy) were significant predictors of childhood problems. However, factor A and some individual scales showed stability from age 3 to age 4 (Bates, in press).

The Thomas et al. research has been extremely important in the study of infant temperament, but there are problems in interpreting the results. First, it is impossible to determine the extent of homogeneity within any given behavior scale: For example, if activity is rarely mentioned by the mother, a high score on activity could result from activity only during the feeding situation. Items intuitively assigned to measure intensity were also combined for a score on that dimension, but without determining whether the combined behaviors are, in fact, positively correlated with each other. Second, a possible source of confounding exists in the fact that both descriptions of the child's temperament and referrals of the child as a behavior problem were done by the parent: The mother's attitudes toward her child may have influenced both her description of the child and her tendency to refer him or her for treatment. Third, the subjects ranged in age from 2 months to 6 months at the time of the first interview, with subsequent interviews held at 3-month intervals. Some of the subjects were thus considerably older than other subjects during all phases of the study, so that age differences possibly confounded the findings of actual individual differences among the children. Finally, the New York sample was highly restricted with respect to SES and ethnic group; a number of subjects in the study came from the same families.

The New York Longitudinal Study has had far-reaching effects on subsequent research on temperament in young children. In fact, since the Thomas et al. research, most of the instruments developed for research in infant temperament have attempted to assess the nine variables originally identified in the New York Longitudinal Study.

Scarr and Salapatek (1970) chose items, based on examples from Thomas et al.'s 1963 book, to which mothers were asked to respond "mostly true" or "mostly false." Children in the study ranged in age from 2 months to 24 months. Item analyses for 70 mothers' responses to these items yielded correlations of items with total scores ranging from .15 to .55; reliabilities of scales were not reported. Scales measuring mood, threshold, adaptability, and rhythmicity showed significant relations with the child's fear reactions as assessed in the laboratory.

The Scarr–Salapatek questionnaire has not been used in subsequent studies of infant temperament, but a questionnaire devised by Carey (1970) has been widely used. Carey developed a 70-item questionnaire primarily as a clinical screening device. Nine scales measured the variables identified by Thomas et al. in the New York study. No item analysis was carried out for the original instrument. Carey administered the questionnaire to 101 mothers of infants between the ages of 4 and 8 months, and reported that the questionnaire was especially useful in detecting babies with the "difficult baby syndrome" as defined by Thomas et al. "Difficult babies" were estimated to comprise approximately 10% of Carey's (1970) sample.

More recently, Carey and McDevitt (1978) revised the original scale, with standardization based on 203 4–8-month-old infants in three suburban pediatric practices. They report internal consistency estimates (statistic unspecified) for the nine Thomas et al. scales ranging from .49 to .71, with a median of .57. Carey and McDevitt also use their scale to classify children as "easy," "difficult," "slow-to-warm-up," and "intermediate." For example, a child is scored "difficult" if four or five scores are greater than the normative means for the categories rhythmicity, approach, adaptability, intensity, and mood. These must include the intensity category, and two of the category scores must be greater than one standard deviation from the mean.

Pederson, Anderson, and Cain (1976) developed a Q-sort measure for assessing parents' perceptions of the nine categories of temperament identified by Thomas et al. (1963, 1968). Both parents from 26 families were given 54 items to sort into categories "Very much like my baby," "Sometimes or occasionally like my baby," and "Not at all like my baby," or "Have no experience with this." Pederson et al. report corrected split-half reliabilities for the dimensions of activity, rhythmicity, adaptability, approach, and positive mood ranging from .54 to .69, with a median of .60. They had less success measuring threshold, persistence, distractibility, and intensity, with corrected split-half correlations ranging from .31 to .48, and a median of .40. The New York Longitudinal

Study variables have also been used as the basis for questionnaires in Swedish (Hagekull, Bohlin, & Lindhagen, 1979; Persson-Blennow & McNeil, 1979) and an interview schedule in Norwegian (Torgersen & Kringlen, 1978).

Bates and his associates (Bates, Freeland, & Lounsbury, 1979) have attempted to further explore the dimension of infant "difficultness" originally identified in the Thomas et al. studies (1963, 1968). Bates et al. have developed a caregiver rating instrument, the Infant Characteristics Questionnaire (ICQ), consisting of 24 items scored on seven-point scales. The responses of 322 mothers of 4–6-month-old infants were factor analyzed, yielding four factors labeled by Bates as: (1) Fussy/Difficult; (2) Unadaptable; (3) Dull; and (4) Unpredictable. Internal consistency reliabilities for the factors assessed through coefficient alpha were computed for a cross-validational sample with coefficients ranging from .39 to .79 for the four factors measured by the test, and a median coefficient alpha of .63. Bates et al. (1979) are the only researchers to have described in detail their study of the correlation between parent-reported temperament and the observed behavior of infants. This research is reported in the later section, *Validation of Parent-Report Measures.*

Not all current research on infant temperament has derived from the dimensions identified by the Thomas et al. (1963, 1968) research. In a 1957 book, *Personality and Temperament,* Diamond reviewed comparative as well as human studies on individual differences in order to extract hypotheses about fundamental dimensions of temperamental variability. On the basis of his review, Diamond identified four dimensions of temperamental variability: fearfulness, aggressiveness, affiliativeness, and impulsiveness. Beginning with Diamond's conceptual work, and after carrying out their own heritability study on a wide age range of children, Buss and Plomin (1975) argued that there are three, possibly four, inherited "temperaments": emotionality (consisting of Diamond's combined fear and aggressiveness), activity, sociability, and perhaps impulsivity. Their criteria for a temperament are that it be stable across the life span and that it has demonstrated heritability.

Buss and Plomin (1975) carried out a behavior-genetics study with 139 pairs of same-sex twins, whose ages ranged from 1 to 9 years. These children's temperamental characteristics were assessed by an inventory involving global parent judgments of children's characteristics (e.g., indicating level of agreement with statements such as "Learning self-control is difficult for the child" and "Child tends to be impulsive"). Factor analysis indicated that the four factors previously described accounted for the majority of the variance on their scale; comparison of the correlations between monozygotic and dizygotic pairs of twins indicated significantly higher concordance for identical twins on emotionality, activity, and sociability scores for both sexes and for impulsivity scores for boys only. One problem with this study is that the pattern of monozygotic and dizygotic correlations would not be predicted by any simple genetic model (Goldsmith & Gottesman, 1977).

We (Rothbart, 1979, 1980, in press; Rothbart, Furby, Kelly and Hamilton, 1977) have based our empirical work on a combination of the dimensions suggested by the New York group, Diamond's work, and other animal heritability work and human twin studies (Fuller & Thompson, 1960; Gray, 1971). The first stage of our research has involved development of a parent-report temperament measure, the Infant Behavior Questionnaire, to be used with 3-, 6-, 9-, and 12-month-old infants. In an attempt to avoid the problems of previous parent-report measures, items on the Infant Behavior Questionnaire were developed that referred to specific behaviors of infants, and caregivers were asked to respond to the items on the basis of the infant's behavior during the previous week (or for some items, the previous 2 weeks). For example, the respondent is asked: "During the past week, when being undressed, how often did your baby: Wave his/her arms and kick?" Response options on a seven-point scale range from Never (1) to Always (7). In a questionnaire item-refinement study (Rothbart, in press), 463 questionnaires were filled out by parents of 3-, 6-, 9-, and 12-month-old infants. Only items correlating .20 or better with scale scores for a given age were retained. Three scales were eliminated because of unsatisfactory item–scale correlations and internal reliability: threshold, rhythmicity, and distractibility. Scales with adequate psychometric and conceptual properties were developed for the following dimensions: activity level, soothability, fear (distress and latency to approach intense or novel stimuli), distress to limitations (anger/frustration), smiling and laughter, and duration of orienting. Coefficient alphas for these scales were computed as a measure of internal reliability. Mean item–scale correlations for the temperament scales ranged from .41 to .77. Coefficient alphas for temperament scales ranged from .67 to .85, with a median of .80.

We now consider some of the current methodological problems in the assessment of infant temperament in the home. In particular, because most research to date has involved the use of parent report, we must consider possible problems associated with parent-report measures.

Characteristics of Parent-Report Instruments

Parent-report instruments differ on the specificity of items. Buss and Plomin (1975) ask parents for highly general judgments about their children, Carey and McDevitt (1978) and Rothbart (in press) use specific behavioral items to assess temperamental characteristics, and Bates et al. (1979) use items varying in the specificity of response required.

Parent-report instruments vary in the extent to which conceptual overlap exists between temperament dimensions. For example, the Thomas et al. (1963, 1968) and Carey and McDevitt (1978) dimensions of approach, mood, and adaptability overlap with each other. Buss and Plomin (1975) have attempted to identify orthogonal temperaments in their factor analytic research, whereas we (Rothbart, in press) have attempted to develop operational definitions of temperament scales that do not conceptually overlap. This allows testing of empirical relations using scales that do not contain overlapping items.

Homogeneity of scale items is a basic criterion for test construction (Nunnally, 1978) and most researchers have attempted to determine the extent to which scales are composed of homogeneous items, usually through computation of coefficient alpha. To date, it is chiefly in connection with the dimension of intensity that items have been combined before item analyses have been performed. Scales of specific dimensions vary, however, in their extent of homogeneity as assessed by item analysis and coefficient alpha.

Parent report instruments also vary in the value connotations of labels they use to describe dimensions of temperament (scale scores), composite ratings (e.g., designation of the "difficult" child), and factor scores. Although the labels assigned to dimension scores generally do not have strong value connotations, dimension labels such as "adaptability," "attention span," and "persistence" may be seen to connote positive characteristics. Buss and Plomin's (1975) "impulsivity" and "sociability" are both value-connotative labels. The most frequent use of value-connotative labels has been in connection with the "difficult" and "easy" composite scores developed by Carey and McDevitt (1978) based on the Thomas et al. work (1968), and the factor scores of Bates et al. (1979) labeled "fussy/difficult," "unadaptable," "dull," and "unpredictable."

The term "difficult" implies a judgment on someone's part that an infant is causing problems for his or her caregiver(s). When Bates et al. (1979) use the term, they are tapping parents' attitudes about the difficulty of their infant's behavior. When Thomas et al. (1968) or Carey and McDevitt (1978) use the "difficult," "easy," and "slow-to-warm-up" labels, they are acting as clinicians making judgments that a child is more or less difficult to care for than other infants. This judgment may or may not correspond to attitudes of the infants' caregivers about the difficulty of the child.

However, a note must be made about the advisability of using the "difficult" label to characterize infants. Such a term may encourage observers of a child thus labeled to focus on negative characteristics of the infant, leading to possible self-fulfilling prophecies of problem behavior. The label "difficult" may also connote the existence of child "difficulty" in areas not intended by the investigators who developed the term. In addition, there is no reason to believe that the same characteristic will connote "difficulty" at all ages and in all situations. The infant who is "easy" because s/he is easily distracted from prohibited activities may at a later age have difficulty finishing tasks as a result of the same characteristic. Finally, Bates' (in press) review of research on difficult temperament suggests that the concept does not have a strong empirical base, and argues that "difficulty" should be seen as an important social perception of the adult informant rather than as an inherent characteristic of the child. This perception may in turn, however, prove to be an important predictor of later problem behavior in the child.

Validation of Parent-Report Measures

As yet, there have been few attempts at external validation of parent-reported infant temperament. Bates et al. (1979), however, report significant correlations between mothers' reports of infant temperament characteristics and fathers' reports on the same infants. In our research (Rothbart, 1980), a subsample of 22 mothers filled out the Infant Behavior Questionnaire along with a second adult in the household (father or babysitter) who spent time caring for the infant. Household agreement product–moment correlations for all six scales were significant, ranging from .45 (smiling and laughter) to .69 (activity level), with a median of .60. Hanson (1979; Rothbart & Hanson, 1980) has also found predicted differences between a sample of Down's syndrome and normal infants on smiling and laughter (greater for normal infants) and duration of orienting (greater for Down's syndrome infants at 6 and 9 months).

Although Thomas et al. (1968) report agreement "at the .01 level" between scoring of parental interviews and direct home observation of the child, Bates et al. (1979) and Rothbart (1980) are the only researchers to have described in detail their study of the correlation between parent-reported temperament and the observed behavior of infants. Bates et al. attempted to predict mothers' perceptions of their infants' difficultness from: (1) independently observed behavior of the infant in the home; (2) mothers' parity; and (3) mothers' personality characteristics. They report low but significant correlations between parent reports and infant behaviors, but found in a multiple regression analysis that mothers' parity and self-reported extraversion and achievement orientation best predicted their perception of difficultness in their infants, with independently observed fussiness of the infant making only a questionable contribution.

When observer *ratings* rather than observed behavior scores were entered into the regression equation, the observer's rating of fussy/difficult did make a positive contribution to the prediction of mothers' ratings of difficultness, in addition to the variables just listed. This might be expected, since the observers' ratings were made on a scale identical to the mothers' ratings, and the scale may have tapped aspects of the child's behavior not measured by the observation codes. For example, it is possible that unpleasant qualities of the infant's cry may have affected mothers' and observers' ratings of "difficulty," but may not have been captured by the observation code. Lounsbury (1978) has reported evidence to suggest that the cries of infants rated "difficult" by their parents are acoustically differentiable from cries of infants rated "average" or "easy." In general, Bates et al.'s findings support the position that parents' perception of "difficult" behaviors in the infant reflect characteristics of the parent as well as observable behavior of the infant.

In the second phase of our own research (Rothbart, 1980), we have collected data on a longitudinal sample, examining the level of convergence between the Infant Behavior Questionnaire and independent home observations of infant temperament, and studying stability of caretaker–reported temperament and observed temperament in 46 infants seen at 3, 6, and 9 months of age. Three home observations were made within a 2-week period for each subject at each age, with infants and their mothers observed during feeding, bathing, dressing, and play. We also gathered reliability data based on a sample of 24 home observations for each of our measures. Home-observation measures were calculated for each day of observation. We then computed the mean across 3 days of observation to use for data analysis. Reliability data is reported in the left-hand side of Table 2.1.

Product–moment correlations between Infant Behavior Questionnaires and home-observations scores are also shown in Table 2.1, uncorrected for the unreliability of the measures. Correlations between questionnaires and home observations were low, with significant correlations for only the two distress scales at 3 months ($r = .44$ and $.24$) and for distress to limitations ($.24$) and activity level ($.34$) at 6 months. Correlations at 9 months were significantly positive for fear ($r = .38$), activity level ($.35$), and smiling and laughter ($.50$). We were not able to reliably measure soothability or duration of orienting in the home.

Although the correlations between home observation and parent report are modest, we did not expect the two measures to show a great deal of overlap. First, the questionnaire covers a much wider range of stimulus situations than we were able to observe in the home. Second, the parents are basing their report on a much longer time period than even our three visits allow. Third, we expect that

TABLE 2.1
Reliabilities and Product–Moment Correlations Between
Home Observation and Infant Behavior Questionnaire (IBQ)

Observation Interrater Correlation	Mean Correlation Across Observations	Mean Coefficient Alpha: IBQ	Dimension	3 Months	6 Months	9 Months
.90	.30	.77	Activity level	.15	.34[b]	.35[b]
.88	.37	.78	Smiling and laughter	.17	.21	.50[b]
.85	.32	.82	Fear	.44[b]	.01	.38[b]
.36	.30	.80	Distress to limitations	.24[a]	.24[a]	.09

[a]$p<.05$ (one-tailed tests).
[b]$p<.01$ (one-tailed tests).

mothers' and infants' reactions to the presence of an observer will influence home-observation scores. Nevertheless, the measures show some convergence and also quite similar patterns of longitudinal stability and developmental change.

In this regard, we have assessed the interindividual stability of temperament scores from one age to another based on both the observation and questionnaire measures; these are reported in Table 2.2. For the observation measures, there are significant but low correlations across all three ages for both activity level and smiling and laughter. Fear showed a significant correlation only from 3–6 months, whereas distress to limitations showed stability only from 6–9 months. Patterns of significant stability correlations were similar for the parent-report measure, with the exception of fear and smiling and laughter between 6 and 9 months, where a positive correlation was found for parent report but not for observational data.

Although this research indicates some agreement between parents and observers concerning temperament in the home and some stability of parent-reported and observed temperament over the first year, we realize that such stability will also reflect the kind of stimulating environment provided for the child as well as the temperamental characteristics of the infant. Some parents and older siblings provide high levels of stimulation for the infant, whereas other home environments are quiet, with emphasis on soothing the infant. Another problem in connection with home observation of temperament is that infants' reactions occur rapidly and a coder might be unable to capture important aspects of an infant's behavior in one viewing.

In order to more precisely assess temperament under controlled conditions, we are now collecting videotaped longitudinal laboratory data on infants' reactivity to stimuli varying in intensity and modality. This allows assessment of infant temperamental characteristics when the child is reacting to controlled stimuli.

TABLE 2.2
Stability Product–Moment Correlations

	3–6 Months		6–9 Months		3–9 Months	
	Home Obs.	IBQ	Home Obs.	IBQ	Home Obs.	IBQ
Activity level	.35[b]	.60[b]	.27[a]	.63[b]	.28[a]	.37[b]
Smiling and laughter	.31[a]	.48[b]	.48[b]	.48[b]	.10	.48[b]
Fear	.31[a]	.37[b]	.18	.37[b]	.12	.21
Distress to limitations	.18	.44[b]	.32[a]	.51[b]	.05	.16

[a]$p < .05$ (one-tailed tests).
[b]$p < .01$ (one-tailed tests).

Summary and Conclusions

Beginning with the work of Thomas and Chess (Thomas & Chess, 1977; Thomas et al., 1963, 1968) on parent interviews, considerable progress has been made in the development of caregiver report instruments for the assessment of infant temperament. These instruments differ in the specificity of items, the conceptual overlap among temperament dimensions, in scale homogeneity, and in value connotations of dimension labels. Validation research indicates moderate agreement between members of the same household reporting on the same infant. Agreement between home observation and parent report shows some convergence, but correlations are not high.

We would argue that parent-report measures show some promise for characterizing the infant's behavioral reactivity and self-regulation as seen in the home environment. This behavior must always be seen as part of a system involving caregivers, siblings, and the physical environment of the home. Caregiver report measures will be especially useful for group comparisons—for example, characterizing the behavior of prematures in comparison with a matched group of full-term infants at different ages. However, we caution against the use of such measures as assessments of child temperament independent of the social environment. For independent assessment of temperament, the presentation of a controlled set of stimuli is necessary. Because it is difficult to administer the number of behavioral items necessary for an independent assessment of infant temperament, however, this will probably rarely be done.

SUMMARY AND CONCLUSIONS

This chapter has attempted to view the development of temperament within psychobiological, maturational, and social–experiential perspectives. These three approaches have been brought together in a focus emphasizing the emergence and continuing development of reactive and regulatory processes. Because temperamental factors underlie so much of the infant's affective, cognitive, and social behavior, the task of adequately describing their development requires a consideration of nearly all aspects of early behavior.

We have argued that previously delineated dimensions of temperament can be viewed as expressions of underlying reactive and self-regulatory processes. These processes differ in their intensive and temporal characteristics, and also in the response modalities through which they are expressed. Such a multivariate approach seems necessary for a description of the full range and influence of individual differences. It also allows for a more adequate consideration of temperament within a psychobiological context. Thus, we have spoken of individual differences in the relative strengths, temporal dynamics, and sequencing of neural systems. The biological framework in turn allows for a maturational perspective. In terms of reactivity, for example, we have mentioned the psychophysical, collative, and meaningful properties of the environment which become influential as the child matures. In considering self-regulation, we have emphasized the importance of approach and avoidance systems, as well as the maturing attentional capacities that allow the child to augment or attenuate ongoing reactivity. The maturational perspective lends itself to a consideration of its complementary aspect, subjective experience. In this respect, we have stressed the importance of the physical and social environment, interacting with temperamental factors, in determining the quality of the infant's experience. Conversely, throughout the discussion we have stressed the importance of the infant's temperament in regulating the caregiver's behavior along with the regulating and stimulating effects of the caregiver.

An important issue underlying much of our discussion involves the active versus passive nature of the child. Although the infant is initially a reactive organism, active regulatory processes soon begin shaping this reactivity. Thus, the eyes, the hands, the body, and the voice come under the voluntary control of attentional mechanisms. As the infant's cognitive processes attain anticipatory capacities, self-regulation is no longer limited to a correctional mode. The reactive substrate, of course, remains and continues to develop, but the active regulatory functions far outweigh its contribution to behavior. In light of these considerations, we have viewed development as the progressive elaboration of higher and finer levels of control.

Another underlying theme has been that of "balance." We have spoken of the balance between approach and avoidance systems, between reactive and regulatory systems, and between the infant and the environment. Although temperament is often conceived of as having a static, enduring influence on behavior, we have attempted to give some idea of the flexibility and adaptability inherent in the regulatory processes, both within the infant and within the environment. Such flexibility appears to preclude the idea that temperament establishes a preset point of optimal equilibrium between the organism and the environment. Instead, a large number of potentially balanced outcomes are possible.

Finally, we have tried to provide some notion of the extent of variability inherent in the human constitution. Even in the relatively immature infant, this individuality is remarkable. The elaboration of these differences, as well as their relation to other aspects of behavior, is a most interesting and challenging topic in development.

ACKNOWLEDGMENTS

The research by the first-named author and the writing of this chapter were supported in part by NIMH Grant SR01 MH 26674–04. The authors are very grateful for the helpful comments of John Bates, Hill Goldsmith, Diana Pien, Michael Posner, Marjorie Reed, and Myron Rothbart on an earlier draft, and to the parents and infants of Eugene, Oregon, who make our research possible.

REFERENCES

Ainsworth, M. D. S. The development of infant–mother attachment. In B. M. Caldwell & H. N. Ricciuti (Eds.), *Review of child development research.* Chicago: University of Chicago Press, 1973.

Bates, J. E. The concept of difficult temperament. *Merrill-Palmer Quarterly,* in press.

Bates, J. E., Freeland, C. A. B., & Lounsbury, M. L. Measurement of infant difficultness. *Child Development,* 1979, *50,* 794–803.

Bell, R. Q. A reinterpretation of the direction of effects in studies of socialization. *Psychological Review,* 1968, *75,* 81–95.

Bell, R. Q. Stimulus control of parent or caretaker by offspring. *Developmental Psychology,* 1971, *4,* 63–72.

Bell, R. Q., Weller, G. M., & Waldrop, M. F. Newborn and preschooler: Organization of behavior and relations between periods. *Monographs of the Society for Research in Child Development,* 1971, *36* (1 and 2, Serial No. 142).

Benjamin, J. Developmental biology and psychoanalysis. In N. Greenfield & W. Lewis (Eds.), *Psychoanalysis and current biological thought.* Madison: University of Wisconsin Press, 1965.

Bergman, D., & Escalona, S. K. Unusual sensitivities in very young children. *The psychoanalytic study of the child* (Vols. 3 and 4). New York: International Universities Press, 1949.

Berlyne, D. E. *Aesthetics and psychobiology.* New York: Appleton-Century-Crofts, 1971.

Birns, B. Individual differences in human neonates' responses to stimulation. *Child Development,* 1965, *36,* 249–256.

Birns, B., Barten, S., & Bridger, W. Individual differences in temperamental characteristics of infants. *Transactions of the New York Academy of Sciences,* 1969, *31,* 1071–1082.

Block, J. H., & Block, J. The role of ego-control and ego-resiliency in the organization of behavior. In W. A. Collins (Ed.), *Minnesota symposia on child psychology* (Vol. 13). Hillsdale, N.J.: Lawrence Erlbaum Associates, 1980.

Brazelton, T. B. Neonatal behavioral assessment scale. *Clinics in developmental medicine* (No. 50). Philadelphia: Lippincott, 1973.

Bruner, J. S. *Processes of cognitive growth: Infancy.* Clark University Press, 1968.

Bruner, J. S. Pacifier-produced visual buffering in human infants. *Developmental Psychobiology,* 1973, *6,* 45–51.

Buss, A. H., & Plomin, R. *A temperament theory of personality.* New York: Wiley, 1975.

Carey, W. B. A simplified method for measuring infant temperament. *Journal of Pediatrics,* 1970, *77,* 188–194.

Carey, W. B., & McDevitt, S. C. Revision of the infant temperament questionnaire. *Pediatrics,* 1978, *61,* 735–739.

Cattell, R. B. *Personality: A systematic and factual study.* New York: McGraw-Hill, 1950.

Charlesworth, W. The role of surprise in cognitive development. In D. Elkind & J. Flavell (Eds.), *Studies in cognitive development.* London: Oxford University Press, 1969.

Clarke-Stewart, K. A. Interactions between mothers and their young children: Characteristics and consequences. *Monographs of the Society for Research in Child Development,* 1973, *38,* (6 and 7, Serial No. 153).

Cohen, L. B. Infant visual memory: A backward look into the future. In N. R. Ellis (Ed.), *Aberrant development in infancy.* New York: Wiley, 1975.

Crow, T. J. Catecholamine-containing neurones and electrical self-stimulation. 2. A theoretical interpretation and some psychiatric implications. *Psychological Medicine,* 1973, *3,* 66–73.

Diamond, S. *Personality and temperament*. New York: Harper, 1957.

Diamond, S. (Ed.). *The roots of psychology*. New York: Basic Books, 1974.

Dittrichova, J., & Lapackova, V. Development of sleep in infancy. In R. J. Robinson (Ed.), *Brain and early behavior*. New York: Academic Press, 1969.

Emde, R. N. Two developmental shifts in infant biobehavioral organization: Two months and seven-nine months. In *Qualitative Transitions in Behavior During Infancy*. Symposium presented at the meeting of the Society for Research in Child Development, New Orleans, 1977.

Emde, R. N., Gaensbauer, R. J., & Harmon, R. J. Emotional expression in infancy. *Psychological Issues*, 1976, Monograph 37.

Emde, R. N., & Metcalf, D. R. An electroencephalographic study of behavioral rapid eye movement states in the human newborn. *Journal of Nervous and Mental Diseases*, 1970, *140*, 376-386.

Escalona, S. K. *The roots of individuality: Normal patterns of development in infancy*. Chicago: Aldine, 1968.

Eysenck, H. J. Personality and drug effects. In H. J. Eysenck (Ed.), *Experiments with drugs*. New York: Macmillan, 1963.

Eysenck, H. J. *The biological basis of personality*. Springfield, Ill.: Thomas, 1967.

Freedman, D. G. An ethological approach to the genetic study of human behavior. In S. Vandenberg (Ed.), *Methods and goals in human behavior genetics*. New York: Academic Press, 1965.

Fries, M. Psychosomatic relations between mother and infant. *Psychosomatic Medicine*, 1944, *6*, 159-162.

Fuller, J. L., & Thompson, W. R. *Behavior genetics*. New York: Wiley, 1960.

Goldsmith, H. H., & Gottesman, I. I. An extension of construct validity for personality scales using twin-based criteria. *Journal of Research in Personality*, 1977, *11*, 381-397.

Goldsmith, H. H., & Gottesman, I. I. Origins of variation in behavioral style: A longitudinal study of temperament in twins. *Child Development*, in press.

Gottesman, I. I. Heritability of personality: A demonstration. *Psychological Monographs*, 1963, *77* (No. 9, Whole No. 572).

Graham, F. K., & Jackson, J. C. Arousal systems and infant heart rate responses. In H. W. Reese & L. P. Lipsett (Eds.), *Advances in child development and behavior* (Vol. 5). New York: Academic Press, 1970.

Gray, J. A. *The psychology of fear and stress*. New York: McGraw-Hill, 1971.

Gray, J. A. The psychophysiological nature of introversion-extraversion: A modification of Eysenck's theory. In V. D. Nebylitsyn & J. A. Gray (Eds.), *Biological bases of individual behavior*. New York: Academic Press, 1972.

Gray, J. A. Causal theories of personality and how to test them. In J. R. Royce (Ed.), *Multivariate analysis and psychological theory*. New York: Academic Press, 1973.

Gray, J. A. A neuropsychological theory of anxiety. In C. E. Izard (Ed.), *Emotions in personality and psychopathology*. New York: Plenum Press, 1979.

Guilford, J. P. *Personality*. New York: McGraw-Hill, 1959.

Hagekull, B., Bohlin, G., & Lindhagen, K. *Individual differences in infant behavior*. Paper presented at the meetings of the International Society for the Study of Behavioral Development, Lund, Sweden, June 1979.

Hall, C. S. The genetics of behavior. In S. S. Stevens (Ed.), *Handbook of experimental psychology*. New York: Wiley, 1951.

Hanson, M. J. A longitudinal, descriptive study of the behaviors of Down's syndrome infants in an early intervention program. *Monograph of the Center on Human Development*. Eugene, Ore.: University of Oregon, 1979.

Horowitz, F. D. (Ed.). Visual attention, auditory stimulation, and language discrimination in young infants. *Monographs of the Society for Research in Child Development*, 1974, *39* (5-6, Serial No. 158).

Jackson, J. H. The Croonian lectures on evolution and dissolution of the nervous system. *British Medical Journal*, 1884, *1*, 591–593, 600–663, 703–707.

Jackson, J. H. Selected writings of John Hughlings Jackson (Vol. 1). In H. Taylor (Ed.), *On epilepsy and epileptiform convulsions*. London: Hodder and Stoughton, 1931.

Kagan, J. *Change and continuity in infancy*. New York: Wiley, 1971.

Kagan, J. Discrepancy, temperament, and infant distress. In M. Lewis & L. A. Rosenblum (Eds.), *The origins of fear*. New York: Wiley, 1974.

Kagan, J., Kearsley, R. B., & Zelazo, P. R. *Infancy: Its place in human development*. Cambridge, Mass.: Harvard University Press, 1978.

Karmel, B. Z., & Maisel, E. B. A neuronal activity model for infant visual attention. In L. B. Cohen & P. Salapatek (Eds.), *Infant perception: From sensation to cognition*. New York: Academic Press, 1975.

Keele, S. W., Neill, W. T., & deLemos, S. M. Individual differences in attentional flexibility. *Center for Cognitive and Perceptual Research Technical Report* (No. 1). Eugene, Oregon: University of Oregon, 1978.

Korner, A. Visual alertness in neonates: Individual differences and their correlates. *Perceptual and Motor Skills*, 1970, *31*, 499–509.

Korner, A. Individual differences at birth: Implications for early experience and later development. In J. C. Westman (Ed.), *Individual differences in children*. New York: Wiley, 1973.

Kramer, Y., & Rosenblum, L. A. Responses to "frustration" in one-year-old infants. *Psychosomatic Medicine*, 1970, *32*, 243–247.

Lacey, J. I. Somatic response patterning and stress: Some revisions of activation theory. In M. H. Appley & R. Trumbull (Eds.), *Psychological stress: Issues in research*. New York: Appleton-Century-Crofts, 1967.

Lewis, M., Wilson, C., Ban, L., & Baumel, L. An exploratory study of the resting cardiac rate and variability from the last trimester of prenatal life through the first year of postnatal life. *Child Development*, 1970, *41*, 799–811.

Lipton, E. L., Steinschneider, A., & Richmond, J. B. Autonomic function in the neonate: Individual differences in cardiac reactivity. *Psychosomatic Medicine*, 1961, *23*, 472–484.

Lounsbury, M. L. *Acoustic properties and maternal reactions to infant cries as a function of infant temperament*. Unpublished doctoral dissertation, Department of Psychology, Indiana University, 1978.

Mason, J. W. Emotion as reflected in patterns of endocrine integration. In L. Levi (Ed.), *Emotions—their parameters and measurement*. New York: Raven Press, 1975.

Matas, L., Arend, R. A., & Sroufe, L. A. Continuity of adaptation in the second year: The relationship between quality of attachment and later competence. *Child Development*, 1978, *49*, 547–556.

McCall, R. B. Attention in the infant: Avenue to the study of cognitive development. In D. N. Walcher & D. L. Peters (Eds.), *The development of self-regulatory mechanisms*. New York: Academic Press, 1971.

McCall, R. B., Eichorn, D. H., & Hogarty, P. S. Transitions in early mental development. *Monographs of the Society for Research in Child Development*, 1977, *42* (3, Serial No. 171).

Mogenson, G. J., & Phillips, A. G. Motivation: A psychological construct in search of a physiological substrate. In J. M. Sprague & A. N. Epstein (Eds.), *Progress in psychobiology and physiological psychology* (Vol. 6). New York: Academic Press, 1976.

Montgomery, K. C. The relation between fear induced by novel stimulation and exploratory behavior. *Journal of Comparative and Physiological Psychology*, 1955, *48*, 254–260.

Moss, H. A., Robson, K. S., & Pedersen, F. Determinants of maternal stimulation of infants and consequences of treatment for later reactions to strangers. *Developmental Psychology*, 1969, *1*, 239–246.

Murphy, D. L., Belmaker, R. H., Buchsbaum, M., Martin, N. F., Ciaranello, R., & Wyatt, R. J.

Biogenic amine-related enzymes and personality variations in normals. *Psychological Medicine,* 1977, *7,* 149-157.

Nebylitsyn, V. D. *Fundamental properties of the human nervous system.* New York: Plenum, 1972.

Nunnally, J. C. *Psychometric theory.* New York: McGraw-Hill, 1978.

Olds, J. Behavioral studies of hypothalamic functions: Drives and reinforcements. In R. G. Grenell & S. Gabay (Eds.), *Biological foundations of psychiatry* (Vol. 1). New York: Raven Press, 1976.

Oster, H. Facial expression and affect development. In M. Lewis & L. A. Rosenblum (Eds.), *The development of affect.* New York: Plenum Press, 1978.

Parmelee, A. H., & Michaelis, R. Neurological examination of the newborn. In G. Hellmuth (Ed.), *The exceptional infant.* New York: Bruner/Mazel, 1971.

Parmelee, A., Wenner, W., Akiyama, Y., Schultz, M., & Stern, E. Sleep states in premature infants. *Developmental Medicine and Child Neurology,* 1967, *99,* 70-77.

Pavlov, I. P. General types of animal and human higher nervous activity. *Selected Works.* Moscow: Foreign Language Publishing House, 1955. (Originally published, 1935.)

Pederson, F. A., Anderson, B. J., & Cain, R. L., Jr. *A methodology for assessing parental perception of infant temperament.* Paper presented at Southeastern Conference on Human Development, Nashville TN, April 1976.

Peiper, A. *Cerebral function in infancy and childhood.* New York: Consultants Bureau, 1963.

Persson-Blennow, I., & McNeil, T. F. A questionnaire for measurement of temperament in six-month old infants: Development and standardization. *Journal of Child Psychology and Psychiatry,* 1979, *20,* 1-13.

Porges, S. W. Peripheral and neurochemical parallels of psychopathology: A psychophysical model relating autonomic imbalance to hyperactivity, psychopathy, and autism. In H. W. Reese (Ed.), *Advances in child development and behavior* (Vol. 11). New York: Academic Press, 1976.

Posner, M. I., & Rothbart, M. K. The development of attentional mechanisms. In J. Flowers (Ed.), *Nebraska symposium on motivation.* Lincoln: University of Nebraska Press, in press.

Rapoport, J. L., Pandoni, C., Renfield, M., Lake, C. R., & Ziegler, M. G. Newborn dopamine-beta-hydroxylase, minor physical anomalies, and infant temperament. *American Journal of Psychiatry,* 1977, *134,* 676-679.

Rheingold, H. L., & Eckerman, C. O. Fear of the stranger: A critical examination. In H. W. Reese (Ed.), *Advances in child development and behavior* (Vol. 8). New York: Academic Press, 1973.

Robson, K. S., & Moss, H. A. Patterns and determinants of maternal attachment. *Journal of Pediatrics,* 1970, *77,* 976-985.

Rose, S. A., Schmidt, K., & Bridger, W. H. Changes in tactile responsivity during sleep in the human newborn infant. *Developmental Psychology,* 1978, *14,* 163-172.

Rothbart, M. K. Laughter in young children. *Psychological Bulletin,* 1973, *80,* 247-256.

Rothbart, M. K. *Continuities and discontinuities in the development of infant temperament.* Paper presented at the meetings of the International Society for the Study of Behavioral Development, Lund, Sweden, June 1979.

Rothbart, M. K. *Longitudinal home observation of infant temperament.* Paper presented at the International Conference on Infant Studies, New Haven, April 1980.

Rothbart, M. K. Measurement of temperament in infancy. *Child Development,* in press.

Rothbart, M. K., & Derryberry, D. Theoretical issues in temperament. In M. Lewis & L. Taft (Eds.), *Developmental disabilities: Theory, assessment and intervention.* New York: S. P. Medical and Scientific Books, in press.

Rothbart, M. K., Furby, L., Kelly, S. R., & Hamilton, J. S. *Development of a caretaker report temperament scale for use with 3, 6, 9, and 12 month old infants.* Paper presented at meetings of the Society for Research in Child Development, New Orleans, March 1977.

Rothbart, M. K., & Hanson, M. J. *A comparison of temperamental characteristics of Down's syndrome and normal infants.* Paper submitted for publication, 1980.

Routtenberg, A., & Santos-Anderson, R. The role of prefrontal cortex in intracranial self-stimulation: A case history of anatomical localization of motivational structures. In L. L. Iversen,S. D. Iversen, & S. H. Snyder (Eds.), *Handbook of psychopharmacology* (Vol. 8). New York: Plenum Press, 1977.

Sameroff, A., & Chandler, M. J. Reproductive risk and the continuum of care-taking casualty. In F. D. Horowitz (Ed.), *Review of child development research* (Vol. 4). Chicago: University of Chicago Press, 1975.

Santostefano, S. *A biodevelopmental approach to clinical child psychology.* New York: Wiley, 1978.

Scarr, S. Genetic factors in activity motivation. *Child Development,* 1966, *37,* 663–673.

Scarr, S., & Salapatek, P. Patterns of fear development during infancy. *Merrill-Palmer Quarterly,* 1970, *16,* 53–90.

Schaffer, H. R. Activity level as a constitutional determinant of infantile reaction to deprivation. *Child Development,* 1966, *37,* 595–602.

Schaffer, H. R., Greenwood, A., & Parry, M. H. The onset of wariness. *Child Development,* 1972, *43,* 165–175.

Schaffer, R. *Mothering.* Cambridge, Mass.: Harvard University Press, 1977.

Schooler, C., Zahn, T. P., Murphy, D. L., & Buchsbaum, M. Psychological correlates of monoamine oxidase in normals. *Journal of Nervous and Mental Diseases,* 1978, *166,* 177–186.

Sostek, A. J., Sostek, A. M., Murphy, D. L., Martin, E. B., & Born, W. S. *Arousal levels and motor functioning in human newborns associated with differences in cord blood amine oxidase activities.* Paper presented at the International Conference on Infant Studies, New Haven, April 1980.

Sroufe, L. A., Stuecher, H. U., & Stutzer, W. The functional significance of autistic behaviors for the psychotic child. *Journal of Abnormal Child Psychology,* 1973, *1,* 225–240.

Sroufe, L. A., & Waters, E. Attachment as an organizational construct. *Child Development,* 1977, *48,* 1184–1199.

St. Clair, K. L. Neonatal assessment procedures: A historical review. *Child Development,* 1978, *49,* 280–292.

Stechler, G., & Latz, E. Some observations on attention and arousal in the human infant. *Journal of the American Academy of Child Psychiatry,* 1966, *5,* 517–525.

Stein, L. Norepinephrine reward pathways: Role in self-stimulation, memory consolidation, and schizophrenia. In *Nebraska symposium on motivation* (Vol. 22). Lincoln, Neb.: University of Nebraska Press, 1974.

Stern, D. H. Mother and infant at play: The dyadic interaction involving facial, vocal, and gaze behaviors. In M. Lewis & L. Rosenblum (Eds.), *The effect of the infant on its caregiver.* New York: Wiley, 1974.

Strelau, J. Reactivity and activity style in selected occupations. *Polish Psychological Bulletin,* 1975, *6,* 199–206.

Tennes, K., Downey, K., & Vernadakis, A. Urinary cortisol excretion rates and anxiety in normal one-year-old infants. *Psychosomatic Medicine,* 1977, *39,* 178–187.

Tennes, K., Emde, R., Kisley, A., & Metcalf, D. The stimulus barrier in early infancy: An exploration of some formulations of John Benjamin. In R. R. Holt & E. Peterfreund (Eds.), *Psychoanalysis and contemporary science* (Vol. 1). New York: Macmillan, 1972.

Tennes, K., & Vernadakis, A. *Behavioral correlates of cortisol in children.* Paper presented at the Meeting of the Society for Research in Child Development, San Francisco, 1979.

Teplov, B. M. Problems in the study of general types of higher nervous activity in man and animals. In J. A. Gray (Ed.), *Pavlov's typology.* New York: Macmillan, 1964.

Thomas, A., & Chess, S. *Temperament and development.* New York: Bruner/Mazel, 1977.

Thomas, A., Chess, S., & Birch, H. G. *Temperament and behavior disorders in children.* New York: New York Universities Press, 1968.

Thomas, A., Chess, S., Birch, H. G., Hertzig, M. E., & Korn, S. *Behavioral individuality in early childhood.* New York: New York Universities Press, 1963.

Torgersen, A. E., & Kringlen, E. Genetic aspects of temperament differences in infants. *Journal of the American Academy of Child Psychiatry,* 1978, *17,* 433-449.

Washburn, R. A study of the smiling and laughing of infants in the first year of life. *Genetic Psychology Monographs,* 1929, *6,* 397-539.

Waters, E. The reliability and stability of individual differences in infant-mother attachment. *Child Development,* 1978, *49,* 483-494.

Willerman, L. Activity level and hyperactivity in twins. *Child Development,* 1973, *44,* 288-293.

Wilson, R. S. Synchronies in mental development: An epigenetic perspective. *Science,* 1978, *202,* 939-947.

Wise, C. D., Berger, B. D., & Stein, L. Evidence of α-noradrenergic reward receptors and serotonergic punishment receptors in the rat brain. *Biological Psychiatry,* 1973, *6,* 3-21.

Yakovlev, P. I., & Lecours, A. The myelogenetic cycles of regional maturation of the brain. In A. Minkowski (Ed.), *Regional development of the brain in early life.* Oxford: Blackwell Scientific Publications, 1967.

Yerkes, R. M., & Yerkes, A. W. Nature and conditions of avoidance (fear) response in the chimpanzees. *Journal of Comparative Psychology,* 1936, *21,* 53-66.

Zuckerman, M. *Sensation seeking: Beyond the optimal level of arousal.* Hillsdale, N.J.: Lawrence Erlbaum Associates, 1979.

3 Social Conflict and Dominance in Children: A Case for a Primate Homology

D. W. Rajecki
Indiana University—Purdue University at Indianapolis

Randall C. Flanery
University of Wisconsin at Madison

Children's groups are a traditional subject matter in developmental psychology. One of the more salient features of such groups is social structure. In his review of the literature, Hartup (1970) said of such organization that "individual differences *inevitably* produce differentiation of status positions; children's peer groups *always* possess a hierarchical structure," and that ". . . status differentiation is a *universal* attribute of group functioning [p. 370, emphases added]." But, although Hartup's review is excellent in every other respect, in dealing with this topic, he makes little reference to the nonhuman primate literature on peer influence. Our thesis, to the contrary, is that a fuller understanding of important aspects of the structure and functioning of children's groups *depends* on a systematic comparative assessment of similar features in nonhuman groups. We firmly believe that animal data of this sort make an important contribution to mainstream developmental psychology. But, what is the proper place of these data in our discipline?

Past evaluations of the utility of nonhuman data in understanding human phenomena have varied widely. At one extreme are overenthusiastic popularizers (e.g., Ardrey, 1966; Lorenz, 1966) who generalize, sometimes uncritically, concepts derived from studies of animal behavior to human affairs. At the other extreme are doctrinaire environmentalists (e.g., Boulding, 1973; Montagu, 1973) who insist that the human experience is unique, and who reject utterly, and sometimes unthinkingly, the notion that cross-species comparisons are meaningful. In addition to the controversial standing of the comparative philosophy, a number of serious attempts at systematic comparison in other domains of psy-

87

chology have foundered (see the critiques of Hodos & Campbell, 1969, and Lockard, 1971).

In the face of such difficulties, what hope is there that our comparative chapter makes a meaningful contribution? Indeed, our attempt to establish that dominance patterns in children and in nonhuman primates are similar, and that the source of this resemblance is a genetic similarity based on common ancestry, is controversial. If the chapter *is* successful in this endeavor, it is so in part because it proceeds carefully along formal and systematic methods of comparison. One of the first issues raised is the matter of the rules or criteria for cross-species comparisons in general. Behavioral homologies, analogies, and models are discussed, and we defend our choice of one type of comparison over the others. Another contribution to the viability of this project is that the concept of dominance relations in nonhuman primates is well documented by research, and well grounded in theory, as shown in our selected review of the literature. Finally, much recent information on children's *and* nonhuman primates' behavior in groups, a conjunction of hard human data and hard nonhuman primate data, lends credence to our comparison. Our conclusion is that, based on their agreement in several unusual characteristics, dominance patterns are homologous in primates. This agreement of unusual characteristics is found at several levels, including fine motor movement, gross motor movement, and behavior at the group level. Following this treatment of dominance among peers, we explore comparative analyses of (1) the origins of individual differences in dominance behavior; and (2) children's social conflicts in the family.

DOMINANCE FROM AN ETHOLOGICAL PERSPECTIVE

William Golding's novel, *Lord of the Flies*, was first published in 1954. It tells the story of a group of innocent British school boys—aged from about 6 to 12—who have been stranded on an uninhabited island. A leader of sorts emerges, and under his youthful command the children begin to cope with the demands of their wilderness environment. However, rivalries soon develop that lead to a brutal struggle for power within the group. Terrorism, torture, and murder become the rule, with the result that one of the competing factions is virtually exterminated.

Golding's story is highly engaging, and within a few years, his book became a popular and critical success. It is interesting to note reactions to his story. In representative reviews from the book's first decade (see Nelson, 1963), literary commentators point to the "evil," "barbarism," "state of darkness," "lower instincts," "savagery," "wickedness," and other unfortunate matters they saw revealed in Golding's allegory. To the contrary, if the story were reviewed by certain of today's developmental psychologists, a rather different interpretation would likely emerge. It might not occur to this more recent crop of analysts to consider the evil, barbarism, savagery, or wickedness of children in conflict. Instead, they might see the disputes in the novel as all very natural (if exaggerated under the license of art), and employ concepts such as "agonistic encounter," "dominance," "submission," and "dominance hierarchy."

This contemporary vocabulary of social conflict and dominance[1] in childhood stems from something of a new look in the study of children's interactions with others. Although work on conflict, status, leadership, and popularity in children's groups goes back to the 1930's, researchers in the late 1960's began to adopt a frame of reference that was different from the traditional psychoanalytic, learning, social-learning, and structural approaches in developmental psychology. The new look was derived from ethology in general, and from the study of the social behavior of nonhuman animals in particular. In what appears to be the first published ethologically oriented research on children's peer relations, Blurton Jones (1967) described his project, and concluded that:

> It became obvious that one can study human behaviour in just the same way as Tinbergen (1953 and 1959), and Moynihan (1955) and others have studied gulls, and van Hooff (1962), Andrew (1963, who also gives comparative data from a child), and others have studied non-human primates. This paper describes the crude preliminary observations which gave rise to this conclusion. It is a provisional, descriptive account, much like a report on the first season's ethological field work on any new species [p. 347].

What advantage is there in regarding children as a "new species"? For one thing, this approach is a way of getting around the potentially confounding problem of existing assumptions about human nature and human function. For another, such an approach immediately focuses the observer on the behavior in question. As McGrew (1972) put it:

> Using such behavioral categories, ethologists directly record the behavior of normal individuals as it occurs. There is no need to resort to indirect measures: ratings, tests, questionnaires, projective techniques, interviews. Consequently, ethologists need not speculate about the applicability of [for example] doll play results or the validity of test scores to ongoing personal behavior. By recording behavior directly, ethologists see it functioning in real-life situations, and by using sophisticated and inconspicuous recording aids, they attempt to avoid disrupting ongoing behavior [p. 19].

---

[1]A discussion of conflict and dominance sooner or later implicates the concept of aggression, and that word is, in fact, used here and there in our chapter. However, because the chapter is not devoted to aggression per se, we would prefer to hedge on the difficult matter of defining it. If pressed, we would fall in line with those (Rosenzweig, 1977) who define aggression as "generic assertiveness [p. 379]" or, simply (Eibl-Eibesfeldt, 1974), as behavior that leads to "spacing or to the establishment of a dominance–subordination relationship [p. 443]."

TABLE 3.1

Behavior Categories from Ethological Research on Monkey, Ape, and Human (Children) Social Conflict and Dominance Patterns[a]

Dominance Behavior

Japanese Monkeys (After Fedigan, 1976)	Chimpanzees (After van Lawick-Goodall, 1972)	Preschool Children (After Abramovitch & Strayer, 1978)
Visual and vocal threat: consists of the following agonistic signals: stare, ..., gape, and growl...	Glare. Lips compressed, animal stares fixedly at another individual.	Threat gestures
	Arm raising... the forearm or the entire arm is raised with a rapid movement: the palm of the animal is normally oriented towards the threatened individual...	Face and body posture
Lunge or bluff charge: a plunge forward towards an opponent in an agonistic encounter...	Hitting away... a hitting movement with the back of the hand directed towards the threatened animal...	Intention hit
Displace: one monkey moves toward another who immediately moves out of the former's way...	Frustrate[b]... fear of another individual prevents [a] chimpanzee from obtaining a desired objective... [as when] a dominant individual takes food in the possession of a subordinate...	Intention kick
Take away: to remove a desirable object, such as a food item from another monkey.		Intention bite
Chase: to pursue another animal with accompanying agonistic signals.		Object/position struggles
Pull or push: to attempt to move another monkey by applying pressure.	Hair-pulling... attacked animals lose fairly large handfuls of hair during a fight.	Displace without contact
Cuff: the first monkey hits the second with the flat of its hand...	Slapping... downward movement of the arm in which the palm of the hand slaps the body of the other...	Displace with contact
Pinch or grab: to take hold of another's body by the hand and squeeze to the point of causing pain.	Stamping on back... attacker seizes the victim by the hair and endeavors to leap onto its back. If this is achieved, attacker then stamps on the victim with both feet.	Physical attack
		Chase
		Push–pull

Bite: to seize another with the teeth.

	Lifting, slamming, and dragging ... the victim ... may be lifted bodily from the ground ... and slammed down again ...	Hit
		Kick
	Biting. During an attack the aggressor often puts his mouth to the body of the victim as though biting.	Wrestle
		Bite

Subordinance Behavior

Fear grimace: a submissive signal in which the lips are retracted from the teeth, with the teeth clenched.	Grinning ... lips are parted, the corners drawn back, and an oblong expanse of closed teeth shown.	Submission
		Cry–scream
Avoid: a monkey notices another in its path or coming in its direction and changes its movement pattern in order to avoid encountering the latter monkey.	Presenting ... in a nonsexual context occurs when a subordinate individual turns its rump toward a higher ranking one.	Cringe
		Hand–cover
	Bowing, bobbing, and crouching ... involve various degrees of limb flexion ... so that [the] body is close to the ground.	Flinch
Seek aid: an animal in a dispute screams and looks repeatedly toward an uninvolved monkey for support ...		Withdrawal
	Screaming ... some screams have a rasping quality, some are long and drawn out.	Requests cessation
	Submissive behavior [help seeking?] ... the subordinate, after being attacked or threatened, approaches a third individual of higher social status than the aggressor and makes gestures similar to appeasement gestures.	Help-seeking
		Seeks adult help
		Seeks child help

[a] The entries are quotes from the original sources, rearranged here under dominance and subordinance categories.
[b] Strictly speaking, the van Lawick-Goodall (1972) paper was about expressions in chimps, and not about social conflict and dominance per se. Therefore, van Lawick-Goodall does not name any response pattern as "frustrate," but her descriptions clearly indicate that object/position struggles do occur in chimpanzee groups.

Having borrowed the ethologists' principles and methodology, certain developmentalists began recording freely emitted responses of children in more or less
naturalistic situations. Researchers went to nurseries, day-care centers, play-
grounds, summer camps, and other places where children typically interact with
one another, and noted just what went on. For example, consider the conflict
depicted in Fig. 3.1. The researcher observing this fracas might carefully note
that the dyad was engaged in a struggle over an object (the ball on the ground),
and that the boy was pushing the girl over and scratching her at the same time.

This is not to say that there were no observational studies of children's conflict
in the past (see, for example, the annotated bibliography of Oetzel, 1966), or that
earlier researchers had not made fine distinctions between various acts related to
dominance (e.g., Gellert, 1961, 1962). The difference was that ethologically
oriented workers were careful to pay attention to the sorts of behavior that *any*
primatologist would find interesting in studying social relations. Table 3.1 lists
response categories from studies of nonhuman primates under seminaturalistic
and natural conditions (Japanese monkeys: Fedigan, 1976; chimpanzees: van
Lawick-Goodall, 1972) and a paper on young children (Abramovitch & Strayer,
1978). Notice that, in many cases, the response categories for monkeys, apes,
and children are virtually interchangeable. It is interesting that these three sets of

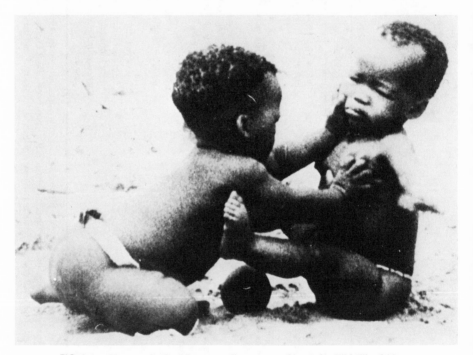

FIG. 3.1.   Photograph of toddlers struggling over an object (after Eibl-Eibesfeldt,
1974; reproduced with the permission of the author and Academic Press).

researchers *independently* developed their own coding categories, which means that similarities in their coding schemes did not result from a simple borrowing of classifications. All three schemes are based on extensive preliminary observations, which enabled the researchers to become familiar with the specific behavioral repertoires of their respective subjects.

Given the enthusiasm for the ethological approach and the resemblances in response classifications, comparisons across phyletic branches seem plausible. Yet, caution is required in making such comparisons because comparative psychology is fraught with difficulties, and these difficulties are not always made clear in papers seeking and reporting "parallels" between human and nonhuman behavior. Accordingly, we now discuss three ways of comparing similar behavior across different species: homologies, analogies, and models. It is our contention that all three forms of comparison are worthwhile and should be pursued, but that each also has its difficulties and limitations. Our aim is to make recommendations regarding the most feasible and stimulating approach given the current state of knowledge.

HOMOLOGIES, ANALOGIES, AND MODELS

At a certain level, it is obvious that there are lawful relationships between features of a variety of species. For example, a glance at the anatomy of fetal development of certain mammals (see Fig. 3.2) provides compelling evidence of biological continuity among members of this class. But what about comparing other features of these species, or species outside the mammal class? If there are methods for determining that anatomies of humans and nonhumans are indeed comparable (or not), can these methods be used to help us formally compare our behavior with that of other animals? For example, imagine that we see a monkey threaten another monkey (visual and vocal threat in Table 3.1), and that on another occasion we see a child threaten another child (face and body posture in Table 3.1). Further imagine that we observe a submissive reaction (fear grimace, or cringe) by the targets of such threats. What are we to make of the relationship of these patterns or sequences? To what extent are they comparable, and how much does one sequence tell us about the other? Various answers to these questions are available in terms of homologies, analogies, and models of human behavior.

Homologies in Behavior

Homologies are genetically based similarities, across two or more species, that can be traced to a common ancestor. Biologists have established explicit rules for determining the existence of morphological homologies. Atz (1970) outlines the principal criteria of the biologist A. Remane:

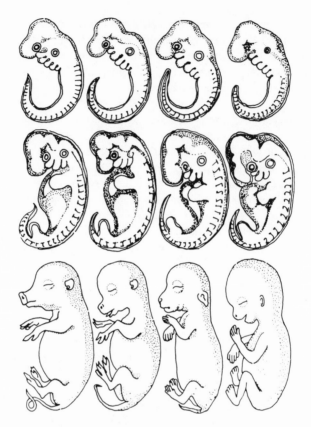

FIG. 3.2.   Sketch of fetal development in (from left to right) the pig, cow, dog, and human child (drawn by J. Rajecki).

1. Criterion of position: Homology results from the same position in comparable systems of structures (that is, structures that occupy the same position within comparable anatomical units are likely to be homologous).

2. Criterion of special quality: Similar structures can be homologized, without regard to position, if they agree in several unusual characteristics. The greater the complexity and degree of correspondence, the more likely the homology.

3. Criterion of constancy or continuity: Even dissimilar and differently located structures can be considered homologous if intermediate, connecting forms can be shown to exist, so that Criterion 1 or 2 can be met by comparing the adjacent forms. The connecting forms may be ontogenetic stages or members of taxonomic groups [p. 57].

As an example of a morphological homology in primates, Washburn and Avis (1958) discuss certain special sensory features that are common in monkeys, apes, and humans (see Table 3.2). Of no small interest here is that these presumed morphological homologies immediately implicate *behavioral* homologies as well. According to Washburn and Avis (1958), "in primates the great change in the special senses apparently came between the prosimians of the Eocene and later forms, since those of monkey, ape, and man are very similar. The latter three all receive the same sensory impressions and *explore* the world with hands rather than with muzzle . . . [p. 425, italics added]." In any event, it can be argued that the similarities listed in Table 3.2 qualify as morphological homologies under Remane's second criterion, that of special quality. These sensory features in monkeys, apes, and humans agree in several unusual characteristics.

Indeed, application of any of Remane's three criteria for morphological homology is a relatively simple matter for the comparative anatomist or biological systematist. He or she can inspect or dissect various living forms, and trace the fossil record of ancestral species. On the contrary, the comparative behaviorist searching for homologies is generally thought to be in a much less attractive position, simply because animal and human behavior is harder to pinpoint. To date, forecasts of the chances for establishing behavioral homologies have been gloomy. Atz (1970), for one, was especially pessimistic in his formal appraisal. He doubted that the essentially morphological concept of homology could be applied to the nonmorphological phenomenon of behavior. First, whereas morphological units are tangible and discrete (have precise boundries), behavior was seen (Atz, 1970) as "immaterial,""evanescent," and "continuous." As Atz put it, "the most difficult task of all is to extract from the continuum of the animal's total behavior, parts to measure, count, and compare [p. 56]." Second, Atz pointed out that behavior itself does not fossilize, so tracing behavior directly to an extinct ancestor is not possible in any precise fashion. Although we might conjecture on an animal's diet based on characteristics of fossilized jaw bones, such remains offer few clues to things like social life. Third, there is the possibility of confusing homologies with analogies (see

TABLE 3.2
Morphological Homologies, Based on the Criterion of
Special Quality, of Certain Sensory Features in
Monkeys, Apes, and Humans[a]

	Group		
Sensory Feature	Monkeys	Apes	Humans
Reduced sense of smell?	Yes	Yes	Yes
Loss of primitive muzzle?	Yes	Yes	Yes
Loss of tactile hairs?	Yes	Yes	Yes
Stereoscopic color vision?	Yes	Yes	Yes
Loss of mobility of external ears?	Yes	Yes	Yes

[a]After Washburn and Avis, 1958, Table 19–3.

the following discussion). Similar behavior in two species might be due to convergent evolution to disparate lines (analogy), rather than to descent from a single ancestral stock (homology). However, Atz did admit that if any of the three criteria for morphological homology were ever to be meaningfully applied to behavior, it would probably be the criterion of special quality—Remane's second standard—whereby agreement in special features is identified.

Analogies in Behavior

Members of different species can share various similarities as a consequence of convergent evolution. Similarities arrived at in this fashion are termed convergences or analogies. If situational demands place severe selection pressures on a variety of types living in that environment, those species may evolve along similar morphological or behavioral lines. A handy example of this principle is the streamlined shape of most aquatic animals. As Lorenz (1974) pointed out, even though they are quite distinct in their genetic makeup, sharks and dolphins look very much alike. Presumably, all species of shark and all species of dolphin evolved in such a way as to maximize their efficiency in moving through water. Therefore, the search for behavioral analogies between humans and animals is a matter of no little importance. If a true behavioral analogy is discovered, then an important basis of human behavior is revealed.

All this sounds very promising, of course, until one considers that there are apparently no rules for specifying whether meaningful analogous behavior really exists. As Lorenz (1974) put it: "ethologists are often accused of drawing false analogies between animal and human behavior. However, no such thing as a false analogy exists: An analogy can be more or less detailed and hence more or less informative [p. 185]." In this light, an analogy between the shape of a naval torpedo and the shape of a dolphin is as legitimate as an analogy between the shape of a shark and the shape of the dolphin (Lorenz, 1974), but one wonders how much could be learned about dolphins via the study of torpedos. Unfortunately, the closest thing to a formal criterion for specifying the meaningfulness of a behavioral analogy is that common sense be used (cf. Hodos & Campbell, 1969; Lockard, 1971).

Caution is necessary in allowing the process of convergent evolution to account for possibly superficial similarities between different species living contemporaneously. It is an error to state that a species' phenotype is the one that is perfectly suited to its current ecological niche. That is, it is merely a tautology to claim that some morphological or behavioral feature of a species is necessary simply because it exists (Brace, 1979). This error is based on the assumption that evolutionary selection results in the best fit of the organism to the environment. The more correct view is that selection results in a *tolerable* solution to environmental pressure (Bernstein & Smith, 1979). Moreover, some current morphological or behavioral characteristics may have been adaptive in the environment of one's genetic ancestor. These ancient adaptations may survive to the present because they are not *mal*adaptive (Bernstein & Smith, 1979; Coelho, Bramblett, & Quick, 1979). In sum, if one observes similarity of behavior across different organisms living in roughly the same ecological niche, this observation, in and of itself, does not constitute proof for convergent evolution within that environment. Such similarities could be due to other factors, or to the influence of some other environments at some other times. They might even be homologies!

Models of Behavior

A third way to deal with comparisons between humans and other species is to seek animal models of human behavior. Do not confuse the term *model,* as used here, with the meaning of the word in other scientific contexts. We do not mean model in the sense that chemists and biologists build oversized assemblies to depict the structures of atoms and molecules. Neither do we mean model in the sense of a mathematical algorithm for, nor a verbal or a symbolic theory of, a phenomenon. Rather, the meaning of *model* in the current sense is roughly equivalent to the meaning of *substitute.* Consider the usage of Corson, Corson, Arnold, and Knopp (1976): "Some of these animal models (but not all) respond favorably to amphetamine . . . , thus these animal models represent suitable subjects for . . . developing rational diagnostic, pragmatic, and therapeutic criteria which might be applicable to . . . children and adults . . . [pp. 133–134]." In this sense, animal models are temporary replacements for humans for purposes of research and development.

The issue surrounding modeling is not whether there are biological continuities or evolutionary parallels between species. Rather, scientists who use animal models simply assume that organisms on this planet can function in only so many ways, and that for whatever reason, certain functions in different animals will happen to be alike. Hence, this is an atheoretical approach wherein commonalities—should they exist—are determined empirically. Appropriate models (i.e., appropriate species) are not defined a priori; they are discovered. Further, models are chosen for their suitability in answering particular research questions. For example, the study of brain chemistry requires the use of a large number of animals, so inexpensive rodents are often the model of choice (Delgado, 1976). On the other hand, it has been suggested that the pig is the best model when human nutrition is concerned (Pichot, 1976).

The obvious advantage of using an animal model for human behavior is that such models are open to forms of investigation, manipulation, or preparation prohibited in the original—humans. But, the dilemma faced by model-seekers is the *choice* of a model (species). Murphy (1976) has argued that in the case of models of psychopathology, for example, it would be desirable to find those with the greatest possible similarity to the disorders of humans. He would seek essential replicas of these disorders. Compared with human problems, these model disorders should (ideally) have a similar etiology, phenomenology, and reactivity to treatment. To the contrary, Hinde (1976) feels that the model should not be *too* similar to the original, because then one might as well work with the original. But where to find such an optimal model?

Choosing among Models, Analogies, and Homologies

The establishment of all three forms of comparison—models, analogies, and homologies—is clearly important, with the preferred approach depending on the behavioral scientist's aims or resources. But, whereas *all* are desirable, it is necessary to maintain a *distinction* between these categories, for the loss of this distinction can only lead to confusion and error. One can be distracted by a failure to specify which comparison category is involved, and this can occur even in a work as imposing as Wilson's (1975) *Sociobiology*. For example, in a discussion of defense against predators as an ecological pressure for social evolution, Wilson (1975) offers close-packed examples from the behavior of fruit bats, arctic ground squirrels, prairie dogs, redshanks, eider ducklings, wood pigeons, starlings, and domestic cattle. Even though this array of animal types is impressive in and of itself, some meaning is lost because Wilson does not consistently label the comparisons as homologies, analogies, or models.

Therefore, in our comparative approach, we sought to establish or seek evidence for a single comparison type. The first advantage of this restriction is that if we are *correct* in our interpretations, the meaning of our comparisons will be that much clearer. The second advantage is that should our interpretations be *incorrect,* the source and extent of our errors will eventually be that much clearer.

We did not seek a primate model of children's dominance behavior, primarily because we judged that the theoretical yield of a comparative approach would be greater if *either* analogy or homology could be demonstrated. Analogies or homologies would identify evolutionary influences on contemporary patterns of child development and behavior, and thus forge a link between developmental psychology and sociobiology. However, by extending our principle of maximum theoretical yield, we did not seek primate analogies of children's peer relations. Analogies are most useful in explaining behavioral similarities in genetically unrelated lines of animals, but it is already known that monkeys, apes, and humans are more or less closely related, as indicated by the traditional fossil record (see Hodos & Campbell, 1969, Figures 1 and 3) and by modern methods of molecular taxonomy (see Washburn, 1978). The biological systematists have thus provided a valuable justification for assuming that certain nonhuman primate dominance behavior might be homologous with that of children. In fact, if the conservative critic Atz (see the earlier discussion) was ever optimistic about finding behavioral homologies, it was through the use of biological systematics.

Atz (1970) said that "in practice, the student of behavior works with animals already classified, and it is natural that he should use the distribution of the behavior patterns he is studying as evidence for or against his proposed behavioral homologies ... [p. 58]." Therefore, on biological grounds alone, it seems meaningful to turn to the other primates in our search for behavioral homologies.

THE CONCEPT OF NONHUMAN PRIMATE DOMINANCE

The first step in a comparison of human to nonhuman dominance patterns is to note that certain primatologists have challenged the importance of dominance relations in the natural life of monkeys and apes and, moreover, have questioned the very concept of dominance itself. To varying degrees, critics have argued that the concept should be modified, limited, or abandoned altogether. Therefore, if a comparison of nonhuman primate behavior to human dominance relations is to be realistic, it is necessary to first establish the standing of the concept of dominance among the other primates.

Dominance versus Subordinance

Certain writers (e.g., Rowell, 1974) claimed that if there were reliable status differences between monkeys in a group, it was not because some individuals were acting in a dominant fashion over others; it was rather that some animals were behaving in a subordinate manner. Rowell's own observations (1974) were that the "subordinate's behavior elicited dominating behavior rather than the reverse," and that "of complete sequences [of attacks] observed those in which the first gesture came from the subordinate are much the more frequent [p. 140]." Thus, Rowell wished to replace the notion of a dominance hierarchy with the concept of a subordinance hierarchy.

However, further examination indicates that Rowell's position on subordinance was only partly correct. In contrast to Rowell's (1974) claim that primate social organization is based solely on subordinance, Deag (1977) provided evidence that hierarchies are maintained by the joint action of *both* dominant and subordinate members. Even though Deag (1977) observed that certain subordinate members of a macaque troop did initiate avoidance responses, he also noted that *dominant* animals initiated many interactions involving threats. Furthermore, the frequency with which some animals avoided others was more closely correlated with the avoided animal's rank than with their own. This means that the subordinate animal was basing the avoidance response on the rank of the dominant animal, and not so much on its own rank. On the other hand, the frequency with which a dominant animal initiated a threat was more closely correlated with its own rank than with the rank of the target of the threat. This pattern indicates that the initiator of the threat was not necessarily paying attention to the other's subordinate rank, or that degree of subordinance was not a factor in eliciting threats. Therefore, even though Rowell (1974) was correct in asserting that patterns of subordinance were important in the social organization of primates, she was wrong in stating that patterns of dominance were not, for Deag (1977) showed that both types of behavior are observable and influential.

Dominance as an Artifact of Captivity

Other critics (e.g., Gartlan, 1968) felt that for historical reasons the emphasis on dominance relations was misplaced. Gartlan argued that early studies—which influenced the form and interpretation of later laboratory and field work—erred in using captive animals, because captivity had artificially increased the rate of aggression within those groups. According to Gartlan (1968), the effects of captivity had masked other social mechanisms, and misled the researchers into thinking aggression was a preeminently important feature of natural primate social behavior.

But Gartlan, like Rowell, was only partly correct. His claim that captivity increases aggression and dominance behavior was right, but his assertion that dominance occurs solely in captivity was wrong. For example, the troop that Deag (1977) observed was in natural circumstances, yet he saw a good deal of dominance (and subordinance) activities. Deag further cites the findings of dominance patterns in natural groups by Hausfater (1975) and Struhsaker (1967), to which can be added the observations of Seyfarth (1976). Yet, it remains true that captivity does increase agonistic behavior in primates, and the proper question is how to interpret this increase. One could argue, in contrast to Gartlan, that the elevation of aggression is not pathological, but may very well be adaptive. It seems reasonable to speculate that primates may be preadapted to react to various forms of environmental stress with an intensification of their social behavior. If the animals' habitat deteriorated occasionally, rigidification of a hierarchy during the lean periods might permit at least some to survive. This hypothesis is partly supported by the findings of Singh (1966, 1969) that city-dwelling (substandard environment) rhesus monkeys are much more aggressive than their forest-dwelling (standard environment) counterparts, and that in mixed groups, the former dominate the latter. In sum, the effects of captivity on aggressive behavior may be adaptive—at least in the short run—rather than necessarily maladaptive.

Correlates of Dominance

Part of the wide interest in the idea of social hierarchies was that in using such an explanatory concept, one could organize in a coherent way a great many different forms of interaction between animals. Because status implies degree of privilege, knowledge of a dominance hierarchy based on some criterion (e.g., face-to-face interaction) might allow the prediction of outcomes in other situations, such as reproductive success, spatial arrangement, or access to limited resources. However, such predictions were not always borne out for all aspects of the animals' social life; thus, a third form of criticism (cf. Bernstein, 1970; Drews, 1973; Kolata, 1976) was that traditional assumptions about the functions or consequences of a primate dominance hierarchy apparently did not hold. Bernstein reported that his research on a number of groups failed to find a general operating principle that related monkeys' (1) aggressive role in agonistic relations with (2) the male role in mounting episodes, or (3) the recipient role in episodes of social grooming.

Still, even if we allow that aggression and dominance-related behavior do not correlate with every activity an animal can undertake, there are additional studies that do show that status can be correlated with a number of activities critical to an animal's functioning. For example, Richards (1974) found that in small groups of laboratory-housed rhesus—each having only a single adult male—the following measures all indicated pretty much the same rank ordering of animals within each group under study: priority of access to solid food, priority of access to liquid, fights, displays, and avoidance responses. As Richards (1974) wrote: "all the measures which ranked all group members were correlated with each other in every experimental group [p. 924]." These results compare favorably with those of Christopher (1972). Therefore, rather than dismissing the importance of outcomes, the more appropriate approach might be to leave the question open, and to empirically determine such correlates.

Review Conclusion

Admittedly, dominance relations are not the only important influence on an individual's behavior (e.g., see Fedigan, 1976, for a discussion of "roles" in primate social organization). But, it does appear that the concept of dominance in nonhuman primates has weathered the several sorts of criticism just noted. Given this viability, we feel justified in using the behavior of such animals as a basis for comparison with children's dominance relations.

COMPARISONS OF DOMINANCE PHENOMENA

It remains to decide just what human behavior to compare with that of nonhumans. Even recognizing Atz' (1970) concern about the problem of abstracting relevant units of behavior at some levels, we simply assume that patterns of social interaction are generally quite obvious to both the participants and the objective observer. Therefore, in our review, we wished to deal with dominance *patterns* rather than the dominance *acts* per se. Although an act may differ from species to species, the social consequence of that act may be functionally equivalent. For example, the social bite of an aggressive monkey, ape, or child must surely differ on a number of anatomical and motoric points, but the bitten animal or child may very well react in a way that is theoretically indistinguishable. Of course, where good records of discrete acts are available, we will not hesitate to include them in our review.

Further, we argue that for the present, at least, the monkeys and apes should serve collectively as the comparison. The basis for this claim is concern about drawbacks in focusing on only a particular subgroup for comparison. The most important problem is the variability of social behavior *within* any given species. Although we disagree with Gartlan's (1968) conclusion that social structure in primates is largely habitat specific (as opposed to being species specific), we agree that local conditions certainly influence their group dynamics. For example, Yamada (1971) observed five natural troops of Japanese monkeys on Shodoshima Island and recorded marked differences in their social behavior (e.g., degree of dispersion while feeding), and in their actual social composition (e.g., classes and subclasses of males per troop). Similarly, Dunbar and Dunbar (1976) studied the social organization of colobus monkeys under natural conditions and noted three distinct types: small one-male, large one-male, and multimale groups. Only in the last category were dominance and a relatively high rate of agonistic behavior expected. Wilson (1975) has applied the term "behavioral scaling [p. 20]" to such genetically based within-species variability. But, whatever the reasons for the differences detected by the Dunbars and by Yamada (see also Kawai, 1965), concentration on any one species, or on any one group or troop would not be completely informative about some other related animals, or about general principles involved. Because we seek *general* principles, it seems reasonable to look for information on antecedents, mechanisms, functions, and consequences of dominance that characterize simians *in general* (cf. Bernstein, 1970).

A final concern is the relevance of data from more or less *mature* animals to more or less *immature* humans. We feel that such comparisons are admissible for our purpose, because this chapter is basically a look at the social psychology of the child, and not strictly at the development of aggression and dominance in childhood. Indeed, we would argue that this particular treatment is appropriate at this particular time, for it would seem important to explicate the nature of dominance before one attempts to trace its ontogeny. In any event, we do consider some developmental antecedents in dominance behavior, but in general, data on developmental trends are scarce (Hartup, 1979).

In the following section, we compare various aspects of dominance patterns across nonhuman primates and children in groups. We proceed by outlining a certain characteristic or facet of social structure or behavior in monkeys and apes, and then seek similar observations in the developmental literature. In this section, we touch on a number of dominance phenomena, including: (1) rank and the allocation of resources; (2) short-term increases in the intensity of dominance in the face of environmental demands or stress; (3) nonverbal communication and its role in dominance patterns; and (4) dominance relations and the patterns of social monitoring (attention structure) in groups. The sequence of discussion of these topics is of no special consequence to us, for in our view, none of them are (a priori) more important than the others in capturing the general idea of dominance relations.

Rank and the Allocation of Resources

Nonhumans. There seems little question that one's rank in a group of nonhuman primates is an important factor in what resources are obtained. Already noted are the findings of Richards (1974) and Christopher (1972) that rank does predict success in priority to dietary items in monkeys; the same can be said of apes (Wrangham, 1974). Other resources are also differentially distributed according to status. Kaufmann (1967) defined the "central group" of a troop of rhesus monkeys as the area encompassed by an imaginary line drawn around all the females. An adult male's rank—independently determined in terms of aggressive and submissive acts shown in another situation—predicted his relation to the central group. High-dominant males spent 90% of their time in the central group, and the remaining 10% on the group's fringe. In contrast, low-ranking males spent only 35% of their time in the central group, and the lowest ranking animals (peripherals) were seen in this area only 14% of the time. Doubtless, time spent in the central group by males is related to access to females (cf. Carpenter, 1942; Kolata, 1976).

Children. In nursery situations, most conflicts between preschoolers are disputes over objects such as toys and apparatus (Blurton Jones, 1967); Smith and Green (1975) estimated that fully 73% of all aggressive incidents can be classified as property fights. Smith and Green (1975) also report that the initiator of a dispute was successful in 63% of the cases in which there was no adult intervention. Successes such as these are related to the child's social status. Abramovitch and Strayer (1978) calculated two types of hierarchies in their preschool subjects—one based on what they termed aggressive interactions (threats or direct physical attacks) and the other based on victories in object-position struggles. They report that the aggressive interaction (social status) hierarchy showed no reversals, and that it correlated +.76 with the hierarchy based on disputes over resources. Further, Strayer and Strayer (1976) found that the outcomes of 76% of object-position struggles were predicted by the attack-threat dominance ranking of their preschool subjects, and McGrew (1972) reported that in his sample, the six most aggressively ranked boys won 77% of their quarrels over objects, whereas the six least aggressively ranked boys won only 38% of their disputes.

In addition to short-term consequences of struggles over objects, long-term allocation of resources based on rank has been observed. For older children (as was the case for monkeys), the use of space becomes an issue, with dominant boys and girls having most control over areas that are deemed desirable. One such area is one's bunk at summer camp. Savin-Williams (1976, 1977) reports that desirable bunk position—in terms of proximity to the cottage counselor's bunk—correlated +.83 with social rank (but, see Savin-Williams, 1979, for a failure to replicate this relationship, and Austin & Bates, 1974, for a conceptual replication of the positive effect in adult males). Similarly, Sundstrom and Altman (1974) found that the high- and medium-dominant boys in their sample used the desirable areas of a cottage more often than did low-ranking boys over many weeks of observation.

Girls also exhibit territoriality-related rank. Deutsch, Esser, and Sossin (1978) computed the number of locations in a girls' residence cottage (e.g., bedroom, playroom, dining area, TV room) in which a subject spent the first 50% of the time she was being observed. These authors reasoned that if a dominant girl could wrest a territory away from another (subordinate) girl, she would spend time there, and would thus be seen in fewer different locations than would a subordinate girl. Rank (defined by the number of aggressive acts given and received) did predict territoriality. The number of locations that were occupied for half of the time by the high-, medium-, and low-ranked subjects were, respectively, 4.5, 5.8, and 10.5.

Rank is also related to spatial arrangement and participation in children's groups in other ways. Recall that in Kaufmann's (1967) study of rhesus monkeys the lowest ranking animals—the so-called peripherals—spent only 14% of their time in the central group, as defined by the presence of females. Low-ranking children are also peripheral and poorly integrated into their respective groups. Ginsburg (1980) defined omega (lowest ranking) boys as those consistently chosen last for team sports, and then sampled the free spatial arrangements of the boys' groups using stop-action video pictures. The omega children were located, on the average, about twice as far from the nearest other child compared with nonomegas, and nonomegas exhibited 10 times the amount of physical contact with others as the omegas. Finally, omegas were literally peripheral to the group, and were found on the group's boundary twice as often as nonomegas (Ginsburg, 1980).

Summary. Obviously, nonhuman primates and children are not competing for the same things. Monkeys might be competing for proximity to females, whereas children might be after preferred bunk positions. Nevertheless, when resources are scarce or when spatial arrangements are at issue, the rank structure of a group has a distinct bearing on who gets what. Low-ranking individuals do not share equally in the resources available to the group, and in some cases actually exist on the fringe of the group.

Short-Term Increases in Dominance Patterns in Reaction to Environmental Demands

Nonhumans. As previously stated, captivity tends to increase the level of aggression in groups of monkeys. This captivity effect is also apparent in apes, as indicated in the work of Wilson and Wilson (cited in Hamburg, 1971). Indeed, it is possible to induce ranking via cramping in some New World species of primates who do not normally show dominance patterns in the wild (Kolata, 1976); these patterns seem related to changes in the organization of natural troops as a result of environmental pressure. Crook and Gartlan (1966) remark on shifts in the social structure of baboons from herds, in good feeding areas, to foraging harem groups when conditions deteriorate.

Deterioration of the environment is not the only thing that can provoke agonistic interactions among simians. Artificial provisioning (feeding) can also produce such effects. Southwick, Siddiqi, Farooqui, and Pal (1976) observed several troops of rhesus who were periodically fed by the local Indian population, and compared the animals' behavior to that in nonfeeding periods. The effect of provisioning (Southwick et al., 1976) was clear:

> In both rural and urban groups, the frequency of aggressive interactions increased two to six times during feeding periods in terms of threats, chases, attacks, and total aggressive interactions. For example, total aggressive interactions in one group increased from .79 per hour per monkey to 5.09 per hour per monkey . . . [p. 12]."

These observers also saw more aggression when there were narrowly scattered large food items (e.g., bananas, carrots) than when there were widely scattered small food items (e.g., rice, peanuts, beans). This contrast is also evident in magabeys in natural settings, who show more aggression when feeding on a few large fruit than when feeding on many small fruit (Chalmers, cited in Wrangham, 1974).

The provisioning effect has also been seen in chimpanzees observed at the Gombe Stream Research Center by Wrangham (1974). Artificial provisioning of bananas resulted in well over a 10-fold increase in the frequency of attacks than on days on which fruit was not provided. Thus, both Southwick et al. (1976) and Wrangham (1974) found that nonhuman primates will avidly enter into disputes when there is something over which to dispute.

Children. Monkeys from substandard environments behave more aggressively than do those in more appropriate settings (Singh, 1966, 1969), and the same may be true of toddlers. George and Main (1979) compared the aggression (reactive hostility, harassment, and teasing) and assault (hitting, kicking, spitting, pinching) rates of abused 1 to 3 year olds to those of normal controls, and found that the abused children showed four times the amount of aggression and twice the amount of assault seen in controls. If an abusive environment is a substandard environment, then the monkey and the toddler data may be comparable.

What is perhaps clearer is that scarcity of toys and other apparatus is linked to the amount of agonistic interactions in children's groups. Smith (1974) used a set of toys that included a table and table toys, a doll house, climbing frame and slide, sand pit, toy chest, and others. In his experiment, he gave groups of children either one, two, or three duplicate sets of toys to play with and also systematically varied room size so that each child had 75, 50, or 25 square feet available. Although the space manipulation did not influence agonistic behavior (responses that hurt or conflicted with the intentions of others), availability of toys certainly did. Smith (1974) reports a fairly linear rate of agonistic interactions as a function of resources: the more toys, the fewer the conflicts.

The general environmental setting also influences overall rates of disputes between children. Certain preschoolers were studied outdoors in the summer at the Langara Preschool Center in Vancouver, and others were observed indoors in the winter at the Early Childhood Education Centre in Waterloo (Strayer & Strayer, 1978). Although the groups were roughly the same size (17–19 children), the Waterloo group showed over twice the rate of object–position struggles when compared with the Vancouver children. Interestingly, Strayer and Strayer (1978) remark that:

> This finding may reflect the effects of setting, since the children of Waterloo were observed during winter in an indoor setting with spatial constraints and many toy-related play activities. Such environmental factors may influence the form of social conflict in a stable group in a fashion roughly analogous to the effects of artificial provisioning on competition and aggression in feral troops of nonhuman primates [p. 176].

A further analysis of differences between the Waterloo and Vancouver groups (carried out by Strayer, Chapeskie, & Strayer, 1978) indicated that counter attacks in reaction to initiated agonism were more frequent at the former site (43%) than at the latter (23%). This difference was also attributed to the settings.

Summary. Changes in the environment evoke changes in the rate of dominance-related activities of primate groups. When the environment becomes spatially restricted, such as in captivity, conflict increases. Further, when members are given a reason to enter into conflict—for example, if food or toys are provisioned—they do so avidly. These patterns are in line with our earlier argument that dominance relations preadapt or predispose the group (as a group) to react in an optimal fashion to an environmental crisis. Here, the species would ultimately benefit at the expense of the lower-ranking members.

Nonverbal Communication, Conflict, and Dominance

Nonhumans.   Primatologists have long appreciated the fact that signals can substitute for acts in simian societies, and students of social conflict and social structure in these animals frequently record postures, gestures, and expressions that reveal dominance (e.g., threat signals) and subordinance (e.g., appeasement signals). Note that such categories are included in Fedigan's (1976) and van Lawick-Goodall's (1972) lists of measures in Table 3.1. Examples of such threat and appeasement signals in rhesus monkeys are shown in the drawing in Fig. 3.3. The topmost depiction is an appeasement grin, and the remaining two depictions are aspects of a threat face. Wickler (1967) provides an interesting example of an

FIG. 3.3.   Sketch of an appeasement grin (top figure) and threat face (two lower figures) of rhesus monkeys (drawn by J. Rajecki).

exchange of such signals between two crab-eating macaques: a dominant male and a subordinate female. Wickler's first picture shows the animals sitting near to one another. In the sequence that followed, the female committed an "offence" (Wickler's term) by placing her hand on the branch that supported the male. The male quickly directed a threat face at the female, who in turn reacted with an appeasement grin (and the removal of the offending hand). The grin seemed to placate the male, whose face quickly relaxed to a resting configuration. In the absence of a threat, the female's face relaxed, and in a total of 4 seconds from the beginning of the exchange, the status quo was restored. The male succeeded in removing a social irritant, not by physical attack, but rather by nonverbal communication. Signals such as these have been catalogued for a wide variety of nonhuman primates, including chimpanzees (van Lawick-Goodall, 1968).

Children.   Studies of the facial expressions of even deaf–blind-born children show that they have a wide repertoire of contextually defined emotional expression. For example, when they are playing, they laugh, and when they are hurt, they cry (Eibl-Eibesfeldt, 1973). It is further known that normal adults are able to identify the expressions of these children without knowing the context in which the face occurred (Rajecki, 1977). Eibl-Eibesfeldt (1974) also provides examples of what he believes are a threat stare and a submissive pout in an agonistic encounter between a boy and a girl, and Blurton Jones (1967) mentions that children's property fights are preceded and accompanied by "what looks like a frown with lowering of the eyebrows and rather little furrowing of the brow ('low frown') and no conspicuous modification of the mouth expression [p. 355]." Camras (1980) has completed a catalogue of components of children's and nonhumans' threat faces from a variety of reports; a summary of these elements is shown in Table 3.3. According to Camras, such expressions in nonhumans are

TABLE 3.3
Features of Monkeys', Apes', and Children's Facial–Threat Patterns
at the Level of Fine Motor Movement[a]

Configuration	Group		
	Monkeys	Apes	Children
Lips thrust forward?	?	Yes	Yes
Lips pressed together?	?	Yes	Yes
Lower lip drop?	Yes	?	Yes
Small mouth?	Yes	Yes	Yes
Lowered brow?	Yes	Yes	Yes
Nose wrinkle?	Yes	?	Yes
Face thrust?	Yes	Yes	Yes
Stare?	Yes	Yes	Yes

[a]After Camras, 1980, Table 1. Note that these features agree in several unusual characteristics.

usually accompanied by some form of aggression (chase, attack) on the part of the signaler, and some form of appeasement (fleeing, avoiding) on the part of the target.

Additionally, Camras (1977) provided a detailed study of these expressions and their relation to children's conflicts; her results made clear that expressions do influence the course of object–position struggles between children. Camras' kindergarten subjects were induced to compete to play with a gerbil in a box. To gain access to the box, a child had to demand it or pull it away from some other child who was already playing with the animal, and who could resist losing the plaything by rejecting the request or by pulling back. Camras (1977) found that aggressive facial expressions (i.e., lowered brows, stare, lips pursed together and thrust forward, among other features) were associated with persistent resistance to the loss of the object on the part of the player. Moreover, percipients of these expressions were relatively hesitant about undertaking subsequent attempts to win the object away from the player.

Zivin (1977a) has extended the investigation of the relation of certain facial configurations to conflict outcomes to naturalistic settings for preschoolers. Her interest was in the so-called "plus face" (raised brows, eyes wide open with eye contact with the opponent, and raised chin) in contrast to the so-called "minus face" (gently furrowed brows, eyes dropped in broken eye contact, and chin lowered). Children were observed in spontaneous interactions, and note was made of wins, losses, and no outcomes as a result of the interaction. Additionally, a record was kept of the sort of face (plus, minus, or other) that accompanied each type of outcome. The relationship of face to outcome at two different schools is shown in Table 3.4. Virtually the same result was obtained at the two locations, with plus faces predicting wins more often than the remaining configurations. On the contrary, minus faces were more predictive of losses than the others.

In a related study, Zivin (1977a) tested some children in the situation employed by Camras (1977), with the modification that whereas on some occasions, the contestants could see one another, at other times, their vision was blocked by a barrier. Plus faces were evident in 60% of the win outcomes when visual contact was possible, but only in 28% of the win outcomes when vision was blocked. Apparently, the plus face was more likely to be expressed when the expresser thought it could be appreciated.

The plus face may work to increase wins for the expresser because it tends to inhibit the behavior of the percipient. In a fine-grained analysis of reactions to the two types of faces, Zivin (1978b) found that the latency of *any* act by the percipient following a plus face was 1.2 seconds, compared with a latency of .64 seconds after a minus face. When *counterconflict* acts on the part of the percipient are considered separately, an even larger difference emerges. Average latency following a plus face for counterconflict reactions was 1.8 seconds, whereas mean latency following a minus face was only .54 seconds. These

TABLE 3.4
Relationship of Outcome Type
to Accompanying Facial
Configuration in Interactions
among Preschoolers[a]

Outcome	Face		
	Plus	Minus	Other[b]
School 1			
Win	67	11	22
Loss	15	51	33
No outcome	19	04	76
School 2			
Win	66	03	29
Loss	11	52	37
No outcome	23	00	76

[a]From Zivin, 1977a. Values in the table are percentages.

[b]The *other* category is comprised of about 18 different expressions, all of which are too infrequent to report separately, and none of which is related to wins or losses.

inhibitory effects seem in line with the effects for threat faces reported by Camras (1977).

Finally, Zivin (1977b) indicates that the rate of emission of the plus face is related to a child's rank in the group. Preschoolers (4–5 year olds) and elementary school pupils (7–10 year olds) were ranked by one another for "toughness" within their respective groups, and their free social interactions were videotaped. The analysis showed that whereas there was no relation of rank to plus-face emission in the younger children, for the older set, a significant positive effect did emerge: +.36. It is difficult to say if one should expect a more robust relationship between these variables than is revealed by a coefficient of +.36, but Zivin (1978a) feels that the plus face and the threat face are not equivalent. Perhaps future research will reveal the relation of the plus face to the threat face, and the relation of the threat face to rank.

The complements to threat signals are appeasement gestures. Ginsburg (1980) has suggested that one such gesture in children might be an overall diminution in physical stature, as in making oneself look smaller via body posture (see "crouching" in chimps in Table 3.1). Ginsburg tested this idea by obtaining videotapes of elementary school boys in free interaction on a playground. With these tapes, Ginsburg was able to identify 72 instances of aggressive attacks, including hitting, jumping upon, pushing, pulling, or kicking. For each aggressive episode, Ginsburg determined when the aggressor *ceased* his attack, defined by the absence of physical contact for at least 2 minutes. Then, he determined what behavior on the part of the victim preceded the aggressor's restraint. He found that about 80% of the time, attack termination coincided with the diminution of stature on the part of the victim. Furthermore, diminution of stature was almost always accompanied by gaze aversion, which, as noted, is a characteristic of the minus face described by Zivin (1977a). Diminution of stature in combination with gaze aversion is apparently a relatively effective signal of appeasement on submission, and works to suspend the actions of an attacker. In fact, this behavior also has meaning for other group members who were not initially involved in the aggression. Ginsburg (1980) extended his observations and identified 36 episodes in which a third child intervened in a dispute and attacked the original aggressor. Seventy five percent of these third-party interventions occurred when the original attacker failed to heed his victim's diminution in stature!

Summary.   Nonverbal communication along several dimensions is definitely related to social conflict and dominance in primates. Dominant or attacking individuals display threats, and subordinates and victims show appeasement. Further, there is evidence that such exchanges not only express established relationships between individuals, but also lend an advantage to the aggressive signaler in situations in which the individuals were previously unknown to one another (as in the studies of children by Camras and Zivin). These patterns are observable in monkeys, apes, and children. In fact, these groups share many common features of facial expression (see Table 3.3). Similar nonverbal communication of dominance is therefore available to all the primates under study. Such communication is a valuable substitute for more violent expressions of dominance relations.

Attention Structure and Dominance

Nonhumans.   The visual monitoring of *certain* animals in nonhuman primate groups is important. An animal that is predictable and controlled, such as a subordinate in a social hierarchy, would not be a cause for concern, and therefore would not draw much attention. On the other hand, dominant animals, whose behavior is out of the control of lesser group members, would warrant a good deal of watching. This is the pattern that is usually found, and it has been termed "attention structure" by Chance (1976). For example, low-ranking talapoin monkeys scanned others in the colony more frequently than did high-ranking members, and when there was a shift in the dominance hierarchy (animals gained or lost in rank), there was a corresponding shift in the monitoring pattern (Keverne, Leonard, Scruton, & Young, 1978). A similar result was obtained by Haude, Graber, and Farres (1976), who found a positive, linear effect between rank and duration of social observing in rhesus monkeys.

A related pattern of responses is seen in monkeys' reactions to social strangers. Strangers, by virtue of their unfamiliarity, are not predictable initially (or necessarily controllable), so those that are physically introduced to established groups get their share of looks, in addition to any direct attacks they may inspire. Rosenblum, Levy, and Kaufman (1968) found that newcomers to squirrel monkey groups received the most social exploration—including visual inspection—on the day of entry, and that such exploration was virtually absent 5 days later. A related finding was made by Scruton and Herbert (1972), who found that both male and female talapoin strangers received most looks by residents on the first day, and that the rate of looks dropped sharply over the 5 days of observation.

Research on apes strongly suggests that such attention structures exist in this phyletic branch. For instance, Chance (1976) reanalyzed Schaller's (1963) data on gorillas in groups, and found that a disproportionate number of interactions of all members involved the dominant male. Chance interpreted this pattern to mean that there was a direct or indirect pattern of attention towards that male. Of a more concrete nature is Bauer's (1980) observation of the social-monitoring patterns of subordinate male chimpanzees:

> The performance of ''arrival-charging'' displays is quite common for alpha [dominant] males joining a party and it is most likely due to this that adult males are often ''glancing around the periphery'' of their visual field when on the ground in open areas. They do this so that they can anticipate and avoid difficult situations before they arise [p. 111].

Similarly, van Lawick-Goodall (1972) reported that subordinate chimpanzees seated near a superior animal constantly watch the face of the other, presumably for changes of expression that may reveal changes in mood.

Children.   A clear relationship between rank and attention structure in children's groups was recorded by Abramovitch (1976). Abramovitch defined the dominance hierarchy among her preschooler sample in terms of property fights won and lost. Next, attention structure was determined by systematically recording the glances of each child at the others. An eye or head movement that oriented the eyes or face of the child towards another child was the operational definition of a glance (attention). Rank and the number of glances received were then compared. The general result was that high-ranking children received more glances than would be expected by chance. Contrarily, low-ranking children received fewer glances than would be expected by chance.[2]

Abramovitch's findings are nicely supplemented by those of Omark and Edelman (1976). The latter authors estimated the dominance hierarchies of first-through third-grade pupils by asking individuals about the toughness of their schoolmates. Fairly reliable and valid hierarchies can be specified using this procedure, and such structures are evident in the Omark–Edelman data. But, their most interesting result was a "statistical" dissimilarity between high- and low-ranked individuals. This statistical property was the amount of variance in the estimates of the toughness of the dominant versus the subordinate children. There was relatively small variance in the distributions of pupils' toughness judgments of the high rankers, and relatively large variance in the corresponding distributions of the low rankers. This difference implies that there was more agreement about the toughness of the dominant children than of the subordinate children, which seems to tie in with Abramovitch's (1976) data on glancing. Because more attention is paid to children of higher status, more will be learned about them, and more accurate estimates can be made by more judges. In fact, accuracy of one's estimate of his or her own rank depends on that individual's rank. Strayer et al. (1978) obtained behavioral measures of rank and preschoolers' self-reports of their own rank. They found that children in the high and medium slots were more accurate in estimating their own relative position (in terms of the behavioral data) than were those in the low ranks. These sorts of findings seem related to Deag's (1977) observations that monkeys' social interactions are based more clearly on the dominant's rank than on the subordinate's rank.

Another confirmation of the relation of attention received to rank is provided by Abramovitch and Strayer (1978). These authors used several conventional methods to rank their preschoolers and to record attention patterns, and found that at a number of preschools, the correlations between various definitions of rank and attention ranged from $+.41$ to $+.96$ with an average correlation of

---

[2]Vaughn and Waters (1980) failed to find a strong relationship between hazing and specific hostility and attention structure ($r = .14$) in their study of children, and found only a weak relationship between success in object struggles and attention structure ($r = .43$). However, before too much is made of this apparent failure to replicate, one should point out that the various measures in the Vaughn–Waters research were made at different times and in different places. Dominance patterns were established outdoors in the spring, and attention structure was recorded indoors in the winter. Because there is good reason to believe that physical locale has a strong influence on patterns of social conflict and dominance in children (see Strayer et al., 1978; Strayer & Strayer, 1978), it may well be the case that Vaughn and Waters' (1980) results are due to shifts in dominance patterns across the two locations in their study, rather than to an absence of a relationship between dominance and attention structure.

+.78. However, a more interesting finding in the Abramovitch–Strayer chapter is a comparison of observations obtained at the Waterloo preschool previously mentioned. Recall that Abramovitch and Strayer (1978) reported a correlation of +.76 between a hierarchy based on object–position struggles and one based on attack–threat interactions (see the section *Children* under the heading *Rank and Allocation of Resources*), which means that those measures are related, but not identical. The average correlation between object–position struggle ranking and attention received was +.45, compared with a correlation of +.63 for attention compared with success in attack–threat interactions. This difference means that rankings based on attack–threat interactions are probably the better standard against which to compare other kinds of measures. In any case, attention structure seems more clearly related to the attack–threat measure than to the object–position struggle index.

Summary.   Animals in groups pay attention to one another. The general finding in monkeys and apes is that subordinates pay more attention to dominants than vice versa. This finding is in line with the notion that subordinates are more in jeopardy than are superiors. Related patterns are seen in children's groups where dominant members receive a disproportionately large number of glances from other group members. Apparently, the powerful members of any group bear watching. Children, like chimpanzees, doubtless want to avoid difficult situations before they arise.

HOMOLOGY: THE CRITERION OF SPECIAL QUALITY

The great advantage of the ethological approach to the study of children's social development and behavior is that workers in this tradition have provided us with a wealth of detailed observations of behavior. Their extensive and precise records therefore allow comparisons with nonhuman primates that were heretofore difficult, or of dubious merit. We have reviewed a good deal of this ethological literature, and feel that it constitutes prima facia evidence that social conflict and dominance in children's groups are generally homologous with social conflict and dominance in groups of nonhuman primates. Our claim is based on an appeal to Remane's criterion of special quality for determining morphological homologies (cited in Atz, 1970). This rule states that similarities in morphology can be homologized, without regard to other criteria, if they agree in several unusual characteristics. In other words, the greater the degree of complexity and correspondence of structures across species, the more likely the homology. There is no reason that the same rule cannot be applied to cross-species comparisons of social conflict and dominance where precise observations are available. We feel that such correspondences—or agreement in unusual characteristics—exist across various phyletic branches of primates at several levels of behavioral organization including: (1) patterns at the group level; (2) gross motor movement; and (3) fine motor movement. Sections of our chapter support this claim.

Agreement in Characteristics at Levels of Behavioral Organization

Behavior Patterns at the Group Level.   Our review indicated that, in general: (1) rank is related to the allocation of resources, with high-ranking individuals having priority to access; (2) environmental demands or stress (such as captivity) tend to produce short-term intensification or rigidification of dominance relations in a group; (3) dominance relations are often expressed via nonverbal communication, with dominant animals signaling threats and subordinates signaling appeasement or fear; and (4) attention (social monitoring) in such groups is structured in such a way that subordinates are more likely to pay attention to individuals that are dominant than vice versa. There is a respectable amount of data that indicates that these four patterns are characteristic of all the groups under study, as indicated in Table 3.5.

Gross Motor Movement.   There are marked resemblances among monkeys, apes, and children in the gross motor movements involved in social conflict and dominance (see Table 3.1). These resemblances are particularly impressive when we remember that the various researchers cited in Table 3.1 did not borrow classifications from one another, but rather worked them out independently, based on extensive observations of their respective subjects. Therefore, we can

TABLE 3.5
Features of Monkeys', Apes', and Children's Dominance
Patterns at the Group Level[a]

Feature	Group		
	Monkeys	*Apes*	*Children*
Rank and the allocation of resources:			
Dominant members have the advantage?	Yes	Yes	Yes
Reaction to short-term environmental change:			
Dominance pattern is intensified?	Yes	Yes	Yes
Nonverbal communication and rank:			
Dominant members threaten and displace?	Yes	Yes	Yes
Subordinate members appease?	Yes	Yes	Yes
Dominance and attention structure:			
Dominant members are monitored?	Yes	Yes	Yes

[a]Note that these comparative features agree in several unusual characteristics.

reliably identify a high degree of correspondence in social behavior across phyletic branches at the level of gross motor movement.

Fine Motor Movement.   Camras' (1980) catalogue of the components of facial expressions of threat (see Table 3.3) indicates a high degree of correspondence among monkeys, apes, and children at a fine-motor-movement level. Although Camras herself (1980) is cautious about labeling these comparisons as homologies, we are more optimistic and feel that this precise level of analysis might even satisfy the stringent demands of the morphological taxonomist (see Atz, 1970). Future discussion of the similarities in primate threat expressions (and other forms of expressions) should point to the musculature involved, and the possibility of morphological homologies of such musculature.

In sum, there is evidence for agreement of special features at several levels of behavioral organization in the primate groups under study, and this degree of agreement lends itself to an argument for homology. Having established that dominance relations are characteristic of all these primates, the next question is: Why dominance?

ADVANTAGES OF DOMINANCE: COMPENSATIONS OF SUBORDINANCE

When children find themselves in on-going groups, they sort themselves out along a dimension of dominance (among, perhaps, others). The question is not why they are in groups, but rather why they manifest this form of social organization. Recognizing the ubiquitousness of such social structures, Hartup (1970) nonetheless doubted that "children have a 'natural' propensity for forming structured groups . . . [p. 371]." Again, we find we must disagree with Hartup. If the claim for homology across primates in social conflict and dominance is correct, then children's propensity towards group structure is indeed natural. Our guess is that humans, along with certain monkeys and apes, inherited tendencies towards small-group social conflict and dominance from a prosimian ancestor who existed prior to the Eocene. This is the same speculation advanced by Washburn and Avis (1958) to account for similarities in special sensory features across modern primates.

But why conflict and dominance? Why not harmony and equality? The answer is that it would be advantageous to the species (if not to every individual) were there a mechanism whereby certain genes could be retained in the gene pool, and others discarded. Obviously, the notion of the survival of the fittest applies here. "Survival of the fittest" and "social conflict and dominance" have a lot in common, as indicated by this passage from Wilson (1975):

In the language of sociobiology, to dominate is to possess priority of access to the necessities of life and reproduction. This is not a circular definition; it is a statement of a strong correlation observed in nature. With rare exceptions, the aggressively superior animal displaces the subordinate from food, from mates, and from nest sites. It only remains to be established that this power actually raises the genetic fitness of the animals possessing it. On this point the evidence is completely clear [p. 287].

The term "genetic fitness" refers to the contribution to the *next* generation of one genotype (individual organism) in a population, relative to the contributions of other genotypes (other individual organisms). As noted in the quote from Wilson, the genetic fitness of dominant animals is maximized by virtue of their rank. On the other hand, subordinance also works to maximize the genetic fitness of even inferior individuals. The existence of a social hierarchy allows dangerous animals (dominants *and* subordinates can inflict injury) to coexist in groups, and to reveal their status not only by damaging attack, but also by social signals of threat and appeasement. Such a social strategy minimizes the loss of fitness on the part of subordinates (Deag, 1977). If, instead, subordinates were killed or injured in disputes, or were forced to live in social isolation, their fitness would be reduced to zero.

The path from zygote to parenthood is dangerous to the developing individual, and, in a real sense, an organism's genetic fitness is at risk all along the way. Therefore, ontogenetic considerations are as important as any others in determining such fitness. In this light, dominance hierarchies in groups of children may be related to an individual's fitness in at least two important ways: First, success in childhood social conflict and dominance may be a *determinant* of one's later fitness when more mature. Second, success in this youthful arena may be a *reflection* of already existing differences in fitness. In either event, our attempt to show that children's dominance patterns are homologous with those of other primates becomes much more than an empirical exercise if it is proper that these comparisons be made from the theoretically unifying principle of genetic fitness.

SPECULATIONS: DOMINANCE-RELATED PHENOMENA

Because dominance behavior is such an important feature of children's social life, it behooves us to identify phenomena that antedate or accompany this behavior. Moreover, in keeping with our comparative approach, it is productive and stimulating to draw parallels to these ancillary phenomena at the animal level. We have identified two potential candidates for such an analysis, familial influences on individual differences in rank and social conflict in the family.

On the Antecedents of Rank

We suggested that success in children's social conflicts and dominance relations could (1) contribute to the individual's genetic fitness; or (2) be a reflection of such fitness. Although these are not mutually exclusive possibilities, the evidence at hand points to the latter. Dominant and subordinate children are very different people because they are usually characterized by quite different profiles. For example, Savin-Williams (1976, 1977) obtained sociometric descriptions of the highest and lowest ranked boys in the hierarchies he observed. These descriptions were provided by the other boys in the groups, and are shown in Table 3.6. As noted, the picture is very different for the alpha (dominant) and omega (subordinate) cabin mates.

The impression that personality is involved in dominance patterns is buttressed by the work of Olweus (1978) on "bullies" and their victims, "whipping

TABLE 3.6
Characterizations of the
Most Dominant (Alpha) and
Most Subordinate (Omega) Boys[a]

Rank	
Alpha (Dominant)	*Omega (Subordinate)*
1976 Study	
Most athletic	Most mature
Most irreligious	Most friendly
Most dominant	Most religious
Most popular	Most quiet
Most stubborn	Most serious
Best "little chief"	Cabin "brownnoser"
1977 Study	
Most athletic	Most shy
Most mature	Most quiet
Most masculine	Most feminine
Most serious	Most submissive
Most handsome	Cabin follower
Most strong	Cabin helper
Most dominant	Cabin smiler
Cabin leader	
Cabin organizer	

[a]Note that these characterizations have been judged by other members of the hierarchies in Savin-Williams' 1976 and 1977 reports.

boys.'' Olweus found that whipping boys were generally more anxious, insecure and nervous, and that they evaluated themselves and their situation rather negatively. On the other hand, bullies were more secure, less afraid and anxious, and generally evaluated themselves and their situation positively. However, the assessment of personality after a rank order has been established is problematic. After all, if one ends up being the omega (subordinate) boy, it may be perfectly reasonable to act in a friendly, quiet, and unobtrusive way, and anyone who is a whipping boy also has a right to feel anxious and evaluate his environment negatively. Therefore, if one's personality determines one's rank, a theorist is still faced with the problem of accounting for the personality. Interestingly, research indicates strong filial influences on the attainment of rank in nonhumans, and the expression of social skills and assertiveness in humans. Success in social conflict and dominance thus do have experiential antecedents.

Experiential Antecedents to Dominance and Subordinance in Nonhumans.   In certain monkey societies, an offspring's rank is determined in large part by its mother's rank. Sade's (1967) observations of rhesus monkeys on Cayo Santiago (off Puerto Rico) indicate that in fights between yearlings, animals defeated peers whose mothers ranked below their own, and in turn were defeated by peers whose mothers ranked above their own (Kawai, 1965; cf. Kawamura, 1965). Hierarchies established in this fashion are stable for several years and more, at least for female offspring. As females mature, they remain in the natal group, and rank near their mothers. As adults, they outrank lesser females who had already become adults while the daughters in question were maturing. For males, the picture is somewhat different. At age 4, or so, most males leave or are forced out of the center of the natal group, and are said to be peripheral to the group. Because of this displacement, males at puberty may gain or lose in rank. Still, Koford (1963) reports that the adolescent sons of high-ranking mothers may remain in the central group and may rise to a high rank as adults without becoming peripheral (cf. Yamada, 1971).

Of course, without its mother, a young monkey could not be dominant over a normal adult. But with the mother present, it is even possible to manipulate a young monkey's rank over other adults. Marsden (1968) caused fluctuations in rank among adult females in a group by removing and replacing certain adult males whose presence favored one or the other of the females. As the females' ranks vis-a-vis one another changed from time to time, the rank of their offspring in the group shifted accordingly. That is, if female X was dominant over female Y at some point, the young offspring of female X also dominated the adult Y. When female Y came to be dominant over X, Y's young offspring also dominated the adult X.

Evidence of any sort of familial influence on social rank in apes is scarce, but nevertheless interesting. For example, van Lawick-Goodall's (1967) impressions were that young chimps sometimes threatened animals older than themselves, but only those who were subordinate to their own mother, and only in the mother's presence. Further, chimp mothers do provide social support for their offspring in conflict situations (cf. Bauer, 1980), but not universally. The observations of van Lawick-Goodall (1967) suggest that high-ranking mothers were more likely to assist their young than were low-ranking individuals, but more evidence is necessary before this point can be made conclusively. Still, the information on apes is at least in line with what is known about filial influences on social rank in young monkeys.

Experiential Antecedents to Social Skills in Children.   Dealing with peers poses problems for the child, and it may well be that the child's general problem-solving abilities, coping styles, and social skills lead to success (dominance) or failure (subordinance) in such situations. An illustration of this idea is Esser's (1968) study of psychiatrically hospitalized boys. Esser found that her measure of social rank was related to the severity of the childrens' disorders. Lower ranked individuals were the most debilitated, and higher ranked boys were discharged sooner.

But, most groups of children are not characterized by a broad range of psychopathology, so other dimensions in their psychological makeup must predict dominance. One promising individual difference that may be specified for this purpose is the child's quality of attachment to the mother. Briefly, Ainsworth (see Ainsworth, Blehar, Waters, & Wall, 1978) has developed a classification scheme for denoting the quality of an infant's attachment to the mother. In this scheme, nominal *A*- and *C*-type babies are said to be anxiously attached, whereas *B*-type babies are securely attached. Classifications are based on a short laboratory test (the strange situation) in which the child is observed in both the presence and the absence of the parent. Apparently, the child's attachment classification is based on the mother's child-rearing attitudes and practices. Observations in the home indicate that mothers of *B*-type babies are more sensitive to their children than are mothers of *A*- and *C*-type babies (Ainsworth, Bell, & Stayton, 1971).

In addition to the variations in their reactions to their mothers, *A*-, *B*-, and *C*-type babies differ in a number of other ways. For our purposes, an important difference is that a child's attachment classification predicts later social behavior among age mates. Compared with those that are anxiously attached, securely attached preschoolers show more social competence. They are better able to deal flexibly with an unfamiliar situation by exchanging information with others nonverbally (and perhaps verbally, as well) in dyads composed of strangers (Lieberman, 1977). Further, Waters, Wippman and Sroufe (1979) provide evidence of a different sort that infantile attachment classification predicts later peer competence even in the mother's absence. In their study, adult observers

TABLE 3.7
Average Scores for Selected Measures of Peer
Competence for Anxiously and Securely Attached
Preschoolers[a]

	Classification	
Measure	Anxious	Secure
Other children seek child's company	3.8	6.2[b]
Socially withdrawn	6.2	3.9
Suggests activities	3.5	6.2
Peer leader	3.3	5.2
Attracts attention	3.4	5.6
Hesitant with other children	5.4	3.4

[a] After Waters, Wippman, & Sroufe, 1979, Table 1.
[b] Scores can range from 1 to 9.

classified preschool children on dimensions using scales that ranged numerically from 1 to 9. The average scores for anxiously and securely attached preschoolers on various dimensions of peer competence are shown in Table 3.7, where differences are quite clear. B-type babies are obviously more socially competent than their A- or C-type counterparts (cf. Easterbrooks & Lamb, 1979).

Therefore, it seems that human mothers, by virtue of their child-rearing practices, have an impact on their children's role in the peer group. We feel that social competence as assessed by Lieberman (1977), Waters et al. (1979) and Easterbrooks and Lamb (1979) will probably prove to be quite predictive of dominance hierarchies as measured by the ethologically-oriented researchers.

Conflict in the Family

That children exhibit dominance behavior seems beyond doubt; that this youthful behavior is indeed related to their genetic fitness requires further validation. However, if success in conflict does promote the winner's fitness, then other types of social conflict might be homologous as well. It is common knowledge that children come into conflict with family members, including parents, and this is also true of young monkeys and apes. Trivers (1974) has placed a sociobiological analysis on certain of these parent–child conflicts. He argues that parental investment in an offspring (e.g., feeding, protecting) serves to ensure the offspring's well being (and hence its fitness). For example, primate mothers nurse their babies at the breast, by which the young survive. Sooner or later, however, conflict between parent and child may develop because of their incongruent wishes. At some point, the mother may wish to wean the offspring, whereas the offspring may wish to continue feeding at the breast. Indeed, weaning can be a traumatic experience for all involved, but the offspring's noisy insistence may gain access to the nipple and more parental investment than would otherwise have been obtained.

Parents can thus provide various kinds of noxious stimulation that reflect a reduction in parental investment. They can be inaccessible, indifferent, or punitive and restrictive, and offspring might react so as to restore their parents' investments. Patterson and his coauthors (e.g., Patterson, 1974, 1976, 1979; Patterson & Cobb, 1973; Patterson & Reid, 1970) have developed a coercion theory of such conflicts. Note that Patterson's coercion theory does not stem from ethology or sociobiology, but more from a family-therapy orientation. Still, it is a handy way to comprehend a phenomenon that has important ethological or sociobiological implications. Basically, the theory says that the child uses his or her own forms of noxious stimulation to place a brake on the noxious stimulation emanating from some family member. In the earlier example, such noxious stimulation on the part of the parent might be denial of the nipple, and the child's coercion might take the form of a temper tantrum. The general sequence of coercive episodes is depicted in Fig. 3.4. As shown in the flow chart, escalation of conflict is possible (up to some point) if the offspring's coercion is initially ineffective.

From the perspective of this chapter, the next question to be asked is whether there might be homologies in offsprings' coercion across phyletic branches. So far, there is at least tentative evidence for this possibility. Table 3.8 presents *recorded* examples from various sources of presumably coercive behavior in a number of primate groups, including monkeys, apes, and children (e.g., monkeys: Hinde & Spencer-Booth, 1967; Ransom & Rowell, 1972; apes: Clark, 1977; van Lawick-Goodall, 1968, 1972; children: Patterson, 1974, 1979). Again, one can only speculate at this point, but if peer conflicts are homologous in primates, it is worthwhile to look for homologies in other forms of conflict, such as those labeled coercion in Table 3.8.

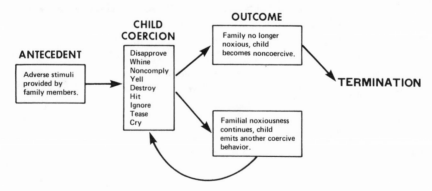

FIG. 3.4.   Flow chart of steps in a coercive episode in intrafamilial social conflict in children.

TABLE 3.8
Observations of Infant Coercion in Mother–Infant Conflicts
in Various Primates (References in Text)

	Steps in Conflict		
Primate	Parental Antecedents	Infant Coercion	Conflict Outcome
Humans	Mother unavailable Disapproval Commands Punishment	Disapproval Negativism Whine Hit	Terminated familial aversive- ness
Apes (chimpanzees)	Denial of nipple	Whimper Scream Tantrum Hit	Occasionally obtained nipple
Monkeys (macaques)	Denial of nipple Threat Maternal bite	Threat face Tantrum Charging Slapping	Obtained proximity and nipple
Monkeys (baboons)	Forced following Denial of nipple Mock bites Hitting	Distress cry Scream Tantrum	Gained nipple or rode on mother

CONCLUSION

*If we had been made directly from clay, the way it says in the
Bible, and had therefore inherited no intermediate characteristics,—if some god, or some principle of growth, had gone
that way to work with us, he or she might have molded us into
much more splendid forms. But considering our simian descent, it
has done very well. The only people who are disappointed in us
are those who still believe that clay story. Or who—
unconsciously—still let it color their thinking.*

Clarence Day, 1920

Our claim in this chapter is that features of social conflict and dominance in
children's groups are homologous with that seen in groups of nonhuman primates. That is, it is our assertion that the similarities in certain social phenomena
across monkeys, apes, and humans (children) are attributable to a genetic similarity across these phyletic branches, based on a common ancestry. To support this
claim, we have appealed to biologists' standards for establishing morphological
homologies of similar structures, and we have applied these standards to conflict

and dominance behavior. In particular, we focused on the criterion of special quality, whereby agreement in several unusual features is the standard for conclusions about homology. Application of this criterion has provided compelling evidence in the case of morphological homologies across monkeys, apes, and humans (see Fig. 3.1 and Table 3.2); we feel that the evidence is no less compelling when this standard is applied to behavior.

There are indisputable agreements on several features of conflict and dominance across primates, both nonhuman and human. One source of agreement is the observation that dominance greatly influences, in similar ways, the social lives of individual monkeys, apes, and human groups (see Table 3.5). Another source of considerable agreement is the details of the gross and fine motor movements in the social structure of primate groups (see Tables 3.1 and 3.3). This picture is simultaneously too complex and too coherent to represent a collection of sheer coincidences or analogies. We feel that it constitutes prima facia evidence for homology according to the criterion of special quality. Were this evidence deemed insufficient, in and of itself, we could also appeal to the relatedness of nonhuman and human primates based on fossil and molecular taxonomies, but given the richness of the behavioral data, such an appeal seems gratuitous.

Unfortunately, we cannot express the mathematical probability that social conflict and dominance are homologous in the groups under study. First, the criterion of special quality does not specify how *many* correspondences or agreements in features are required before homology can be concluded. Second, if there were a great deal of disagreement in special features, then one would doubt homology existed. At present, we have no way of knowing about the *lack* of correspondence of as yet undetermined but important features of social organization in one or another primate group, because these may have been overlooked or ignored by researchers. However, we are not overly pessimistic on this last point, because past advances in the quality and quantity of research in this area have revealed more and more, rather than less and less, similarity.

What is gained in demonstrating that there are homologies in behavior across humans and nonhumans? Are humans elevated or debased by such comparisons? Neither, we think. Discoveries of homologies (or analogies, for that matter) inform us of humanity's true place in the scheme of things, much in the same way that fossil and molecular taxonomies are fundamentally informative. Montagu (1973) recounts an anecdote from the time when Darwin's controversial ideas about evolution burst on the scene in Victorian England. On being informed of the theory of humanity's kinship with other primates, the horrified wife of an English Bishop said that she certainly hoped that the theory was not true, but if it *were* true, that not many people would find out about it. To the contrary, most people these days, including developmental psychologists, want to know the truth about humanity. To paraphrase Clarence Day, the only people who will be disappointed in the discovery of primate homologies are those who still believe in that clay story.

REFERENCES

Abramovitch, R. The relation of attention and proximity to rank in preschool children. In M. R. A. Chance & R. R. Larsen (Eds.), *The social structure of attention*. New York: Wiley, 1976.

Abramovitch, R., & Strayer, F. Preschool social organization: Agonistic, spacing, and attentional behaviors. In L. Krames, P. Pliner, & T. Alloway (Eds.), *Aggression, dominance, and individual spacing*. New York: Plenum Press, 1978.

Ainsworth, M. D. S., Bell, S. M. V., & Stayton, D. J. Individual differences in strange-situation behaviour of one-year-olds. In H. R. Schaffer (Ed.), *The origins of human social relations*. New York: Academic Press, 1971.

Ainsworth, M. D. S., Blehar, M. C., Waters, E., & Wall, S. *Patterns of attachment*. Hillsdale, N.J.: Lawrence Erlbaum Associates, 1978.

Andrew, R. J. The origin and evolution of the calls and facial expressions of the primates. *Behaviour*, 1963, *20*, 1–109.

Ardrey, R. *The territorial imperative*. New York: Atheneum, 1966.

Atz, J. W. The application of the idea of homology to behavior. In L. R. Aronson, E. Tobach, D. S. Lehrman, & J. S. Rosenblatt (Eds.), *Development and evolution of behavior*. San Francisco: Freeman, 1970.

Austin, W. T., & Bates, F. L. Ethological indicators of dominance and territory in a human captive population. *Social Forces*, 1974, *52*, 447–455.

Bauer, H. R. Chimpanzee society and social dominance in evolutionary perspective. In D. R. Omark, F. F. Strayer, & D. G. Freedman (Eds.), *Dominance relations*. New York: Garland STMP Press, 1980.

Bernstein, I. S. Primate status hierarchies. In L. A. Rosenblum (Ed.), *Primate behavior: Developments in field and laboratory research* (Vol. 1). New York: Academic Press, 1970.

Bernstein, I. S., & Smith, E. O. Editors' introduction. In I. S. Bernstein & E. O. Smith (Eds.), *Primate ecology and human origins: Ecological influences on social organization*. New York: Garland STMP Press, 1979.

Blurton Jones, N. G. An ethological study of some aspects of social behaviour in children in nursery school. In D. Morris (Ed.), *Primate ethology*. Chicago: Aldine, 1967.

Boulding, K. E. Am I a man or a mouse—or both? In A. Montagu (Ed.), *Man and aggression*. New York: Oxford University Press, 1973.

Brace, C. L. Biological parameters and pleistocene hominid life-ways. In I. S. Bernstein & E. O. Smith (Eds.), *Primate ecology and human origins: Ecological influences on social organization*. New York: Garland STMP Press, 1979.

Camras, L. Facial expressions used by children in a conflict situation. *Child Development*, 1977, *48*, 1431–1435.

Camras, L. Animal threat displays and children's facial expressions: A comparison. In D. R. Omark, F. F. Strayer, & D. G. Freedman (Eds.), *Dominance relations*. New York: Garland STMP Press, 1980.

Carpenter, C. R. Sexual behavior of free ranging rhesus monkeys. *Journal of Comparative Psychology*, 1942, *33*, 113–142.

Chance, M. R. A. Attention structure as the basis of primate rank orders. In M. R. A. Chance & R. R. Larsen (Eds.), *The social structure of attention*. New York: Wiley, 1976.

Christopher, S. B. Social validation of an objective measure of social dominance in captive monkeys. *Behavior Research Methods and Instrumentation*, 1972, *4*, 19–20.

Clark, C. B. A preliminary report on weaning among chimpanzees of the Gombe National Park, Tanzania. In S. Chevalier-Skolnikoff & F. E. Poirier (Eds.), *Primate bio-social development: Biological, social, and ecological determinants.* New York: Garland STMP Press, 1977.

Coelho, A. M., Bramblett, C. A., & Quick, L. B. Activity patterns in howler and spider monkeys: An application of socio-bioenergetic methods. In I. S. Bernstein & E. O. Smith (Eds.), *Primate ecology and human origins.* New York: Garland STMP Press, 1979.

Crook, J. H., & Gartlan, J. S. Evolution of primate societies. *Nature,* 1966, *210,* 1200–1203.

Day, C. *This simian world.* New York: Knopf, 1920.

Deag, J. M. Aggression and submission in monkey societies. *Animal Behaviour,* 1977, *25,* 465–474.

Delgado, J. M. R. Animal models for brain research. In G. Serban & A. Kling (Eds.), *Animal models in human psychobiology.* New York: Plenum Press, 1976.

Deutsch, R. D., Esser, A. H., & Sossin, K. M. Dominance, aggression, and the functional use of space in institutionalized female adolescents. *Aggressive Behavior,* 1978, *4,* 313–329.

Drews, D. R. Group formation in captive *Galago crassicaudatus:* Notes on the dominance concept. *Zietschrift fur Tierpsychologie,* 1973, *32,* 425–435.

Dunbar, R. I. M., & Dunbar, E. P. Contrasts in social structure among black-and-white colobus monkey groups. *Animal Behaviour,* 1976, *24,* 84–92.

Easterbrooks, M. A., & Lamb, M. E. The relationship between quality of infant–mother attachment and infant competence in initial encounters with peers. *Child Development,* 1979, *50,* 380–387.

Eibl-Eibesfeldt, I. The expressive behaviour of the deaf-and-blind-born. In M. von Cranach & I. Vine (Eds.), *Social communication and movement.* New York: Academic Press, 1973.

Eibl-Eibesfeldt, I. The myth of the aggression-free hunter and gatherer society. In R. L. Holloway (Ed.), *Primate aggression, territoriality, and xenophobia.* New York: Academic Press, 1974.

Esser, A. H. Dominance hierarchy and clinical course of psychiatrically hospitalized boys. *Child Development,* 1968, *39,* 147–157.

Fedigan, L. M. A study of roles in the Arashiyama west troop of Japanese monkeys (*Macaca fuscata*). In F. S. Szalay (Ed.), *Contributions to primatology* (Vol. 9). Basel: S. Karger, 1976.

Gartlan, J. S. Structure and function in primate society. *Folia Primatologica,* 1968, *8,* 89–120.

Gellert, E. Stability and fluctuation in the power relationships of young children. *Journal of Abnormal and Social Psychology,* 1961, *62,* 8–15.

Gellert, E. The effect of changes in group composition on the dominant behaviour of young children. *British Journal of Social and Clinical Psychology,* 1962, *1,* 168–181.

George, C., & Main, M. Social interactions of young abused children: Approach, avoidance, and aggression. *Child Development,* 1979, *50,* 306–318.

Ginsburg, H. J. Playground as laboratory: Naturalistic studies of appeasement, altruism, and the omega child. In D. R. Omark, F. F. Strayer, & D. G. Freedman (Eds.), *Dominance relations.* New York: Garland STMP Press, 1980.

Golding, W. *Lord of the flies.* New York: Coward-McCann, 1962. (Originally published, 1954.)

Hamburg, D. A. Crowding, stranger contact, and aggressive behaviour. In L. Levi (Ed.), *Society, stress and disease.* London: Oxford University Press, 1971.

Hartup, W. W. Peer interaction and social organization. In P. H. Mussen (Ed.), *Carmichael's manual of child psychology* (3rd ed.). New York: Wiley, 1970.

Hartup, W. W. The social worlds of childhood. *American Psychologist,* 1979, *34,* 944–950.

Haude, R. H., Graber, J. G., & Farres, A. G. Visual observing by rhesus monkeys: Some relationships with social dominance rank. *Animal Learning & Behavior,* 1976, *4,* 163–166.

Hausfater, G. Dominance and reproduction in baboons (*Papio cynocephalus*). A quantitative analysis. In F. S. Szalay (Ed.), *Contributions to primatology* (Vol. 7). Basel: Karger, 1975.

Hinde, R. A. The use of differences and similarities in comparative psychopathology. In G. Serban & A. Kling (Eds.), *Animal models in human psychobiology.* New York: Plenum Press, 1976.

Hinde, R. A., & Spencer-Booth, Y. The behaviour of socially living rhesus monkeys in their first two and a half years. *Animal Behaviour,* 1967, *15,* 169–196.

Hodos, W., & Campbell, C. B. G. Scala Naturae: Why there is no theory in comparative psychology. *Psychological Review,* 1969, *76,* 337–350.

Kaufmann, J. H. Social relations of adult males in a free-ranging band of rhesus monkeys. In S. A. Altmann (Ed.), *Social communication among primates.* Chicago: University of Chicago Press, 1967.

Kawai, M. On the system of social ranks in a natural troop of Japanese monkeys. In S. A. Altmann (Ed.), *Japanese monkeys.* Edmonton, Alberta: Stuart A. Altmann, 1965.

Kawamura, S. Matriarchal social ranks in the Minoo-B Troop. In S. A. Altmann (Ed.), *Japanese monkeys.* Edmonton, Alberta: Stuart A. Altmann, 1965.

Keverne, E. G., Leonard, R. B., Scruton, D. M., & Young, S. K. Visual monitoring in social groups of talapoin monkeys (*Miopithecus talapoin*). *Animal Behaviour,* 1978, *26,* 933–944.

Koford, C. B. Rank of mothers and sons in bands of rhesus monkeys. *Science,* 1963, *141,* 356–357.

Kolata, G. B. Primate behavior: Sex and the dominant male. *Science,* 1976, *191,* 55–56.

Lieberman, A. F. Preschoolers' competence with a peer: Relations with attachment and peer experience. *Child Development,* 1977, *48,* 1277–1287.

Lockard, R. B. Reflections on the fall of comparative psychology: Is there a message for us all? *American Psychologist,* 1971, *26,* 168–179.

Lorenz, K. Z. *On aggression.* New York: Harcourt, Brace, & World, 1966.

Lorenz, K. Z. Analogy as a source of knowledge. *Science,* 1974, *185,* 229–234.

Marsden, H. M. Agonistic behaviour of young rhesus monkeys after changes induced in social rank of their mothers. *Animal Behaviour,* 1968, *16,* 38–44.

McGrew, W. C. *An ethological study of children's behavior.* New York: Academic Press, 1972.

Montagu, A. The new litany of "innate depravity," or original sin revisited. In A. Montagu (Ed.), *Man and aggression.* New York: Oxford University Press, 1973.

Moynihan, M. Some aspects of reproductive behaviour in the black-headed gull (*Larus ridibundus L.*) and related species. *Behaviour Supplement 4,* 1955.

Murphy, D. L. Animal models for human psychopathology: Observations from the vantage point of clinical psychopharmacology. In G. Serban & A. Kling (Eds.), *Animal models in human psychobiology.* New York: Plenum Press, 1976.

Nelson, W. (Ed.). *William Golding's lord of the flies.* New York: Odyssey Press, 1963.

Oetzel, R. M. Annotated bibliography. In E. E. Maccoby (Ed.), *The development of sex differences.* Stanford, Calif.: Stanford University Press, 1966.

Olweus, D. *Aggression in the schools.* Washington, D.C.: Hemisphere, 1978.

Omark, D. R., & Edelman, M. S. The development of attention structures in young children. In M. R. A. Chance & R. R. Larsen (Eds.), *The social structure of attention.* New York: Wiley, 1976.

Patterson, G. R. A basis for identifying stimuli which control behavior in natural settings. *Child Development,* 1974, *45,* 900–911.

Patterson, G. R. The aggressive child: Victim and architect of a coercive system. In E. J. Mark, L. A. Hamerlynk, & L. C. Handy (Eds.), *Behavior modification and families.* San Francisco: Bruner/Mazel, 1976.

Patterson, G. R. A performance theory for coercive family interaction. In R. B. Cairns (Ed.), *Social interaction: Method, analysis, and illustration.* New York: Halsted Press, 1979.

Patterson, G. R., & Cobb, J. A. Stimulus control for classes of noxious behaviors. In J. F. Knutson (Ed.), *The control of aggression.* Chicago: Aldine, 1973.

Patterson, G. R., & Reid, J. B. Reciprocity and coercion: Two facets of social systems. In C. Neuringer & J. Michael (Eds.), *Behavior modification in clinical psychology.* New York: Appleton-Century-Crofts, 1970.

Pichot, P. New perspectives in psychiatry: Relevance of the psychopathological animal model to the human. In G. Serban & A. Kling (Eds.), *Animal models of human psychobiology*. New York: Plenum Press, 1976.

Rajecki, D. W. Ethological elements in social psychology. In C. Hendrick (Ed.), *Perspectives on social psychology*. Hillsdale, N.J.: Lawrence Erlbaum Associates, 1977.

Ransom, T. W., & Rowell, T. E. Early social development of feral baboons. In F. W. Poirier (Ed.), *Primate socialization*. New York: Random House, 1972.

Richards, S. M. The concept of dominance and methods of assessment. *Animal Behaviour*, 1974, *22*, 914–930.

Rosenblum, L. A., Levy, E. J., & Kaufman, I. C. Social behaviour of squirrel monkeys and the reaction to strangers. *Animal Behaviour*, 1968, *16*, 288–293.

Rosenzweig, S. Outline of a denotative definition of aggression. *Aggressive Behavior*, 1977, *3*, 379–383.

Rowell, T. E. The concept of social dominance. *Behavioral Biology*, 1974, *11*, 131–154.

Sade, D. S. Determinants of dominance in a group of free-ranging rhesus monkeys. In S. A. Altmann (Ed.), *Social communication among primates*. Chicago: Aldine, 1967.

Savin-Williams, R. C. An ethological study of dominance formation and maintenance in a group of human adolescents. *Child Development*, 1976, *47*, 972–979.

Savin-Williams, R. C. Dominance in a human adolescent group. *Animal Behaviour*, 1977, *25*, 400–406.

Savin-Williams, R. C. Dominance hierarchies in groups of early adolescents. *Child Development*, 1979, *50*, 923–935.

Schaller, G. B. *The mountain gorilla: Ecology and behavior*. Chicago: University of Chicago Press, 1963.

Scruton, D. M., & Herbert, J. The reaction of groups of talapoin monkeys to the introduction of male and female strangers of the same species. *Animal Behaviour*, 1972, *20*, 463–473.

Seyfarth, R. M. Social relationships among adult female baboons. *Animal Behaviour*, 1976, *24*, 917–938.

Singh, S. D. The effects of human environment on the social behavior of rhesus monkeys. *Primates*, 1966, *7*, 33–40.

Singh, S. D. Urban monkeys. *Scientific American*, 1969, *221* (1), 108–115.

Smith, P. K. Aggression in a preschool playgroup: Effects of varying physical resources. In J. de Wit & W. W. Hartup (Eds.), *Determinants and origins of aggressive behavior*. The Hague: Mouton, 1974.

Smith, P. K., & Green, M. Aggressive behavior in English nurseries and play groups: Sex differences and response of adults. *Child Development*, 1975, *46*, 211–214.

Southwick, C. H., Siddiqi, M. F., Farooqui, M. Y., & Pal, B. C. Effects of artificial feeding on aggressive behaviour of rhesus monkeys in India. *Animal Behaviour*, 1976, *24*, 11–15.

Strayer, F. F., Chapeskie, T. R., & Strayer, J. The perception of preschool social dominance. *Aggressive Behavior*, 1978, *4*, 183–192.

Strayer, F. F., & Strayer, J. An ethological analysis of social agonism and dominance relations among preschool children. *Child Development*, 1976, *47*, 980–989.

Strayer, J., & Strayer, F. F. Social aggression and power relations among preschool children. *Aggressive Behavior*, 1978, *4*, 173–182.

Struhsaker, T. T. Social structure among vervet monkeys (*Cercopithecus aethiops*). *Behaviour*, 1967, *29*, 83–121.

Sundstrom, E., & Altman, I. Field study of territorial behavior and dominance. *Journal of Personality and Social Psychology*, 1974, *30*, 115–124.

Tinbergen, N. *The herring gull's world*. London: Methuen, 1953.

Tinbergen, N. Comparative studies of the behaviour of gulls (*Laridae*): A progress report. *Behaviour*, 1959, *15*, 1–70.

Trivers, R. L. Parent–offspring conflict. *American Zoologist*, 1974, *14*, 249–264.

van Hooff, J. A. R. A. M. Facial expressions in higher primates. *Symposia of the Zoological Society of London*, 1962, *8*, 97-125.

van Lawick-Goodall, J. Mother–offspring relationships in free-ranging chimpanzees. In D. Morris (Ed.), *Primate ethology*. Chicago: Aldine, 1967.

van Lawick-Goodall, J. The behaviour of free-living chimpanzees in the Gombe Stream Reserve. *Animal Behaviour Monographs*, 1968, *1*, 161-311.

van Lawick-Goodall, J. A preliminary report on expressive movements and communication in the Gombe Stream chimpanzees. In P. Dolhinow (Ed.), *Primate patterns*. New York: Holt, Rinehart, & Winston, 1972.

Vaughn, B. E., & Waters, E. Social organization among preschool peers: Dominance, attention, and sociometric correlates. In D. R. Omark, F. F. Strayer, & D. G. Freeman (Eds.), *Dominance relations*. New York: Garland STMP Press, 1980.

Washburn, S. L. Human behavior and the behavior of the other animals. *American Psychologist*, 1978, *33*, 405-418.

Washburn, S. L., & Avis, V. Evolution of human behavior. In A. Roe & G. G. Simpson (Eds.), *Behavior and evolution*. New Haven: Yale University Press, 1958.

Waters, E., Wippman, J., & Sroufe, L. A. Attachment, positive affect, and competence in the peer group: Two studies in construct validation. *Child Development*, 1979, *50*, 821-829.

Wickler, W. Socio-sexual signals and their intra-specific imitation among primates. In D. Morris (Ed.), *Primate ethology*. Chicago: Aldine, 1967.

Wilson, D. O. *Sociobiology*. Cambridge, Mass.: Belknap Press, 1975.

Wrangham, R. W. Artificial feeding of chimpanzees and baboons in their natural habitat. *Animal Behaviour*, 1974, *22*, 83-93.

Yamada, M. Five natural troops of Japanese monkeys on Shodoshima Island: II. A comparison of social structure. *Primates*, 1971, *12*, 125-150.

Zivin, G. Facial gestures predict preschoolers' encounter outcomes. *Social Science Information*, 1977, *16*, 715-730. (a)

Zivin, G. On becoming subtle: Age and social rank changes in the use of a facial gesture. *Child Development*, 1977, *48*, 1314-1321. (b)

Zivin, G. *The relation of facial gestures to conflict outcomes*. Paper presented at the Meetings of the International Society of Political Psychology, New York, 1978. (a)

Zivin, G. *Stopped cold: Sight of two facial gestures differentially affects children's latencies during conflict*. Paper presented at the Meetings of the Animal Behavior Society, Seattle, 1978. (b)

4

Generalized Event Representations: Basic Building Blocks of Cognitive Development

Katherine Nelson
City University of New York Graduate Center

Janice Gruendel
Yale University

What do young children remember about their everyday experiences? Is the structure of these memories similar to or different from that of older children and adults? Does their representation of reality based on everyday experience have implications for other—presumably more abstract—cognitive structures and processes?

For several years, we have been studying what young children (ages 3–8) know about routine events with the intent of finding answers to these questions. We began our investigations within the framework of *scripts* as discussed by Schank and Abelson (1977). According to their definition, a script is "a structure that describes an appropriate sequence of events in a particular context. A script is made up of slots and requirements about what can fill those slots. The structure is an interconnected whole, and what is in one slot affects what can be in another [p. 41]." They claim that scripts enable people to infer unstated propositions from events and statements, to interpret simple stories, to predict the probable sequence of events to guide decision making. Work with adults (e.g., Abelson, 1976; Bower, 1978; Bower, Black, & Turner, 1979; Martin, Patterson, & Price, 1979) has supported these claims and has affirmed the proposed structure of script representations.

There are several important characteristics of scripts that are relevant to understanding young children's knowledge structures. First, they are temporal and causal *sequences* of actions. Second, they are general schemas or frames within which *variable elements* may be inserted in appropriate contexts. Third, they form *structural wholes*. If young children's event representations share these characteristics, we would need to reconsider the widely held assumption that the young child's thought is atemporal, acausal, idiosyncratic, unorganized,

131

and particularistic. There is, in fact, increasing evidence that these attributions are inaccurate in a number of domains (e.g., A. L. Brown, 1976; Donaldson, 1978; Gelman & Gallistel, 1978). If we are to find the beginnings of order and understanding in children's thought, however, the most obvious place to look would seem to be knowledge about events with which they have had personal experience. In addition, we believe, as the title of this chapter indicates, that event representations may be basic to many other cognitive structures and processes. The script model, therefore, seems quite appropriate as a framework for these investigations.

In our first script studies, we simply asked preschool children to tell us or to act out with props "what happens when you have lunch at the day-care center" or "dinner at home" or "go to McDonald's"? On the basis of the children's responses, we were able to model the structure of their prototypical meal scripts, and subsequently we have used the data from these studies to design more systematic investigations of the structure and use of scripts in early childhood.

In this chapter, then, we describe some of the most important outcomes of this research. First, we review in more detail the background of the research; next, what we have discovered about the structure and function of children's scripts thus far; and finally, what we see as the implications of the script model for understanding cognitive process in young children.

SCRIPT RESEARCH: BACKGROUND

When we began investigating the cognitive and linquistic abilities of preschool children (that is, children between 2 and 5 years) several years ago, the prevailing wisdom was that children of this age were cognitively incapacitated. In contrast to the research coming out of infant-studies laboratories, which tended to show that babies were growing smarter every day and were clearly more intelligent than they had been given credit for by (for example) Piaget (e.g. Cohen & Salapatek, 1975), studies of preschool children continued to show them as deficient in all regards—preconceptual, prelogical, even preverbal. One of the reasons for this was that preschool children served as a contrast group to grade-school children in most studies in which they took part, and thus it was almost a foregone conclusion that they would turn out to be less capable by comparison. (The ideal developmental study, in fact, has often been defined as one that compares children at ages 5 and 8, because with this design, one is bound to get significant age differences!) Few studies were concerned with development within the preschool years (few still are) and virtually none compared preschoolers to infants below the age of 2, or tried to show how developments in these two age ranges were related to one another.

In order to understand the development of language and thought in early childhood, we felt it important to consider young children from the standpoint of their strengths rather than from their weaknesses. Language ability was an obvious area of strength. Indeed, many theorists had speculated that language ability must be wired in to the organism because, among other reasons, language ability was so much more sophisticated in the young child than any other cognitive system (see, for example, Bruner, Olver, & Greenfield, 1966; Chomsky, 1965; McNeill, 1970). In terms of a grammatical system, 3 year olds appeared to have a good command of a very complex classification and rule-applying system at the same point that they could not combine apples and oranges and get fruit, or decide whether there were more apples or more fruit in a collection—in other words, at a time when they were sadly deficient in general categorizing ability. But language skills require first and foremost the ability to categorize (see, for example, R. W. Brown, 1956, 1958); thus the discrepancy seemed anomalous.

In contrast to language skills, the memory research that was then underway showed young children to be sadly deficient (see A. L. Brown, 1975a, in press). They could remember a few words or numbers in a list; appeared to remember no more whether they tried or not; had no concept of metamemory or the deployment of remembering skills. Moreover, neither children nor adults appeared to remember much from their own lives during the preschool years. There appeared to be an absolute cut-off in terms of autobiographical memory somewhere around 3 years of age (Nelson & Ross, in press; White & Pillemer, 1979). Yet paradoxically, somewhat as in the case of language, it was obvious that children remembered episodes, people, and objects from their own experiences. What did they remember, in what form, and why? Was remembering simply a matter of motivation, or were there other aspects to be understood with respect to this problem? Because what children remembered and talked about was primarily personal experience, it seemed relevant to study what they knew about these events directly.

Recently, there have begun to appear a number of reports attributing more capability to the young child than previously thought. For example, new studies of discourse (e.g., Ervin-Tripp & Mitchell-Kernan, 1977; Garvey, 1975) showed that 3 and 4 year olds have acquired procedures for carrying on conversations and getting things done with words that belied Piaget's (1923/1926) claim that they spoke in egocentric exchanges and collective monologues. Shatz and Gelman (1973) showed that 4 year olds were adept at modifying their speech to take account of their listeners. Along a different line, A. L. Brown and her colleagues (A. L. Brown, 1975b, 1976) demonstrated that children who had been thought incapable of ordering things along a temporal dimension were actually quite good at ordering narrative sequences when the sequences were short and simple enough for them to comprehend.

Towards the end of the 1970's, Donaldson (1978) put forth well-articulated arguments for the importance of the study of cognitive capabilities rather than cognitive deficits in young children. Donaldson especially detailed her own departure from Piaget and presented research evidence to show that when thinking in context, the young child was not at all as limited as had been thought. Gelman and Gallistel (1978) made similar arguments in the context of delineating the child's acquisition of number skills. In addition, the work of Soviet psychologists, particularly in their studies of memory, emphasized that in "natural" contexts, the young child displayed far more competence than in the abstract, contrived situations that the American laboratory (or its counterpart, the schoolroom corner) presented (see Meacham, 1977).

In each of these areas, it seemed that when children were operating in a familiar, well-understood context, they appeared more competent than previously thought. Therefore, the importance of understanding context became clear. The questions of what is context, why is it important to the young child, and what is different about older children that they can operate successfully without the supporting "ecologically valid" context then become important research topics in their own right.

It has been generally agreed that the young child seems bound to the context of the concrete here and now and cannot abstract from it to consider problems that are not motivated by the immediate situation. That is, context for the young child is constrained to the spatially and temporally present. The script model of cognitive representation is, as noted previously, a model that is spatially and temporally defined; therefore, it seemed to provide a highly relevant model for studying how young children acquired and used structured knowledge of the events in which they take part.

But note that the script is a *cognitive model of experienced events*. The implication of this is that if young children represent experience in terms of scripts, they should not be bound to the immediate situational context even though they might be constrained to a model of reality that is spatially and temporally ordered. If this is the case, they should be able to talk about events that they are not presently taking part in, and to use this knowledge also for other purposes and in other contexts. The *context* to which the young child is bound, then, would not be the immediate situation, but *cognitive representations* of familiar situations—that is, available scripts.

SCRIPT RESEARCH: FINDINGS

Our first foray into script research was an exploration to determine whether children's knowledge of events fit the script model as outlined by Schank and Abelson (1977). As previously noted, we interviewed 3 and 4 year olds in a day-care center, asking them "what happens" during three familiar eating events (Nelson, 1978b). At the outset, we were intrigued with the notion that young children might *develop* scripts, or at least develop the ability to organize their verbal output in script form. That is, we expected that 3 year olds would give us disjointed, unordered, idiosyncratic accounts, and that they would gradually move towards a more ordered, more conventional, less idiosyncratic script. Instead, we found that whatever the children gave us appeared to fit an ordered script model. We were genuinely surprised at this outcome. It changed our minds about the nature of young children's thought structures and has led subsequently to a rather detailed proposal about the structure of children's memory representations.

In our first study (Nelson, 1978), we first asked 20 preschool children to tell us "what happens when you have lunch at the day-care center" or "have dinner" or "go to McDonald's." Depending on the child's response, this was followed up with a general probe—for example, "anything else?" Subsequently,

TABLE 4.1
Examples of Cookie and Birthday-Party Scripts from 3–8 Years

Making Cookies
Well, you bake them and eat them. (3;1)

My mommy puts chocolate chips inside the cookies. Then ya put 'em in the oven... Then we take them out, put them on the table and eat them. (4;5)

Add three cups of butter... add three lumps of butter... two cups of sugar, one cup of flour. Mix it up... knead it. Get it in a pan, put it in the oven. Bake it... set it up to 30. Take it out and it'll be cookies. (6;9)

First, you need a bowl, a bowl, and you need about two eggs and chocolate chips and an egg-beater! And then you gotta crack the egg open and put it in a bowl and ya gotta get the chips and mix it together. And put it in a stove for about 5 or 10 minutes, and then you have cookies. Then ya eat them! (8;8)

Birthday Party
You cook a cake and eat it. (3;1)

Well, you get a cake and some ice cream and then some birthday (?) and then you get some clowns and then you get some paper hats, the animal hats and then and then you sing "Happy Birthday to you," and then then then they give you some presents and then you play with them and then that's the end and then they go home and they do what they wanta. (4;9)

First, uhm... you're getting ready for the kids to come, like puttin' balloons up and putting out party plates and making cake. And then all the people come you've asked. Give you presents and then you have lunch or whatever you have. Then... uhm... then you open your presents. Or you can open your presents anytime. Uhm... you could... after you open the presents, then it's probably time to go home. If you're like at Foote Park or something, then it's time to go home and you have to drive all the people home. Then you go home too. (6;7)

Well, first you open your mail box and you get some mail. And then you see that there's an invitation for you. Read the invitation. Then you ask your parents if you can go. Then you... uhm... go to the birthday party and you get a ride there, and after you get there you usually wait for everyone else to come. Then usually they always want to open one of the presents. Sometimes then they have three games, then they have the birthday cake, then sometimes they open up the other presents or they could open them up all at once. After that they like to play some more games and then maybe your parents come to pick you up. And then you go home. (8;10) more specific questions were asked—for example, "What happens next?" "How do you know when it's lunchtime?" In another session, the child was asked to act out the event in question using props. In follow-up studies, we concentrated on the verbal reports for lunch and dinner, comparing the response of children new to the day-care center with those who were more experienced there and contrasting the context of questioning at school and in the home. Finally, we asked preschool children about six different events on two different occasions: going to a restaurant, getting dressed, grocery shopping, having a birthday party, making cookies, and having a fire drill.

Table 4.1 gives examples of some of the responses we received from children of different ages. What can we make of such responses? Are they evidence for scripts? Do they show interesting developmental trends? To address these questions, we need first to have a better understanding of what would be evidence for script structure as well as how the task itself can be interpreted.

The Task Structure and Interpretation

When the young child is asked to tell what happens in a given situation, we need to evaluate what processes are involved in producing an answer before we can interpret the meaning of that answer in terms of our questions. Children begin with an interpretation of the discourse situation in terms of their own understanding of adult–child interactions. They can identify this as an unfamiliar, unknowable situation and refuse to answer or say "I don't know." Or, they (even in preschool) can identify it as a test situation, become nervous and shy, and mumble an answer that they hope is right. If at ease, they still must decide what the adult means by the odd question; often, a number of probes will be needed to elicit relevant responses.

Assume that a child responds to the situation appropriately in the adult's terms and interprets the question correctly. What processes are involved in making an appropriate response? The child must first access a store of information about situations of the type that are being queried. It is the nature of that store that we are interested in:

1. Does it consist of randomly stored bits and pieces of information picked up on one occasion or another?

2. Does it consist of layers of experiences laid down one at a time, each of which might be accessed?

3. Does it consist of a prototype of the situation based on the child's first experience, perhaps updated as new bits of information are added from time to time?

4. Does it consist of a general frame within which recurrent but varying elements are stacked or otherwise arranged?

The first alternative is the one that in the past was usually suggested in discussions about the mind of the preschooler; that is, children's thought was said to be idiosyncratic, fragmented, disorganized, tending to substitute the part for the whole. In this case, we would expect to find in script output a good deal of uninterpretable detail randomly drawn up from this disorganized store.

The second alternative would be expected to lead to a more organized account, but the account would be given in specific terms, such as, "I had (or have) applesauce and milk and mommy read me a story about the three bears and I brush(ed) my teeth and went to bed." The third case, the prototype structure, would also probably produce a quite specific report based primarily on the original experience or on the central tendency. The frame structure, on the other hand, would be reported in general terms, allowing for the possibility of varying details, or "slot fillers."

Before considering the evidence for or against any of these, we need to note the final step in the process involved in our task—that is, the verbal recount. Whatever the nature of the underlying representation, a child might or might not be able to report in words what has been accessed in memory. For example, a single detail might be produced from structures of types (1), (2), or (3), even though in actuality the child was able to "think" about the entire event. Or, the child might produce a general account, very skeletal, such as "I eat" to stand for the layers of (2), the prototype of (3), or the general frame of (4). Thus, the screen between us and the child in this situation is verbal translation ability. Ultimately, therefore, we need a number of converging techniques that will at least reveal the effects of this screen. Although we have some convincing evidence to indicate that the verbal recount accurately reflects the underlying representation, as we report here, we must still interpret with caution until all the evidence is in.

Characteristics of Scripts

Because scripts represent contextually based knowledge, they are content determined. That is, although we can specify a general form for the organization of a script, it is not an abstract structure that is applied to any given content, but, rather, it is representative of many different kinds of content. Script structure presumably emerges from the application of general organizing and analyzing processes to event representations, rather than existing a priori as an abstract structure. Because of this, we can talk about typical scripts, but the characteristics of a script may differ depending on the event that is being modeled. For example, in the cases discussed here, some events have a tighter causal structure than others, and some have more clearly defined goals.

Can we say what is and is not a script in order to determine if children "have" them? There are certain basic characteristics that differentiate scripts from other kinds of schematic organizations, as well as characteristics that are shared with schematic structures in general. The most important of the general characteristics is that the script, like other schemas, is an organized body of knowledge such that a part implies the whole and the whole is more than the sum of the parts. It is this characteristic that gives the script its inferential power. When a situation is understood sufficiently well that an adequate script has been developed for it, the script user can predict all of the *necessary* components and has expectations about optional components even when they are not explicitly stated. Those that are not specified in a particular instantiation will be filled in with "default values." That is to say, the user will assume that the standard components apply, whether the missing component is a role filler, a situation prop, or an action.

Another important characteristic is that scripts are *generalized* structures. Whether the script knowledge is based on only one or a repeated series of the same events, the resulting structure is expected to apply to all such events. It is not specific to a single experience. This characteristic is extremely important for the theory of memory development and is considered in more detail later in this chapter.

What differentiates the script structure from other schematic structures is its temporal causal connections. That is, scripts represent events that occur over time and thus the links between its component acts are temporal links, one act following another; in the most tightly woven structures, they are causal as well. The most important characteristics to look for in children's event representations, then, are correct temporal sequencing; evidence of logical causal links; general specification of roles, actions, and props when these are variables; and consistency over time in what is included, because such consistency is evidence for a relatively permanent representation of the whole event.

Temporal and Causal Structure.   In every study that we have undertaken, we have found that children reproduce component acts in the order in which they occur in the real world. Three year olds mention fewer component acts than do 5 or 7 year olds, but when they string two acts together, they are nearly always mentioned in the correct order. One measure of the power of the underlying order is the consistency of sequencing over time. In several of our studies, we repeated the interview after a lag of 1 to 4 weeks and compared the child's output for which acts are mentioned and for sequencing consistency. The latter is measured in terms of conditional probability—that is, given that two acts are mentioned on both occasions, what is the probability that they will be produced in the same order on each occasion? This consistency index varies between .85 and 1.00 over different studies and different events. It does not vary across the age range from 3–8.

The repeated finding that children are virtually errorless in recounting the correct sequence of acts in an event raises an interesting question: Given the generally expected poor sequencing ability of preschoolers, what accounts for such accuracy? One might expect that a child's familiarity with the event would encourage correct sequencing; yet, in the study (Nelson, 1979a) of script structures of six events that varied across a number of dimensions, we found that it was *not* repeated exposure alone that led to high sequencing ability. Rather, the causal structure of the event appears to determine at least partially how accurate and consistent a child is in producing the sequence.

In order to understand the basis for sequencing accuracy more fully, we have conceptualized the underlying script structure in the hierarchical form illustrated in Fig. 4.1. The lunch script illustrated is based on the most common acts mentioned in the ''lunch at the day-care center'' study. In this structure, certain lower-level specifications (e.g., riding tricycles) and open slots indicated by (...), such as particular teachers' names, are embedded in the main acts, which appear at the top level. The main acts were empirically derived as those mentioned most frequently by the children (of these, the central act and the end anchor are mentioned most often). Main acts in this structure are linked together either because of simple temporal contiguity (*T*) or because one act sets up a state that enables (*E*) the next to take place. This analysis illustrates the degree to which at least some of the events the child is familiar with are bound by causal, as well as spatial and temporal, connections.

In examining the role of causal structure in events in relation to children's ability to generate correct sequences, we drew on the analysis of Schank and

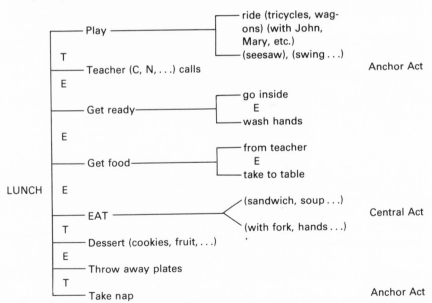

FIG. 4.1.   Script structure based on the most common acts mentioned in Lunch at the Day-Care Center Studies (*T* = Temporal Link; *E* = Enabling Link).

Abelson (1977), who argue that elements of a script are bound together by five types of causal connections. Most basic among these are "actions that bring about a new state" and "states that enable actions." Other types of causal connections include "actions that disable states," "mental states that initiate actions," and "actions that result in a new mental state." Although we found many of the connections between acts in children's scripts to be of the first two basic types, as illustrated in Fig. 4.1, we also found sequences of acts that were not causally connected. This was true in two general types of cases: first, when a number of lower-level acts could be produced in a variable order—for example, in varying the sequence of putting on particular clothes or selecting particular grocery items; second, when the essential components could be joined in different orders—that is, not through causal connectedness, but through social convention.

Consider the birthday-party event depicted in Fig. 4.2. This structure is based on the frequency of act mention in Gruendel's (1980) dissertation study. We see here that there is relatively little causal structure to the birthday-party script. Moreover, even though "Opening presents" is an essential component of the script, it may occur at or near the beginning, in the middle, or at the end (see examples in Table 4.1). "Singing Happy Birthday" and "Blowing out candles" are essential elements that invariably occur prior to cutting and eating the cake. However, the potential causal relation of each to cake eating is different. "Blowing out candles" results in a state of "no fire" enabling the cake cutting, which in turn enables eating. In contrast, only in the sense of satisfying a social convention does "Singing Happy Birthday" enable anything at all to occur; there is no true causal link between it and cake eating. Thus, the relation between temporal sequence and causality in some children's scripts is more problematic that the analysis in Schank and Abelson (1977) suggests.

FIG. 4.2.   Structure of BIRTHDAY PARTY showing alternate position of "open presents."

In our own research, we have analyzed children's scripts in terms of the following relations: causal (act results in state), enabling (state enables act), temporally invariant (for example, Happy Birthday before blowing out candles), and temporally variant (for example, opening presents before or after eating) sequences. We found that children link together acts that stand in a causal or enabling relation more frequently and at a younger age than they do sequences that are merely temporally linked (Nelson, 1979b). The use of verbal markers accompanying temporal and causal links begins with "and then" and moves on to "after," "before," "when," and "because." Both temporal and causal terms are used first in causal or enabling contexts. The correct use of causal terms occurs much earlier in our script protocols than expected by Piaget (1930/1972) or by much current psycholinguistc research (e.g., Blank & Allen, 1975) although it is in accord with recent findings by Hood and Bloom (1979). This usage suggests that script representations may be an important source of the child's understanding of causal relations, as well as an opportunity for learning the correct application of appropriate causal and temporal terms. We are currently analyzing these uses in greater detail (French & Nelson, in preparation).

Recent work on story understanding (Mandler & deForest, 1978; Mandler & Johnson, 1977; Rumelhart, 1975; Stein & Glenn, 1979) has employed the notion of a story schema that people—children or adults—utilize in representing a story that they hear or read. The story schema (or grammar) incorporates expectations that the story will contain a setting, goals, intentions, problem-solving attempts, consequences, and the like. Work with adults (e.g., Bower, Black, & Turner, 1979) has demonstrated that scripts operate in a similar way to shape expectations about a narrative, and to determine in part what will be remembered from it and in what form. Story memory, then, seems a very promising paradigm for testing some propositions about the underlying structure of scripts. If children's memory for story episodes accords with what one should expect on the basis of a canonical script for that event rather than on the basis of what was actually presented, we have further evidence for the strength of the script structure as a basic representational form.

On this reasoning, following up the evidence that young children know and rely on temporal order in familiar scripts, we presented stories to preschool children about making cookies and having a birthday party that either preserved canonical order or violated it. A sample story and recall is presented in Table 4.2.

Preliminary analyses have shown that children tend to repair the temporal violation either by omitting the act that was out of order or by reordering it to its correct place in the sequence.

Although work with story recall has shown similar restructuring of distorted material (e.g., Mandler & deForest, 1978), we believe that the children in this experiment are the youngest who have been found to restructure presented narrative material in the direction of canonical form.

TABLE 4.2
Example of Story Recall from Pilot Subject (age 5;2):
Temporal Variation

Story
1. A little girl and her mother were in the kitchen.
2. They decided to do something.
3. So they put the pan in the oven.
4. They got out the flour and sugar.
5. They stirred in the chocolate chips.
6. They spooned the dough into the pan.
7. They beat the dough until it was all mixed.
8. Then they took it out and ate them all up.

Immediate recall
1. A little girl and a mother were in the kitchen.
2. And they decided to do something.
3. They took the pan and put it in the oven.
4. They took out the flour.
5. And they mixed in the chocolate stuff.
8. And they took then out and ate them all up.
   E: What were they doing?
   C: Making chocolate chip cookies.

Delayed recall after 15 hours
1. A little girl and her mother were in the kitchen.
2. And they decided to do something.
4. They got out the flour and sugar.
5. And stirred in the chocolate chips.
7. And beat the dough until it was all done.
8. And took them out and ate them all up.

Generality of Children's Scripts.   One of the most striking findings in all of our script studies has been the level of generality of children's reports. Even the youngest children report events in a general form that provides a frame and specifies some slots to be filled, but does not necessarily specify what will or can fill those slots on a given occasion. Indeed, development of scripts takes place in the direction of specifying optional paths that may require particular slot fillers, as we discuss in the next section.

There are two linguistic indicators of this general format that are rather surprising to find very young children using. First is the use of the general "you" (in the sense of "one") to report on what happens. As illustrated in the reports in Table 4.1, this use is very common, even among 3 year olds (about 25% of the time across studies). When "you" is not employed, children are most likely to say "we" and least likely to say "I." Thus, when asked to report what generally happens in an event, they employ appropriate general terms; they do not, as one might have expected, personalize and particularize the report.

Another linguistic indication of generality is the use of the tenseless verb—for example, "you eat" or "we throw away plates." This use is virtually universal, appearing in 80–98% of the reports in various studies. The use of the "timeless" form of the verb by 3 year olds contrasts with Cromer's finding (cited in McNeill, 1979) that such use appears "quite suddenly" at 4 years of age. We believe that questioning children in the way that we do reveals some types of linguistic knowledge that observing children at play does not.

In order to study the question of general form more systematically, and to ensure that the youngest children were not using the present tense and the general pronoun in an undifferentiated way—that is, perhaps modeling the form used by the experimenter without distinguishing between a general and specific account—we designed a follow-up study. In this experiment (Hudson & Nelson, in preparation), we compared preschool children's script reports with their recall for specific experiences of the same routine events. Each child was asked to tell "what happens when you have dinner at home (or "snack at camp") on one occasion and on a second occasion, a week earlier or later, "what happen*ed* when you had dinner one time (or yesterday)?" Order of questions within and between sessions was counterbalanced. The results were striking. Significantly *less* material ($p<.05$)was reported in the specific condition (mean of 3.9 acts) than in the general (5.1 acts) and more children were unable to answer the specific question. When they did answer, they tended to include general as well as particular material in the specific condition and to use the general tenseless form of the verb, typical of script reports, in addition to the past tense. In the general condition, however, only the tenseless verb form was used and very little specific information (such as what was eaten) was provided. Comparison of both verb form use and inclusion of specific details showed a significant difference ($p<.01$) across conditions. In other words, 3-year-old children especially, but also the 5 year olds, were able to give good general accounts appropriately formulated, but they had difficulty with specific accounts and tended to slip into the general format. Order of condition did not affect this result, although children who got the specific question first gave significantly less material on the general question than the group that got the general question first. The results appear unequivocal: Young children distinguish between the two types of questions and find the specific inquiry more difficult than the general.

A study by McCartney & Nelson (1981) is also relevant to the issue of generality. Like the temporal-order study described previously, this experiment employed a story-recall paradigm.

Two groups of children—5 and 7 year olds—were presented with stories that were based on the combined scripts for dinner and bedtime. The stories were constructed to contain either skeletal or elaborated dinner or bedtime scripts respectively. Children were asked to retell the story after a short delay. One major finding was that the acts most likely to be recalled were those that had been identified *a priori* as "main acts," including achor acts—that is, those that began or ended the sequence. Main acts were those that had been identified on the basis of pilot work as the most common and basic—for example, eating and going to sleep. Although younger children recalled as many main acts as older children, older children recalled more "filler acts"—those that were not essential to the script. Again, this accords with the findings of story-understanding research, which finds that propositions that fit the story schema are best remembered. It thus supports the claim that the script structure is basic to children's understanding. As in the other studies, memory for sequence was virtually perfect at both ages in this experiment.

Consistency.   One alternative to the notion that children's script recounts reflect underlying structure is the claim that they are producing accounts more or less randomly on the basis of current situational context and/or specific memories. To test this, in a number of studies, we compared the content and structure of scripts for the same events recalled on different occasions, separated by 1 to 3 weeks. Consistency of mention of a component on both occasions in the correct sequence is evidence that the account reflects an underlying representation. Overall, we find few age differences in the degree of consistency, which ranges around 60% (i.e., percent of acts mentioned on both occasions in relation to the mean number mentioned). As noted earlier, sequence consistency is much higher—generally over 90%. The situational context—whether the child is questioned at home or in the school—makes no difference to either the content or the amount recounted.

A stronger test of the representational question was constructed as part of Gruendel's dissertation (1980). In her study, there were two conditions—a script production condition in which standard script instructions were given, and a story condition, in which children were asked to tell stories about events. Children 4, 6, and 8 years old took part and talked about making cookies, building a campfire, having a birthday party, and planting a garden. After the child produced scripts or stories on one occasion, the interviewer returned 3 weeks later and asked each child to repeat the narrative just as s(he) had earlier. Under these instructions, consistency was high (.63) for the script condition, but it was significantly lower (.40) for the stories in the story condition. Children who told stories usually did not *remember* what they had said previously and did not construct the same story a second time. We assume that children in the script condition also did not remember, but, guided by their script representation, produced similar scripts the second time around. Of equal interest is that most of the younger children produced simple scripts in response to the story instructions.

How do Scripts Develop?   Schank and Abelson (1977) state: "Plans are where scripts come from [p. 72]." In their model, a plan is generated when an obstacle is encountered on the way to a goal. They postulate a variety of "plan-boxes" that can be instantiated in standard circumstances. When a particular plan has been carried out in a given situation a number of times, it, in effect, becomes a script. Thus, in this model, scripts develop from plans.

As we have noted elsewhere (Nelson, in press, a), Schank and Abelson's view, with its emphasis on goals and its conception of plans as more abstract than scripts, poses some problems for developmental theory. In particular, the child's goal in an event may be very different from that conceived of by Schank and Abelson in postulating a model for mature information processors. For example, in everyday events, the child's goal may be simply to get through the day by following the adult's lead, or to use a particular event, such as eating lunch, as a source of fun or amusement. It is also possible that young children do not have goals in mind at all as they engage in some early events. Given these possibilities, it is clear that the child's goal may differ from what is assumed by adults to be the orienting goal of the script. This is not to deny that at some point the child has plans for achieving goals; that proposition is not at issue here. Rather, the question is: Does the child's script evolve from a plan based on the goal? We think not, and in fact, we tend to believe the reverse—that plans may evolve from scripts. Our data show that children readily accumulate scripts that are in no sense plans, but rather are routines presented as part of the child's daily experience (e.g., the accomplishments of getting dressed, eating, bathing, grocery shopping). This suggests to us that scripts are not dependent on the child's planfulness, but instead can be built up simply through observation and through participation in someone else's script or plan.

How, then, do scripts develop? There are two parts to this question, one of them partially answerable at this point and the other not. First, we have suggested that children derive scripts from their experiences in events and from observation, but we do not at this point have good evidence about how this process proceeds, what the essential components are, when a child will build a script and when not. We are currently working on these problems.

The other part refers to the course of development of scripts with age and experience. Here we have some evidence. Not surprisingly, older children are able through verbalization to reveal more about their script knowledge than are younger children. Yet, as noted earlier, subject and verb analyses performed on the scripts of even young children suggest that scripts are timeless, general structures early on. With age and experience, children's scripts become more complex and capable of specificity rather than becoming even more general. The examples in Table 4.1 illustrate this. To document these developments more specifically, Gruendel (1980) categorized children's scripts as simple sequences of acts or as conditional sequences. Conditional sequences were identified when the child specified alternative acts or orders within an event or qualified the event using an ''if-then'' or ''when'' clause.

These analyses revealed that simple sequences accounted for 85% of all 4 year olds' scripts, but only 61–62% of those of the 6 and 8 year olds. The percentage of conditional scripts rose accordingly, suggesting that structural complexity is one important facet of script development. Fig. 4.3 illustrates the increasing complexity of the campfire script with increasing age, showing how alternative paths are constructed.

Another aspect of development is the use of increasing specificity to qualify the description. Whereas the youngest child will respond to the request for a restaurant script, "we eat and go somewhere," the older child will say "when I go to Macy's Restaurant," or "It will be about Curious Jane's." In addition, as shown in the McCartney (McCartney & Nelson, 1981) study of dinner and bedtime stories, previously described, the older child will remember more of the various specific script components, whereas younger children will concentrate on remembering main acts.

There is clearly a trade-off here between explicitness and redundancy. Neither children nor adults tell all they could about an event. Some "optimal" level of general recounting defined in terms of basic events seems to emerge.

A recent study by Fivush (in preparation) indeed showed that although, as in all our work, older children (age 6) gave longer script accounts for the birthday party, when given the opportunity to choose pictures showing basic acts and to use the pictures to tell a story, there were no age differences between 4 and 6 year olds. Children of both age levels chose the same number of pictures and incorporated the acts chosen into their stories. Thus, the development apparent in pro-

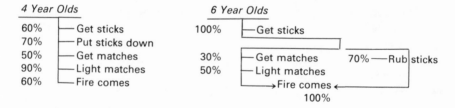

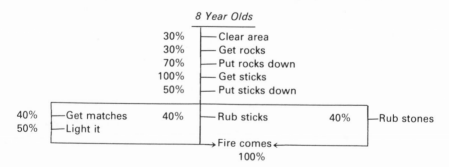

FIG. 4.3.   Age changes in the structure of children's action paths and frequency of act mention for the campfire event. Percentages indicate how many children in each group mentioned a particular act.

duction may be at least in part due to verbal skills rather than underlying representations. Further study is needed on this question.

THE ROLE OF SCRIPTS IN MEMORY

Memory is generally understood to refer either to a memory for some specific episode or fact, such as a particular experience ("Remember the time we went camping in Maine?"), or to a bit of general knowledge ("In what year did Lincoln give his Gettysburg Address?"). These two (possibly distinct) types of memory are typically referred to as episodic and semantic respectively, after Tulving (1972). However, they differ along a number of dimensions and do not exclude other formulations and distinctions (Nelson & Brown, 1979). In particular, episodic, as it is usually used, refers to a *specific* event, whereas semantic refers to *general* knowledge. It has not usually been proposed that the latter is organized around events, but around semantic hierarchies or networks of propositions. But, note that scripts are a form of what we are calling General Event Representation—that is, memory for events that is not specific to a particular experience, but is a kind of generalized knowledge.[1] For this type of distinction, the episodic–semantic dichotomy does not work well. Instead, we prefer to think of the specific (whether of that camping trip or of the color of a particular dress) versus the general (trip scripts or dress colors). It is obvious that this is not *the* correct division to make, either; that is, it will not serve all purposes. Moreover, it is difficult in some cases to decide whether a bit of remembered material is specific or general. Let us evade these questions for the moment, however, and take up the question of scripts and memory.

Scripts according to this analysis are a form of generalized memory structure. They serve to guide action, discourse, and, no doubt, thought in particular contexts. They are not usually the subject of memory discussions among adults (although they sometimes are among children, as we discussed in Nelson & Gruendel, 1979a). People do not query "Do you remember how to go to a restaurant?" although they may ask "Do you know how to get to Leon's?" When scripts are the topic of conversation, among children as well as among adults, it is usually in the form of shared knowledge of how to do something. Memory in the specific sense seems quite unrelated.

Yet, this background knowledge that does not "feel" like memory must have been learned, and it seems inevitable that it was learned through experience—an experience that was probably remembered for at least a time as a specific experience. We speculate, then, that GERs are derived from episodic memory. That seems logical enough until, on further reflection, we run into difficulties. Do

---

[1]The increasing specificity with age just discussed reflects growing complexity of knowledge with respect to what *can* fill slots and alternative pathways; the structure itself remains general.

episodic memories fade as they become GERs? Probably sometimes: but, on the other hand, we can remember specific trips as well as trip scripts. Is it possible then that specific episodic memories only emerge after GERs are established? We consider this relationship to be one of the most fascinating in the developmental consideration of GERs and scripts. Even though we only have fragmentary evidence to bring to bear on it, it still seems worth examining. The study comparing specific memories and general scripts among 3 and 5 year olds described earlier showed that for preschool children (and especially the younger ones), general accounts were easier—that is, more material was recalled—than specific memories. However, another aspect of this study qualifies the interpretation of these findings. Most children were asked at the end of the second session to recount an interesting episode that had happened one time, and some topics were suggested, such as going to the zoo, or going on a trip, or having a birthday party. Under these conditions, although some children were unable to remember any such event, those who did tended to give long and quite vivid accounts. That is, even those who had trouble with specific memories of *recurrent* events seemed to be able to remember and retell salient *novel* events. Moreover, a study of the memories of 2 year olds (Nelson & Ross, in press) has recently revealed that even 2 year olds remember novel events over periods longer than 6 months and can verbalize these memories.

A formulation that can handle these facts (and that may also help in explaining the common phenomenon of infantile amnesia) is as follows: Young children (probably as young as 1 year) represent their experiences in formats that are conducive to script formation. That is, they tend to include information about actors, actions, props, and causal–temporal links between actions and states. An experience that is so coded may be entered into long-term memory and held there available for use in another similar situation, involving the same location, actors and props, or some number of these. When such a situation is encountered, the protoscript (i.e., the representation of the first experience) becomes activated and an expectation is set up for a repetition of the first event. To the extent that relevant parts of the first experience are repeated, the two experiences are *fused*. When fusion takes place, the specific memory for an experience is no longer available. To the extent that the second experience differs from the first, some modifications and additions may take place. Fusion may still occur, although the priority of first experience seems to ensure that the first representation will dominate if the two are in conflict. Repeated experiences lead to well-known scripts. Variations produce open slots and default values. There will then emerge a standard script with options that can be instantiated on any given occasion: to the extent that any occasion is like any other, with ample space for expected variations, specific instances of that scripted event will be difficult to recall. All occasions of it will be fused.

According to this theory, in early childhood there is really no difference between the specific memory and the GER. All specific event memories are in the process of becoming generalized. There is no evidence that the young child who remembers an episode remembers it as having taken place at a particular time in a particular temporal context—that is, that it constitutes an autiobiographical memory of the type that older children and adults are able to draw on. Indeed, it seems quite probable that with very few exceptions, the latter memories are the product of a further process or processes, involving, on the one hand, the ability to identify novelty within familiar experiences—that is, novel variations from the script that do not become fused but are remembered as specific events—and, on the other hand, the ability to recount such experiences and thus to share with self and others, establishing the experiences as part of the personal historical account.

This formulation draws support from the research that we have reported here and it also fits Linton's (1979) description of the fate of her own autobiographical memories. Linton posits—on the basis of a longitudinal study of memory for specific experiences—that with time and repeated experience, episodic memory fades and semantic memory increases for information about the same events. This proposal does, however, raise a number of all-too-familiar problems, such as the recognition of similarity and difference. These problems are not unique to our formulation, however, and further research along these lines may help to elucidate them.

GERS AS BUILDING BLOCKS

The notion of a basic organizing device producing generalized event structures is implicit in the discussion of general and specific memories for experienced events. However, the form that knowledge representation takes also dictates what other processes and structures are necessary to understand the functioning of the developing cognitive system as a whole. At any given level in the system, there may be elements represented and also operators operating on those elements. The nature of the elements is not independent of the nature of the operators or the operations.

The proposal put forth here suggests a series of levels of representations with accompanying operations at each level. The proposal implies that what gets in—gets represented—at the highest initial level is determining for all that comes after. It further suggests that the nature of that representation changes with development. In this general sense, the proposal is not inconsistent with widely shared assumptions about cognitive growth (see Flavell, 1980).

What is partially novel are the following elements: First, the concern is with naturally occurring events in all their complexity. This is taken as a domain, because if we are to understand development from its beginnings, we have to understand how the child selects from complexity and how complexity is represented in the cognitive system. Selecting for the child—in the laboratory or in the schoolroom—is a perfectly valid manipulation if we are interested in some stage of processing after selection has taken place. However, because what processing takes place depends on what is selected from experience, the study of selection would seem to be a prior step. Much of the work that we have done thus far is an attempt to study the results of the child's selection.

A second novelty related to the first is that we are not concerned with discrete elements, but with events (see Jenkins, 1977). That is, we assume that young children observe the panorama before them and encode it in a connected (analogue) rather than discrete (digital) form. Indeed, the achievement of discreteness is assumed to be a developmental step of some importance. The meaning of context is precisely the notion that elements are not separable from their surroundings. The young child's knowledge is context bound in this sense. Within the script model, events are defined at different levels of generality. What we have designated as acts (e.g., in Fig. 4.1) are also events that relate elements to one another in time and space and that may, in turn, specify actions at a more detailed level. For example, eating may be carried out by raising a food-laden fork to one's mouth, followed by chewing and swallowing. Thus, eating has a number of scripts as well as being an event and an action. The elements that are related to one another in these structures also differ in accord with the level being considered. In each structure, however, there are people and objects (elements) that are bound together through causal action and state relationships and it is the set of defining relationships that comprise the script.

It is our contention in this chapter that Generalized Event Representations (GERs) are basic building blocks of cognitive organization. The script is the prototypical form of the GER. We now need to consider how scripts may be useful to children in varying situations and tasks and to suggest how and in what way they may be basic building blocks for other processes.

Story Structure

We have discussed several studies of children's memories for script-based stories. The stories we have used in these studies have incorporated just those events that occur frequently in the children's own output for a given event. The result in most cases is a very dull story indeed, as the example in Table 4.2 illustrates. Oddly, most young children do not seem to be put off by the dullness of the story, but instead attempt to remember it as asked. Of course, young children are told more interesting stories on other occasions, and they watch television with its story-like visual narratives. However, they are also notorious for wishing to have the same story told over and over again. It would appear that they demand less novelty in the story framework than do older children and adults. It could even be that for the young child, a new story is not conceived of within the schema of problem-resolution framework (as described by Mandler & Johnson, 1977; or Stein & Glenn, 1979), but simply as a recounting of another event. Then, the repetition of the story serves to establish it in the same sense that the repetition of an event establishes a script. If stories are not viewed by young children within a problem-resolution schema, then our "boring little stories" would not be viewed as deviant.

In the case of a "real" story—one that meets the standards that older children and adults impose—the script serves as the *context* for the story, within which the action can be interpreted in terms of an implied background. (This is the usefulness of scripts to story understanding for adults.) Real stories rarely recount scripts, although they may make explicit the particular values to be entered into particular slots in an instantiated script.

The relation between scripts and stories can be studied in children's story productions as well as in their story understanding. In Gruendel's (1980) study, 4-, 6-, and 8-year-old children in one condition were asked to tell a story about four events—building a campfire, making cookies, planting a garden, or having a birthday party. Of considerable interest was the finding that the younger children (the 4's and most of the 6's) gave simple scripts when asked to tell a story about the event. Stories emerged only gradually, with children first inserting magical or humorous components, then using story markers (e.g., "once upon a time" and "the end"), and then transforming a bit of the basic script in some way. Real problem-resolution constructions were very rare, even among 8 year olds. Thus, it appeared that stories were emerging from scripts in a gradual fashion, with the script serving not as context for the story, but as central structure itself.

Other research with children's story constructions (e.g., Applebee, 1978; Botvin & Sutton-Smith, 1977) has found more elaborate constructions earlier than Gruendel did. Gruendel suggests that one reason for this may be that children find it more difficult to construct stories about *particular* events than simply to respond when asked to tell a story about anything. This proposal certainly deserves further investigation. It is possible that when the child is given a "scripty" topic, the topic calls up the script and the script is simply read off, whereas when no event is suggested, the child accesses more easily both a story constructor and some materials for constructing. This is reminiscent of the problem that children appear to have in remembering particular episodes of familiar events, as previously reported in the Hudson and Nelson (in preparation) study. In both cases—specific memories and stories—the script appears to preempt the recall or transformation, both of which can operate in the case of less familiar or less highly specified material.

Another obvious use of scripts by young children is in fantasy play. In Nelson and Gruendel (1979a), we analyzed several dialogues that took place during joint play episodes in a preschool setting. In each case, the dialogues incorporated obvious scripts—for example, making dinner plans over the telephone, playing school, having snack, going on a trip. Scripts were used in different ways in each situation: to set up action, to guide pretense in a dialogue, or to serve as a topic for discussion. This study used examples of play, but did not sample play situations systematically. It would be useful to assess the degree to which preschoolers rely on scripts in pretense play and the extent of development that takes place in possible transformations of scripts as was seen in story constructions. This is likely to be a fruitful area for further research.

If scripts become autonomous representational structures, they may also become useful to children in problem-solving situations; that is, they should become available for reflective thought as well as for guiding action, expectations, and inferences. When such manipulation of script knowledge becomes possible is an important developmental question that may make it feasible to relate this knowledge more directly to other areas of cognitive growth.

Implications

It is not possible at this time to spell out a complete model of cognitive development that would specify how and where script knowledge fits into the system. However, we can emphasize what we believe to be the important consequences of our investigation for the development of such a model.

First, we recognize that what gets represented from an experience is apparently a partial copy of that experience. Such a representation provides the input to further cognitive processing. It also provides the *context* for the child's cognition and action in that and similar situations. In the mature system, there are thought to be at least three levels of representation along the continuum from more direct and specific to more abstract and general. At the first level (first in terms of closeness to the experienced event) is a fairly direct representation of something that happened. In asserting that it is a ''direct'' representation, we do not mean to deny that the person's understanding of an event is in all cases at least partially a function of how that event fits into previously established perceptual and cognitive schemas. For this reason, ''direct'' representation of precisely the same event by different people will also vary. In developmental terms, there will also be changes over time with respect to how much of an event it is possible to represent, as well as what aspects of the event will be represented.

These complexities aside, whatever is represented at this first level is subject to schematization over time and thus the production of a more generalized event representation—in the case of highly routinized events, a script. This GER structure is, in turn, the basis for interpretation of similar future events.

The second (generalized) level, however, is subject to still further analysis and abstraction to produce categories based on the GER, such as social roles, categories of objects, problem-solving strategies, discourse procedures, word meanings, and many others. These abstract representations obviously do not form a homogeneous category, but rather raise the possibility of a large number of cognitive abstracting mechanisms, each producing its own store of conceptual categories or schemas. In order for such a system to perform, therefore, one must posit a series of powerful operators that are primarily concerned with scanning for patterns in the accumulated experiential representations. Fortunately, it is not a particularly strange or wild notion that our basic cognitive operations are in fact carried out in terms of pattern extractors.

What does seem both important and unusual in the present conception is that all of these more abstract systems (some explicit and conscious, some implicit and unconscious) are derived from the initial representation of experience. That is (and although this seems obvious, it also appears to be an important and often overlooked consideration), *cognitive processes do not operate on objects in the world, but on cognitive representations.* Therefore, the structure and content of these representations are crucial to our models of cognitive development.

Let us emphasize two other points in this connection. First, we conceive of scripts and other GERs as existing at a fairly high level in the operational hierarchy. They are readily accessible and appear to have bidirectional connections. That is, they determine in part what is perceived and understood of an experience; and they serve as input for further processing and abstraction mechanisms. Although we are neutral with respect to the development of abstracting mechanisms, it seems likely that under any model (and in light of relevant empirical findings), a younger child will have formed fewer abstract structures than an older child. For this reason alone it can be asserted that the young child's cognitive context is to a large extent event based, whereas the older child may take advantage of a fairly rich store of abstract categories.

A second point to emphasize here is that the script-producing process need not be based on an *a priori* structure. It isn't necessary to propose that there is something like an innate "script acquisition device." Scripts as we have observed them in our research are outcomes of the analysis of representations of experience. They are neither the experience itself nor an abstract universal structure. A School script is very different from a Going-Fishing script, but both are formulated in spatial–temporal–cultural terms. We can see that both incorporate notions of who, what, where, when, why, and how in sequentially structured relationships. A novel event will be formulated similarly with the same categorical elements. There seems to be nothing particularly mysterious about this; these are simply the analytical categories that we use—and very young children use—in understanding events. In brief, scripting is a process and an outcome, not a structure.

If scripts are outcomes of representational analysis, it follows that not all experiences need result in a script. In particular, there may be units smaller than we would like to term scripts represented by the very young child or infant; there may be affective or esthetic units; there may be units that are less sequential and more spatial. Even though we see the script as a very basic building block for further processing, we do not claim it is the *only* block.

This conception emphasizes the script as a stable product of a continuously active cognitive process. The stability is not final in any sense, but rather is subject to change with new experience. The model sketched here shares many assumptions with the Soviet theorists (Meacham, 1977), as well as with Bartlett's (1932) theories. Memory is an active, constructive process deriving from culturally embedded experiences. The product at any point is an individual representation derived from previous experiences that are for the most part structured by the social world.

In this conception, memory is not a thing apart (see also Flavell, 1971). Representation of past experience, interpretation of present events, and prediction of future happenings are all involved in the on-going cognitive process. Thus, generalized event representations of all kinds play important roles in all of the child's social and cognitive functioning. In particular, we—like Schank and Abelson—see them as important to the interpretation of discourse as well as in the acquisition of language itself. We previously discussed the use of scripts in play (Nelson & Gruendel, 1979a) where it appears that much of children's fantasy and role play are simply the playing through of scripts. We have further hypothesized that children's problem-solving schemas can also be viewed as types of scripts. All of these possibilities remain to be explored further in future studies. In general, it appears that scripts are but one outcome of the reproduction and analysis of experience. Although cultural schemas of the type suggested by Bartlett play a role in these representations, they do not necessarily dominate.

Table 4.3 summarizes some of the structures, both individually constructed and shared, that appear to be the outcomes of different types of cognitive analysis and construction. We hypothesize that each of these is the product of a particular type of operation on the initial event representation. The left-hand column in this table lists some of the presumed cognitive processes that operate on the initial representation of experience. The products listed are illustrations at the individual and social–cultural level of the types of products that may result from a particular type of operation. In this discussion, cultural refers to those forms that may be shared as well as to those that may be defined by cultural forces.

Pattern analysis of the representation of an experience will yield a generalized form that relates elements through actions and states—that is, the scripts that

TABLE 4.3
Hypothesized Cognitive Operations and Products

Operations	Product	
	Individual	Cultural
Patterns	Scripts/GERs	Stories
Reproductions	Memories	History
Categories	Collections, object and action concepts	Social roles, logical classes
Transformations	Fantasy, dreams	Games, drama

have been the subject of our research thus far. Individuals within a culture produce and the culture reproduces narratives based on these patterns. As story analysts since Bartlett (1932) have emphasized, narrative structures may vary from one culture to another and they certainly vary developmentally, as we have seen. However, the basic story form is likely to remain close to the typical script form in a given culture or at a given age.

Reproductions of the initial experiential representation lead to autobiographical memories in the individual and to the writing of history in the culture. It is interesting that, if our analysis is correct, specific memories are a later product than scripts in the individual, just as valid historical accounts are a later invention than stories in cultures.

Category analysis involves comparing elements within and across GERs (see Nelson, in press b). Ontogenetically, this process produces object and action concepts, collections (Markman & Seibert, 1976), and hierarchical categories. Culturally, such categories are reinforced and rationalized through social structures such as roles and through logical and scientific structures.

Various transformations on GERs and concepts produce fantasy and dreams in the individual, whereas in the culture they produce more elaborated or abstract forms of narrative or uses of class structures such as novels, drama, poetry, and games. We have not attempted to specify particular types of transformations that might operate on lower-level products to produce various forms.

Although these suggestions are exceedingly speculative and farreaching, they seem to us to lend some credibility to the suggestion that GERs are indeed basic cognitive building blocks that serve as the foundation for more complex cognitive structures. Although they posited somewhat different structures (e.g., plans and themes) Schank and Abelson (1977) make a similar claim. Obviously, the evidence that would be needed to sustain this claim is far from complete and the relations among the suggested levels are not well-enough specified to lead to testable predictions. However, we hope that we have provided sufficient evidence for the reality and utility of GERs in the thought of young children to encourage others to follow up some of the implications regarding their importance to cognitive growth in general.

ACKNOWLEDGMENTS

Research reported in this chapter was supported by NSF Grants BNS 78-25810 and BNS 79-14006. We would like to thank the following people who contributed to the research program in various ways: Kathleen McCartney, Lindsay Evans, Robyn Fivush, Margo Morse, Judith Hudson, Joan Lucariello, Jayne Berrier, and Peter Feigenbaum. We would also like to thank the children and school personnel who made the research possible, in particular those at the Calvin Hill Day Care Center, and the Gesell Pre-School in New Haven, CT and Park East Summer Camp Program, Rodeph Shalom Summer Camp Program, and Hunter College Elementary School in New York.

REFERENCES

Abelson, R. P. Script processing in attitude formation and decision making. In J. S. Carroll & J. W. Payne (Eds.), *Cognition and social behavior*. Hillsdale, N.J.: Lawrence Erlbaum Associates, 1976.

Applebee, A. N. *The child's concept of story*. Chicago: University of Chicago Press, 1978.

Bartlett, F. C. *Remembering*. Cambridge, England: Cambridge University Press, 1932.

Blank, M., & Allen, D. Understanding "why": Its significance in early intelligence. In M. Lewis (Ed.), *Infant intelligence*. New York: Plenum Press, 1975.

Botvin, G. J., & Sutton-Smith, B. The development of complexity in children's fantasy narratives. *Developmental Psychology*, 1977, *13*, 377–388.

Bower, G. Experiments on story comprehension and recall. *Discourse Processes*, 1978, *1*, 211–231.

Bower, G., Black, J. B., & Turner, T. J. Scripts in memory for text. *Cognitive Psychology*, 1979, *11*, 177–220.

Brown, A. L. The development of memory: Knowing, knowing about knowing, and knowing how to know. In H. W. Reese (Ed.), *Advances in child development and behavior* (Vol. 10). New York: Academic, Press 1975. (a)

Brown, A. L. Recognition, reconstruction, and recall of narrative sequences by pre-operational children. *Child Development*, 1975, *46*, 156–166. (b)

Brown, A. L. The construction of temporal succession by pre-operational children. In A. D. Pick (Ed.), *Minnesota symposium on child psychology* (Vol. 10). Minneapolis: University of Minnesota Press, 1976.

Brown, A. L. Learning and development: The problems of compatibility, access and induction. *Human Development*, in press.

Brown, R. W. Language and categories. Appendix to J. S. Bruner, J. J. Goodnow, & G. A. Austin, *A study of thinking*. New York: Wiley, 1956.

Brown, R. W. *Words and things*. New York: Free Press, 1958.

Bruner, J. S., Olver, & Greenfield, P. *Studies in cognitive growth*. New York: Wiley, 1966.

Chomsky, N. *Aspects of a theory of syntax*. Cambridge, Mass.: M.I.T. Press, 1965.

Cohen, L. B., & Salapatek, P. (Eds.). *Infant perception: From sensation to cognition* (Vols. 1 and 2) New York: Academic Press, 1975, 1976.

Donaldson, M. *Children's minds*. Glasgow: William Collins & Sons, 1978.

Ervin-Tripp, S., & Mitchell-Kernan, C. (Eds.). *Child discourse*. New York: Academic Press, 1977.

Fivush, R. *Children's recognition of basic acts*. Manuscript in preparation.

Flavell, J. H. First discussant's comments: What is memory development the development of? *Human Development*, 1971, *14*, 272–278.

Flavell, J. H. *Structures, stages and sequences in cognitive development*. Paper presented at the Minnesota Symposium on Child Psychology, Minneapolis, October 1980.

French, L. & Nelson, K. *Children's use of linking terms in scripts*. Manuscript in preparation.

Garvey, C. Requests and responses in children's speech. *Journal of Child Language*, 1975, *2*, 41–64.

Gelman, R. & Gallistel, C.R. *The child's understanding of number*. Cambridge, Mass.: Harvard University Press, 1978.

Gruendel, J. *Scripts and stories: A study of children's event narratives*. Doctoral dissertation, Yale University, 1980.

Hood, L., & Bloom, L. What when and how about why: a longitudinal study of early expressions of causality. *Monographs of the Society for Research in Child Development*, 1979, *44* (No. 6).

Hudson, J., & Nelson, K. *Scripts and autobiographical memories in pre-school children*. In preparation.

Jenkins, J. J. Remember that old theory of memory? Well, forget it! In R. Shaw & J. Bransford (Eds.), *Perceiving, acting, and knowing*. Hillsdale, N.J.: Lawrence Erlbaum Associates, 1977.

Linton, M. *Cuing events in adults' and children's autobiographical memory.* Paper presented at American Psychological Association meeting, New York, September 1979.

Mandler, J. M., & deForest, M. Developmental invariance in story recall *(Chip Report 78).* La Jolla, Calif.: University of California at San Diego, 1978.

Mandler, J. M., & Johnson, N. S. Remembrance of things passed: Story structure and recall. *Cognitive Psychology,* 1977, *9,* 111–151.

McCartney, K., & Nelson, K. Children's use of scripts in story recall. *Discourse Processes,* 1981, *4,* 59–70.

McNeill, D. *The acquisition of language.* New York: Harper & Row, 1970.

McNeill, D. *The conceptual basis for language.* Hillsdale, N.J.: Lawrence Erlbaum Associates, 1979.

Markman, E., & Seibert, J. Classes and collections: Internal organization and resulting holistic properties. *Cognitive Psychology,* 1976, *8,* 561–577.

Martin, J., Patterson, K. J., & Price, R. L. The effects of level of abstraction of a script on accuracy of recall, predictions and belief. Unpublished manuscript, Graduate School of Business, Stanford University, 1979.

Meacham, J. A. Soviet investigations of memory development. In R. V. Kail, Jr. & J. W. Hagen (Eds.), *Perspectives on the development of memory and cognition.* Hillsdale, N.J.: Lawrence Erlbaum Associates, 1977.

Nelson, K. How young children represent knowledge of their world in and out of language. In R. S. Siegler (Ed.), *Children's thinking: What develops?* Hillsdale, N.J.: Lawrence Erlbaum Associates, 1978.

Nelson, K. *Children's long-term memory for routine events.* Paper presented at American Psychological Association symposium on Natural Memory Development, New York, September 1979. (a)

Nelson, K. *The use of temporal and spatial terms in children's narrative descriptions.* Paper presented to the New York Child Language Group, Teachers College, Columbia University, May 1979. (b)

Nelson, K. Social cognition in a script framework. In L. Ross & J. Flavell (Eds.), *The development of social cognition in children.* Hillsdale, N.J.: Lawrence Erlbaum Associates, in press. (a)

Nelson, K. The syntagmatics and paradigmatics of conceptual development. In S. Kuczaj (Ed.), *Language development: Language, cognition, and culture.* Hillsdale, N.J.: Lawrence Erlbaum Associates, in press. (b)

Nelson, K., & Brown, A. L. The semantic–episodic distinction in memory development. In P. Ornstein (Ed.), *Development of memory.* Hillsdale, N.J.: Lawrence Erlbaum Associates, 1979.

Nelson, K., & Gruendel, J. At morning it's lunchtime: A scriptal view of children's dialogues. *Discourse Processes,* 1979, *2* 73–94. (a)

Nelson, K., & Gruendel, J. *From personal episode to social script: Two dimensions in the development of event knowledge.* Paper presented at meeting of the Society for Research in Child Development, San Francisco, March 1979. (b)

Nelson, K., & Ross, G. The general and specifics of long-term memory in infants and young children. In M. Perlmutter (Ed.), *Naturalistic approaches to memory.* San Francisco: Jossey-Bass, in press.

Piaget, J. *The language and thought of the young child* (Trans. from French by M. Garbain). London: Routledge & Kegan Paul, 1926. (Originally published, 1923.)

Piaget, J. *The child's conception of physical causality.* Totowa, N.J.: Littlefield, Adams, 1972. (Originally published, 1930.)

Rumelhart, D. E. Notes on a schema for stories. In D. G. Bobrow & A. M. Collins (Eds.), *Representation and understanding: Studies in cognitive science.* New York: Academic Press, 1975.

Schank, R. C., & Abelson, R. P. *Scripts, plans, goals, and understanding*. Hillsdale, N.J.: Lawrence Erlbaum Associates, 1977.

Shatz, M., & Gelman, R. The development of communicative skills: Modifications in the speech of young children as a function of the listener. *Monographs of the Society for Research in Child Development*, 1973, *38*(5).

Stein, N. L., & Glenn, C. G. An analysis of story comprehension in elementary school children. In R. Freedle (Ed.), *New directions in discourse processing*. Norwood, N.J.: Ablex, 1979.

Tulving, E. Episodic and semantic memory. In E. Tulving & W. Donaldson (Eds.), *Organization of memory*. New York: Academic Press, 1972.

White, S. H., & Pillemer, D. B. Childhood amnesia and the development of a socially accessible memory system. In J. F. Kihlstrom & F. J. Evans (Eds.), *Functional disorders of memory*. Hillsdale, N.J.: Lawrence Erlbaum Associates, 1979.

5 The Role of Taxonomy in Developmental Psychopathology

Thomas M. Achenbach
University of Vermont College of Medicine

Because developmental psychology is the study of behavioral ontogeny, it should contribute to our understanding of children's behavior disorders. G. Stanley Hall, the founder of American developmental psychology (Kessen, 1965), envisioned it as a guide to child rearing and the prevention of maladaptive behavior. Child mental-health services, from their inception early in this century, have also stressed the developmental origins of psychopathology (cf. Achenbach, 1981). Yet, experience in child clinical settings and perusal of the developmental literature show little connection between current clinical practice and developmental research. Why?

Research on children's behavior has been dominated by developmental and educational psychologists concerned more with normative and theoretical questions than with disturbed children. Clinical research, on the other hand, usually centers on particular disorders, assessment procedures, or therapies rather than on the behavioral ontogeny of interest to developmentalists. Do these divergent enterprises have anything to offer each other?

Clinical and developmental thinking draw on similar theoretical sources. The psychodynamic and S–R paradigms, for example, have shaped views of both behavioral development and deviance, as well as clinical practice. Organismic-developmental and ethological theories have also been rich heuristic sources for clinicians and researchers concerned with developmental adaptation.

The metaphors embodied in developmental theories form perhaps the strongest links between developmental research and clinical practice. Such metaphors imply that there is something more profound to development than operationalized variables and the measurable relations among them. The essence of the ''something more'' is a Gestalt-like notion of the whole being more than

159

the sum of its parts and this whole undergoing progressive reorganization and elaboration as it develops. Organic growth and the infant behavioral *schemes* described by Piaget (1970) graphically illustrate this aspect of development. Piaget has amassed evidence that later cognitive development likewise entails progressive reorganization, but on a more covert level. Although difficult to operationalize, the organismic metaphor is exquisitely compelling to those concerned with children's growth, normal or abnormal.

A compelling metaphor can serve not only as a stimulus to creative theory but also as a seductive distraction from the more empirical aspects of science. Clinical and developmental psychology both possess a rich heritage of metaphors encompassing a wide range of phenomena. However, as these fields have progressed from all-encompassing theories to ever-increasing specialization, the gap between their guiding metaphors and their empirically based knowledge has widened. In clinical psychology, for example, the explosion of research touched off by the behavioral revolution of the 1960's engendered a vast body of findings that can no longer be subsumed by S-R metaphors. Instead, purely S-R interpretations of behavior disorders are giving way to efforts to combine behavioral methods with cognitive, pharmacological, and other approaches. Unsatisfying as this may be to theoreticians in general and S-R purists in particular, it reflects a growing awareness of gaps between the metaphors of S-R theory and the phenomena to which they refer.

The explosion of developmental research inspired by Piagetian and psycholinguistic theory in the 1960's has likewise engendered findings too diverse to be accommodated by the original metaphors. Like clinical research, developmental research has therefore spawned numerous miniature paradigms, although these are not focused on particular disorders the way current clinical paradigms are.

THEORETICAL NEEDS OF A DEVELOPMENTAL PSYCHOPATHOLOGY

The importance of viewing children's maladaptive behavior in relation to their developmental course seems obvious. Less obvious, however, are the means for linking the study of psychopathology and development. Psychoanalytic, S-R, and some organismic-developmental theories encompass both normal and deviant functioning. Yet, as developmental research and clinical research have advanced along their separate paths, it has become clear that the classical theories cannot handle all the relevant data within either domain, much less synthesize the two. If there is to be a developmental psychopathology, we therefore need to seek other conceptual structures.

Although not acknowledged as formal theories, certain ways of organizing data on psychopathology and development have provided conceptual structures with which to guide theory and research. In adult psychopathology, for example, disorders such as schizophrenia are central foci of theory and research. General theories may aim to subsume schizophrenia under their own overarching principles, but the construct of schizophrenia has a life of its own, independent of these theories. The diverse interpretations of schizophrenia and the less-than-perfect reliability of diagnosis make it no less useful as a hypothetical construct than most constructs emanating from psychological theories. Other major diagnostic categories likewise function as hypothetical constructs on which research and theory are focused.

In developmental psychology, normative–developmental approaches have yielded organizing concepts that function like the diagnostic constructs of adult psychopathology. Beginning with Binet and Simon (1905/1916), for example, intelligence tests have consisted of items selected and scored according to age norms for performance. These tests have fared better than most other psychological measures in terms of reliability and relations to diverse validity criteria. A normative–developmental approach has likewise proven useful in the construction of infant tests such as the Gesell and Bayley, screening instruments such as the Denver Developmental Screening Test, and scholastic achievement tests.

Because no single developmental or clinical theory is likely to encompass all aspects of deviant development, taxonomic and normative–developmental constructs are needed to guide the developmental study of psychopathology. In other words, before we can expect much progress in developmental psychopathology, we need at least a provisional system for reliably identifying disorders, discriminating among them, and relating them to the typical course of development. These may seem like prosaic goals, but the lack of a viable taxonomy has severely handicapped training, treatment, communication, and research related to psychopathology in children. Furthermore, efforts to devise taxonomies have raised dilemmas not resolvable solely on theoretical grounds, but requiring trial-and-error tinkering with concepts and data to obtain optimal compromises.

Although the task of constructing a developmental psychopathology has many facets, I focus here on taxonomic problems as a central issue. I do this both because the lack of a coherent taxonomy has hindered the cumulative evolution of research and because empirically based taxonomic efforts have begun to show sufficient convergence to warrant a close look at the conceptual issues they raise.

Despite lingering questions about how precisely the findings converge, it seems time to move beyond the aggregation of these findings in favor of a fuller delineation of the conceptual choices to be made. Because extensive reviews of the findings are available elsewhere (e.g., Achenbach & Edelbrock, 1978; Quay, 1979), I do not review them again here, but instead, I concentrate on the practical and theoretical questions involved in formulating taxonomies of psychopathology in children.

In addition to issues raised by the empirical findings, we also need to consider issues raised by the official taxonomy of psychopathology, which in the United

States is the American Psychiatric Association's (1952, 1968, 1980) *Diagnostic and Statistical Manual* (the "DSM"). Because the DSM represents both the conventional psychiatric wisdom and an officially mandated mold for clinical practice in this country, it inevitably shapes American concepts of psychopathology. After outlining problems pertinent to taxonomic efforts in general, I illustrate tentative solutions to these problems as they have evolved in a program of multivariate research on psychopathology in children.

TAXONOMIC CONSTRUCT SYSTEMS

The dilemmas encountered in formulating taxonomies can be posed in terms of a series of contrasting alternatives. These alternatives are not necessarily mutually exclusive, however. In many cases, the most productive solutions may be those that combine various alternatives and promote empirical tests of contrasting approaches.

Provisional or Final?

A basic dilemma concerns the life expectancy of a taxonomy: Should it be a relatively temporary expedient or a model that is expected to survive indefinitely? Although a permanent model would be highly desirable, it also seems highly unlikely. In order to be final, a taxonomy would have to discriminate among disorders in terms of criterial attributes so optimal that no better ones and no better way of codifying them could ever be found.

Because no taxonomy of child psychopathology has undergone sustained formal testing under naturalistic conditions, it is hard to document the major faults and virtues of existing systems, much less to specify the form of an ultimate system. Moreover, taxonomic needs are likely to change with increased knowledge of etiologies and changes in clinical practices. Because an effective taxonomy must do more than guide research and theory, even one that retains its heuristic power over a long period may need revision to keep pace with changing clinical practices. However, it is also likely that no single taxonomic system will be able to serve all needs at even one point in time. Although a single core system would be highly desirable as a framework for research, theory, and clinical communication, finer differentiations would be needed for research within specific taxa; collateral ways of grouping children would also be needed for the management of particular groups. In residential treatment settings, for example, children often have to be grouped according to such factors as self-care skills, potential dangerousness, and educational needs, which would be of less concern in other clinical settings.

Provisional Approaches.   If we accept the impossibility of devising a permanent system, we must nevertheless be clear about the historical role of a provisional system: Should it be a codification of prevailing practice or should it aim to advance the field? The three editions of the DSM (DSM-I, 1952; DSM-II, 1968; DSM-III, 1980) have generally taken the former approach, whereby authorities in the field negotiate a consensus on how to systematize prevailing custom. The DSM-III has departed somewhat from this tradition by imposing research diagnostic criteria on the major adult disorders and finer distinctions on the childhood disorders than have prevailed. Yet, it remains more a codification of conventional wisdom than a new heuristic model. Efforts to derive systems either empirically or theoretically, by contrast, typically aim to advance knowledge beyond the status quo.

Codifying prevailing custom offers continuity with the past and protection against costly errors risked with a new system that may fail miserably. It also reduces the retooling and training needed to accommodate new concepts and procedures. However, it may not only preserve error, but by dominating clinical practice, it may also stifle alternative approaches.

DSM Adult Categories.   Because taxonomies of the foreseeable future will inevitably be provisional, it is important to consider how conventional wisdom can be combined with new ideas and data to advance knowledge and services. The committees responsible for the DSM-III tried to do this for the major adult disorders by defining them in terms of the Research Diagnostic Criteria (RDC) evolved to increase the reliability of research diagnoses (Spitzer, Endicott, & Robins, 1978). In doing so, the committees have purged some diagnostic categories of unsupported theoretical inferences in favor of descriptive criteria. The disorders previously designated as neuroses, for example, are no longer defined in terms of psychoanalytic theory. Nevertheless, the general procedure has been to start with assumptions about what disorders exist and then to formulate criteria for diagnosing them and discriminating among them. Most prevailing taxonomic constructs are thus taken for granted, with revisions primarily in the criteria for operationalizing them. Considering the long history of constructs like schizophrenia and affective disorders, and the large body of research, theory, and practice centered on them, this seems a defensible approach. It would be difficult indeed to promote taxonomic changes that did not retain these constructs.

DSM Child Categories.   The situation with respect to behavior disorders of childhood and adolescence is quite different. Here, we lack venerable diagnostic constructs analogous to adult schizophrenia and affective disorders. Starting with Childhood Schizophrenia and Adjustment Reaction in the DSM-I, the DSM-II added several behavior reactions of childhood and adolescence, but the DSM-III has replaced these with Attention Deficit Disorders, Conduct Disorders, Anxiety

Disorders, and Pervasive Developmental Disorders, each of which is divided into subcategories. Here, the job of the DSM committees was not to codify accepted constructs in terms of research-based diagnostic criteria; diagnostic constructs for children's disorders are not entrenched like the major adult taxa, nor have research diagnostic criteria been developed to operationalize even the most accepted of child diagnostic constructs.

To take the most researched and publicized childhood disorder as an example: What DSM-II called the Hyperkinetic Reaction, DSM-III designates as one of three types of Attention Deficit Disorder, the criteria for which are shown in Table 5.1. Although the DSM-III version reflects changes in thinking beyond the DSM-II's construct of the Hyperkinetic Reaction, and the criteria for diagnosis are more explicit than in DSM-II, neither the DSM committee's choice of taxa nor their criteria for diagnosis are dictated by either prevailing custom or empirical research. There is no evidence, for example, that children having Attention Deficit Disorders without Hyperactivity are reliably discriminable from children having Attention Deficit Disorders with Hyperactivity or Residual Type. Neither is there any firm basis for requiring three out of five symptoms of inattention or two out of five symptoms of hyperactivity to diagnose Attention Deficit Disorder with Hyperactivity, nor for the quantitative judgments implied by the terms "often," "easily," "frequently," and "excessively."

The proof of this type of pudding is in the eating, of course. It remains to be seen whether significant numbers of cases can be discriminated into the different attention deficit disorders and whether, once discriminated, they are found to differ in other important ways. Likewise, it remains to be seen whether the diagnostic criteria can be used reliably. Preliminary studies have shown even less interjudge reliability for DSM-III child diagnoses than for DSM-II child diagnoses (Mattison, Cantwell, Russell, & Will, 1979; Mezzich & Mezzich, 1979). Furthermore, data reported in the DSM-III show lower reliability for the final version of its child diagnoses than for an earlier draft version (American Psychiatric Association, 1980).

Heuristic Systems.   Contrasting with the DSM are efforts to devise new systems according to criteria other than prevailing custom. Such efforts tend to fall into two main categories: those intended to embody the constructs of a particular theory, such as Anna Freud's (1965) Developmental Profile, and those intended to reflect empirically derived groupings, such as syndromes derived from multivariate analyses of behavior checklists (cf. Achenbach & Edelbrock, 1978; Quay, 1979).

Another approach is to accumulate taxa that have been formulated one by one to embody particular clinical phenomena, such as Kanner's (1943) syndrome of early infantile autism. Although this resembles classical approaches to the identification of medical syndromes, it is unlikely to be fruitful for most children's behavior disorders, which are less strikingly distinctive than most physical

TABLE 5.1
DSM–III Diagnostic Criteria for Attention Deficit Disorders
(American Psychiatric Association, 1980)

Attention Deficit Disorder with Hyperactivity

A. *Inattention*. At least three of the following:
   1. Often fails to finish things he or she starts
   2. Often doesn't seem to listen
   3. Easily distracted
   4. Has difficulty concentrating on schoolwork or other tasks requiring sustained attention
   5. Has difficulty sticking to play activity
B. *Impulsivity*. At least three of the following:
   1. Often acts before thinking
   2. Shifts excessively from one activity to another
   3. Has difficulty organizing work (not due to cognitive impairment)
   4. Needs a lot of supervision
   5. Frequently calls out in class
   6. Has difficulty awaiting turn in games or group situations
C. *Hyperactivity*. At least two of the following:
   1. Runs about or climbs on things excessively
   2. Has difficulty sitting still or fidgets excessively
   3. Has difficulty staying seated
   4. Moves about excessively during sleep
   5. Is always "on the go" or acts as if "driven by a motor"
D. *Onset before age 7*
E. *Duration of at least 6 months*
F. *Not due to Schizophrenia, Affective Disorder, or Severe or Profound Mental Retardation*

Attention Deficit Disorder without Hyperactivity

The criteria for this disorder are the same as those for Attention Deficit Disorder with Hyperactivity except that the individual never had signs of hyperactivity (criterion C).

Attention Deficit Disorder, Residual Type

A. The individual once met the criteria for Attention Deficit Disorder with Hyperactivity. This information may come from the individual or from others, such as family members.
B. Signs of hyperactivity are no longer present, but other signs of the illness have persisted to the present without periods of remission, as evidenced by signs of both attentional deficits and impulsivity (e.g., difficulty organizing work and completing tasks, difficulty concentrating, being easily distracted, making sudden decisions without thought of the consequences).
C. The symptoms of inattention and impulsivity result in some impairment in social or occupational functioning.
D. Not due to Schizophrenia, Affective Disorder, Severe or Profound Mental Retardation, or Schizotypal or Borderline Personality Disorders.

anomalies or autistic children's peculiar development. Furthermore, even when an astute clinician like Kanner builds a strong case for a new syndrome, it must still be assimilated into a general taxonomic system embodying rules for discriminating it from other syndromes. This may take a long time, as shown by the lapse of 37 years between Kanner's (1943) classic paper and DSM-III's (1980) adoption of early infantile autism as a diagnostic category. The occasional clinical identification of new syndromes does not, therefore, obviate the need for general systems that apply consistent taxonomic principles to a wide range of disorders.

To return now to general heuristic systems, the lack of entrenched taxonomic constructs for children's disorders has stimulated numerous such efforts (cf. Hobbs, 1975). Contrasts between empirical and theoretical approaches are discussed in more detail later, but they both aspire to capture underlying truths more than prevailing custom. In doing so, they seek to highlight relations among signs and symptoms that will promote better understanding of the disorders. This means that they must be judged more in terms of research than the consensus of authorities; the more new knowledge they foster, the more valuable they are. However, they are continually subject to revision or rejection according to research findings. Heuristic taxonomies are thus always provisional; being provisional, they require decisions about how heavily to invest in a particular taxonomic paradigm and how to accommodate new findings.

Whereas the DSM approach involves periodic organizational decisions to revise an official system through committee consensus, heuristic systems are at the mercy of market forces that make their fate unpredictable. Whether good or bad, the DSM system at least serves in a recognized official capacity for a significant period, whereas even the best heuristic system risks quick consignment to obscurity, a risk faced by all research and theoretical endeavors. Yet, even systems that prove to be short-lived may play a constructive role by demonstrating that certain promising possibilities are not in fact upheld in practice. Like other scientific constructs, the more explicitly taxonomies are formulated and tested, the more they can aid the growth of knowledge, even when their effect is to help disprove the notions on which they are based.

Classification or Diagnosis?

The ambiguity of the term *diagnosis* has been a source of confusion about the function of taxonomies. One dictionary definition of diagnosis (Woolf, 1977) is "the art or act of identifying a disease from its signs or symptoms [p. 313]." An even sparer version put forth by a leader in psychiatric taxonomy is that diagnosis (Guzé, 1978) is "the medical term for classification [p. 53]." In other words, diagnosis is the assignment of a particular individual or disorder to a class within a taxonomy. A slightly broader dictionary definition of diagnosis (Woolf, 1977) is "a concise technical description of a taxon [p. 313]." Besides assignment to a class, diagnosis can thus imply description of the attributes that define the class.

Confusion arises mainly from the contrast between these narrow definitions and a much broader definition of diagnosis (Woolf, 1977) as (1) "investigation or analysis of the cause or nature of a condition, situation or problem; and (2) "a statement or conclusion concerning the nature or cause of some phenomenon [p. 313]." This concept of diagnosis concerns *diagnostic workups* and *diagnostic formulations* (Roth, 1978) undertaken to obtain all information relevant to a plan of action, including the individual's history, possible etiology, special strengths and vulnerabilities, treatment options, and prognosis. The broad concept of diagnosis implies much more than the "act of identifying a disease," which is also known as making a *differential diagnosis* or *formal diagnosis* (Roth, 1978).

Taxonomies cannot possibly serve as diagnostic formulations; yet, the conceptual framework they provide for making a formal diagnosis is a necessary prerequisite for the diagnostic formulation. The formal diagnosis abstracts from an individual's uniqueness those characteristics common to a previously identified taxon. The more correlates that have been verified for that taxon, in terms of etiology, appropriate treatment, and so on, the more a formal diagnosis can contribute to a plan of action.

The term *diagnosis* in the *Diagnostic and Statistical Manual* refers to formal diagnoses rather than diagnostic formulations. Efforts to broaden the DSM–III beyond a syndromal classification by adding physical disorders (Axis III), psychosocial stressors (Axis IV), and impairment of adaptive functioning (Axis V) supplement the formal diagnosis, but it remains to be seen how the additional axes will aid the diagnostic process. It also remains to be seen whether assessment on all five axes will converge to form multiaxial taxa, or whether Axis I (syndromes) and Axis II (developmental and personality disorders) will function as a psychiatric nosology, while the other three axes function as supplementary descriptors. Issues raised by uniaxial versus multiaxial approaches are discussed later; the crucial point here is that the multiaxial approach has certainly not elevated the DSM's categories from formal diagnoses to diagnostic formulations. This is especially true of the child and adolescent categories, because they have few known correlates and the Axes IV and V ratings of stress and impairment may be less informative than for adults.

To summarize, taxonomic construct systems are essentially classification systems. Their value increases with the number of important correlates found for their classes. They provide rules for formal diagnosis, but do not serve as diagnostic formulations. No matter how good a taxonomy is, it may still need to be supplemented with idiographic diagnostic formulations to guide the treatment of individual cases. To capitalize on accumulated knowledge in a field, a diagnostic formulation must draw on established taxonomies, but these may be multiple, such as a syndromal taxonomy for behavioral deviance, a medical taxonomy, a taxonomy of educational needs, and a taxonomy of family patterns. Although we are primarily concerned with behavioral taxonomies, diagnostic formulations of behavior disorders almost always require other taxonomies as well.

Empirical or Theoretical?

Empirical and theoretical approaches were mentioned earlier as the main kinds of heuristically oriented taxonomic efforts. This distinction is not absolute, however, as all empirical efforts entail theoretical decisions about the data domain, sampling, instrumentation, and analytic strategies. Conversely, theoretical efforts should be based on empirical observations of the phenomena to which they refer. The distinction rests mainly on whether formal data-analytic strategies are used to generate taxa or whether taxa are generated from the constructs and inferences of a preexisting theory.

Anna Freud's (1965) derivation of taxonomic principles from psychoanalytic theory is probably the most purely theoretical effort in recent decades, although the classification system proposed by the Group for the Advancement of Psychiatry (GAP, 1966) also defines some disorders in terms of psychoanalytic and developmental theory. Neither of these systems has progressed towards operational definitions of variables and testable distinctions among disorders. The Developmental Profile proposed by Anna Freud (1965) has been popular in psychoanalytic circles, but research efforts have been confined mainly to demonstrations of how it or its derivatives can be applied to a single case, with no assessments of reliability, discriminative power, validity, or correlates (e.g., Greenspan, Hatleberg, & Cullander, 1979). Studies of the GAP system have shown mediocre reliability, especially for diagnoses involving fine-grained theoretical inferences (Beitchman, Dielman, Landis, Benson, & Kemp, 1978; Freeman, 1971).

Probably because no theory has generated a consensual framework for child and adolescent disorders, most recent taxonomic efforts have been empirically oriented. They have typically derived taxonomic constructs from statistically identified associations among observable behaviors, primarily through factor analysis. Following a few earlier efforts, the growing need for a taxonomy and the availability of electronic computers spurred numerous multivariate studies in the 1960's and 1970's. Despite differences in subject samples, instruments, raters, and methods of analysis, multivariate studies have shown considerable convergence in the identification of certain behavior problem syndromes (cf. Achenbach & Edelbrock, 1978; Quay, 1979).

Nearly all studies whose methodology permitted it have identified two broad-band syndromes. One—comprising aggressive, defiant, and delinquent behavior—has been variously labeled *conduct disorder, externalizing,* and *undercontrolled.* The other broad-band syndrome—comprising withdrawal, fearfulness, and somatic complaints—has been variously labeled *personality disor-*

der, internalizing, and *overcontrolled.* In addition, studies whose methodology permitted more finely differentiated syndromes have repeatedly identified narrow-band syndromes that can be summarized with the following labels: *aggressive, delinquent, hyperactive, schizoid, anxious, depressed, somatic,* and *withdrawn.* Several other syndromes have also been replicated in a few studies (cf. Achenbach & Edelbrock, 1978).

The convergence of findings despite methodological differences shows that multivariate approaches can yield replicable syndromes of behavior disorders. Furthermore, the multivariate groupings thus produced can be treated as structural entities (cf. Baltes & Nesselroade, 1979), subject to further test both in relation to each other and over the course of children's development.

Categories or Dimensions?

Classical medical nosologies are composed of categorical disorders. Formal diagnoses within such systems require yes–no judgments as to whether a person has a disorder and forced-choice judgments as to which disorder it is. The choice of formal diagnosis is important because it determines the choice of specific therapies; for many organic disorders, the correct therapy will be curative, whereas an incorrect therapy will be harmful.

The apparent elegance of even well-validated categorical constructs masks ambiguities arising when crucial criterial attributes of a disorder are present without symptoms of illness, such as in typhoid carriers. Ambiguities also arise in disorders, such as essential hypertension, that are defined primarily in terms of cut-off points on quantitative dimensions of functioning rather than by the presence of a specific etiological agent. Other ambiguities arise in drawing categorical distinctions among disorders that are not sufficiently understood to have clear-cut boundaries. Nevertheless, categorical constructs and those defined by dimensional cut-off points seem to serve organic medicine reasonably well, and they are probably easier for most practitioners than purely dimensional constructs would be.

DSM Categories. Nineteenth-century efforts to construct psychiatric taxonomies adopted the categorical format of organic medicine (e.g., Kraepelin, 1883). This was consistent with the view that good categorical distinctions and descriptions would facilitate discovery of a specific organic etiology for each psychiatric disorder. Although few specific etiologies have been confirmed, the differential responsiveness of adult schizophrenia and affective disorders to organic therapies such as electroconvulsive shock, phenothiazines, lithium, and antidepressants suggests that at least these categories correspond to categorical organic differences among patients.

There is little evidence for categorical organic differences among most behavior disorders of childhood and adolescence, however. In fact, even the specific organic etiology implied by hyperactive children's responses to stimulant drugs has become dubious in light of findings that normal children show similar responses (Rapoport, Buchsbaum, Weingartner, Zahn, Ludlow, Bartko, Mikkelsen, Langer, & Bunney, 1980). Furthermore, as illustrated by the diagnostic criteria for even this relatively well-established category (Table 5.1), the effort to operationalize DSM–III diagnoses has made use of dimensional approaches. The three categories of symptoms relevant to the diagnosis of Attention Deficit Disorder with Hyperactivity (namely, Inattention, Impulsivity, and Hyperactivity) represent dimensions on which cut-off points are specified in terms of an arbitrary number of items (three symptoms of inattention, three of impulsivity, and two of hyperactivity). In addition, most of the specific symptoms imply quantitative judgments, such as "often," "easily," "excessively," "a lot," and "frequently" (see Table 5.1).

Other diagnostic categories are likewise based on quasidimensional lists of symptoms, of which an arbitrary number are required to make a diagnosis. Yet, the quantitative gradations implied in the assessment of individual symptoms and the cut-off points for number of symptoms are obscured when the formal diagnosis is made. If the diagnostician's assessments of the specific symptoms summate to the specified cut-off point, the child has the disorder; otherwise, he or she does not.

If the aim were to determine which etiological agent was present or which treatment was optimal, a categorical diagnosis would be appropriate. However, lacking knowledge of specific etiologies, treatments, or even correlates to validate either the cut-off points or the boundaries between disorders, we may lose critical information when we impose categorical diagnoses on dimensional assessments.

The categorical DSM–III criteria also make it likely that children will qualify for more than one diagnosis, especially if variations in their behavior across settings are noted. The DSM handles this by permitting multiple diagnoses and providing exclusion criteria for some diagnoses. For example, Criterion F in Table 5.1 states that Attention Deficit Disorder with Hyperactivity is not to be diagnosed if the symptoms are "due to Schizophrenia, Affective Disorder, or Severe or Profound Mental Retardation." Thus, we should dismiss the hyperactivity of a child who also happens to be schizophrenic, depressed, or retarded. Potentially valuable descriptive data required to make DSM diagnoses are therefore jettisoned in favor of forced choices among disease-like categories, with certain categories preempting others.

In short, DSM–III's operational criteria for diagnosis employ quasiquantitative, dimensionalized assessments of behavior. Yet, the childhood disorders provided by the DSM, the dimensions used to assess them, and the cut-off points on these dimensions are arbitrary rather than being systematically derived from research or theory. Furthermore, the DSM's quasiquantitative, dimensionalized, descriptive assessments are ultimately superceded by the categorical diagnoses derived from them. This means that: (1) potentially important differences in the intensity and content of symptoms within a category are lost; (2) important characteristics subsumed by other categories are ignored unless multiple diagnoses are made; (3) multiple diagnoses convey a picture of multiple categorical disorders rather than a comprehensive picture of the child's overall pattern; (4) certain disorders are given preemptory status as assumed causes of others without evidence for the causal relations implied; (5) the preemptory power of certain disorders dismisses diagnostic data regarded as criterial for other disorders and potentially important in all cases.

Dimensional Approaches. Most multivariate efforts have been dimensional in the sense that they yield dimensions of items on which individuals can receive quantitative scores. Dimensional approaches have also been adopted for research on predefined categories of disorders, as exemplified by behavior-rating scales for scoring hyperactivity (e.g., Conners, 1973). Scores on these scales have been assessed in relation to other variables, and normative data have been used to establish cut-off points for children considered clinically hyperactive.

When factor analysis is used to identify groups of covarying items, several issues arise in translating factors into taxonomic constructs. Table 5.2 summarizes influences on factor-analytically derived taxa; all these and more can affect factor-analytic findings. Yet, as mentioned earlier, there has been considerable convergence in the identification of two broad-band and several narrow-band syndromes through factor analysis and related approaches, despite wide variations in methodology. So far, however, there has been less progress in deriving formal taxonomies from the multivariate results.

In order to move from multivariate analysis of signs and symptoms to a taxonomy of individuals or disorders, several further steps are needed. These entail decisions like those required in a purely categorical approach, although the choices and alternatives can be made more explicit and testable than has been

TABLE 5.2
Methodological Influences on Factor–Analytically Derived Taxa

1. *Items Analyzed: N;* redundancy; exhaustiveness; molecular versus molar; descriptive versus inferential; simple versus complex; time spanned; reliability.
2. *Response Scales:* Present–absent versus multistep; anchor points; instructions; response distributions.
3. *Subject Samples: N;* age; sex; demographic distribution; clinical status.
4. *Informants:* Self; parents; teachers; clinicians; trained observers; peers.
5. *Analytic Method:* Criteria for retaining items to analyze; measure of association among items; type of factor analysis; communality criterion; number of factors retained; rotational criteria.
6. *Derivation of Taxa:* Selection of factors; selection of items on factors; decisions about items loading on multiple factors; scoring of items on each factor—e.g., factor scores versus raw sum of high-loading items.
7. *Standardization:* Type of normative data; type of standard scores.

typical of categorical approaches. I use factor analysis to illustrate multivariate dimensional approaches, but the implications are similar for cluster-analytic approaches to formation of nondimensional groupings of items.

Without minimizing the effects of the methodological influences summarized in Table 5.2, let us assume that (1) we have completed an analysis yielding factors that remain intact through a variety of rotations; and (2) the factors inspire further confidence because they resemble the results of other studies despite methodological differences. How can these multivariate groupings of items be used to describe, classify, or discriminate among individual children?

A first decision concerns the number of robust factors to be retained. Part of the information to be gleaned from a factor analysis is the number of distinctive groupings identifiable among items assessed in a particular sample. However, even after the choice of how many factors to rotate, it is still necessary to decide which factors are the best candidates for retention in a taxonomy. This decision is linked to decisions about how many items to retain from each factor. For example, if only items having high loadings are to be retained, a factor that is robust but is defined primarily by one or two high-loading items would be a poor candidate for a concise taxonomy. The specific items and correlations between pairs of items may be important to recognize in the assessment of individuals, but such a factor is unlikely to add much reliable information beyond the scores on the one or two high-loading items themselves. In our factor analyses, for example, we have repeatedly found a robust factor having high loadings on Overeating and Overweight (Achenbach, 1978; Achenbach & Edelbrock, 1979). However, the unsurprising correlation between these items has not been accompanied by consistent covariation with enough other items to warrant taxonomic recognition as a syndrome.

After excluding factors having only one or two high-loading items, finer discriminations must be made on the basis of how syndromes are ultimately to be scored. If orthodox factor scores are used (i.e., the sum of the products of a child's score on each item multiplied by the item's loading on the factor), then the variance accounted for by the entire factor (i.e., its eigenvalue) is an important criterion. However, because rotation to simple structure typically produces factors that each have a relatively small proportion of items with high loadings, using all items on a factor to compute factor scores can allow the many items with low loadings to contribute as much variance to the factor scores as the few items with high loadings. Because it is the few items with high loadings that are of interest as a syndrome, an alternative is to compute the factor score from them alone.

If a minimum cut-off point (such as .30) is set for the loadings of items to be retained, then all items loading above that cut-off on a particular factor can be retained to define the syndrome identified by that factor. Syndrome scores are then computed for this reduced set of items, either like factor scores (i.e., by summing the products of a child's score on each retained item multiplied by the item's loading), or by simply summing the child's scores on these items without differentially weighting them by their loadings. Although the latter procedure may appear to lose the information implicit in the loadings, the fact that the retained items have a relatively small range of (high) loadings means that the difference between the sums of weighted and unweighted item scores is much less than if all the items on a factor were retained (Cattell, 1978). Furthermore, once items have substantial loadings on a factor, the absolute differences between their loadings are likely to be unreliable (Wainer, 1976).

In brief, when factor analysis is used to detect groups of covarying items, and only the best discriminated groups of items are retained, then it is a short logical step to treat these items as a syndrome quantitatively assessable in terms of the sum of unweighted item scores. Once assembled, such syndromes serve as constructs subject to further test. Note, however, that they differ from the categorical constructs of the DSM in being derived and scored quantitatively. Although subjective choices are required (e.g., the number of factors to retain; orthodox factor scores versus unit weighting; cut-off points for items retained), they are choices among explicit alternatives whose contrasting consequences can be worked out in detail and compared. This degree of formalization and quantification can be an important aid in bringing at least provisional order out of the primeval chaos of child and adolescent psychopathology.

From Dimensions to Individuals. Once factor-analytically derived syndromes are selected and a scoring procedure is adopted, choices must be made about how to integrate scores on the syndromes into a system for discriminating among individual cases and classes of cases. The opportunity to score every case quantitatively on a collection of syndromes offers the possibility of individualized summary descriptions. However, if these descriptions are to contribute meaningful discriminations, they must: (1) be referrable to known base lines in order to determine how the individual compares with a particular standard; and (2) form classes having differential relations to other important variables.

If we wanted our taxonomy to predict scores on a single criterion variable, such as a particular index of outcome under a standard treatment, then scores on each syndrome could be put into a multiple regression equation to find optimal weights for predicting our chosen criterion. After this was done and was cross-validated on large samples representative of our target population, the regression equation would grind out predictions for each new case with no further need for standardization or classification. Such is the procedure for predicting the gradepoint averages of college applicants from high school grades and entrance exams. Similar procedures are possible in many other situations in which taxonomic data can be quantitatively combined to predict a specific criterion.

Alas, we have no such criterion against which to compute regression equations or to validate taxonomic approaches. Instead, we need a taxonomy that facilitates the *discovery* of differential treatments, etiologies, and so on, which can then provide criteria against which to validate taxonomic revisions. Even when we obtain such criteria, a taxonomy will have to serve functions too diverse for the multiple-regression format. Rather than serving only as a predictor in a multiple regression, an omnibus taxonomy must permit individual cases to be assessed in terms of norms and classes. Norming can be done by standardizing raw syndrome scores in relation to normative samples in order to show how much a particular child differs from typical agemates on each syndrome. The problem of translating dimensional syndromes into taxonomic systems for discriminating among groups is more complex and will be taken up after we consider other prior issues.

Cross-Sectional or Longitudinal?

Some of the most crucial questions from a developmental perspective concern the segment of development spanned by a taxon. Does the taxon reflect characteristics of the individual that persist across long periods? Or is it peculiar to one period? If it is peculiar to one period, is it correlated with other characteristics apparent in earlier or later periods? These questions are also important from the clinical perspective, although clinicians are more likely to view them in terms of the etiology, course, and outcome of disorders than in terms of developmental changes per se.

The Age Variable in DSM-III. The enormous changes in the prevalence and patterning of behaviors from birth to maturity must be recognized by any taxonomy of behavior disorders. DSM-III does this by specifying a presumed typical age of onset for each disorder, providing occasional supplementary comments about age differences, and making age part of the criterion for the diagnosis of some disorders.

To continue our example of Attention Deficit Disorder, the DSM (American Psychiatric Association, 1980) places the onset "typically by the age of three, although frequently the disorder does not come to professional attention until the child enters school [p. 42]." The diagnostic criteria (Table 5.1) are prefaced with: "The number of symptoms specified is for children between the ages of eight and ten, the peak age range for referral. In younger children, more severe forms of the symptoms and a greater number of symptoms are usually present. The opposite is true of older children [p. 43]." Age is also an explicit criterion for diagnosis, as Criterion D requires "onset before the age of seven [p. 44]."

The DSM thus acknowledges the importance of age differences in defining this and other childhood disorders. Yet, the use of the age dimension is rather haphazard: When it is stated that "onset is typically by the age of three," does this mean that the defining criteria are already met by age three? Or does the prefatory remark regarding greater severity and number of symptoms in younger children mean that the defining criteria must be altered for younger children? Similarly, does the requirement of onset before age seven mean that the criteria for diagnosis at ages eight to ten also had to be met before age seven, or that the symptoms must be more severe and numerous before age seven to warrant diagnosis as Attention Deficit Disorder, even if the diagnosis is not made until a later age?

The general description of the disorder hints at the DSM committee's intent (American Psychiatric Association, 1980):

> The child displays, for his or her mental and chronological age, signs of developmentally inappropriate inattention, impulsivity, and hyperactivity. The signs must be reported by adults in the child's environment, such as parents and teachers. Because the symptoms are typically variable, they may not be observed directly by the clinician. When the reports of teachers and parents conflict, primary consideration should be given to the teacher reports because of greater familiarity with age-appropriate norms [p. 43].

In short, the committee seems to have thought of the age dimension in terms of descriptive norms for children's behavior in their customary environments. However, no normative data are employed to judge the degree of deviance. Furthermore, the references to age just quoted fail to show how age variations in the composition and intensity of the syndrome should determine diagnostic decisions. Instead, it appears that the disorder is assumed to be an enduring entity defined by the criteria for 8–10 year olds, but also recognizable at other ages if the admonitions about age trends are heeded. Yet, there are few data to support the longitudinal assumptions implied (see Achenbach, 1981). A lack of longitudinal and normative data also plagues DSM assertions about the age patterns of other childhood disorders.

Normative–Developmental Approaches. DSM–III pays more attention to age than DSM–I or DSM–II. But can the age dimension not be used with any greater precision? Age is but a proxy for a host of developmental variables; longitudinal relations among developmental variables would be of greater interest than age data per se. However, the normative–developmental approach adopted in the standardization of intelligence, achievement, and social competence measures could greatly increase the precision with which age is used as a reference point. Although these are all phenotypic measures, adequate phenotypic assessment is a prerequisite for identification of underlying developmental processes.

One way to apply a normative–developmental approach would be to obtain prevalence data for age-graded representative samples on each criterial sign and symptom used in a taxonomy. To obtain prevalence data, the assessment of signs and symptoms must be well standardized. Furthermore, there should be an objective procedure for combining the signs and symptoms into a formal diagnosis. If the diagnoses are categorical like those of the DSM, the prevalence of each diagnosis can then be judged for each age.

Better use could be made of normative–developmental data if they were employed to help set standards for what is considered a disorder at each age. Although prevalence figures alone are inadequate for judging the pathological significance of most behaviors, a finding, for example, that most typical 6 year olds met the DSM criteria for Attention Deficit Disorder should spur either revision of the criteria or more explicit constraints on their application to 6 year olds. Quantifiable diagnoses, such as those based on dimensional scales, could make especially good use of normative–developmental data, because cut-off points can be based on scores found to discriminate between normal children and children independently judged to be clinically deviant. This contrasts with the a priori assertions about age and deviance that characterize the DSM child categories.

Still fuller use could be made of the normative–developmental approach by assessing age differences not only in the intensity but also in the composition of taxa. This can be done best by empirically determining the association among signs and symptoms at each age in order to detect age-related patterns. If there are age differences in the composition of taxa, a taxonomy should reflect these as precisely as possible. Although longitudinal research is needed to discriminate genotypic continuities in disorders from phenotypic changes with age and from disorders peculiar to particular developmental periods, cross-sectional multivariate analyses would yield a far more explicit basis for a normative–developmental taxonomy than the DSM does. This could then serve as a conceptual framework within which to undertake longitudinal research to identify the typical antecedents, developmental course, and outcome of each type of disorder, as well as the reasons for differences among disorders.

Narrow Band or Broad Band?

In the absence of a final taxonomy, decisions must be made about the level of differentiation appropriate for taxonomic constructs. Among taxonomists of all fields, there is an inevitable tension between ''splitters'' and ''lumpers''—that is, those who split phenomena into many molecular taxa and those who lump phenomena into a few molar taxa. The DSM taxonomies of childhood disorders show a progression from extreme lumping in DSM–I to rather extreme splitting in DSM–III. Although splitting is often a by-product of increasing knowledge, many of DSM–III's splits seem to reflect a desire to cover all possibilities rather than new knowledge of differences. It is not known, for example, whether distinctions among DSM–III's three types of Attention Deficit Disorders or four types of Conduct Disorders can be made reliably; or, if they can, whether they relate to any other important variables.

In multivariate studies, a continuing contrast has been evident between those yielding two or three broad-band syndromes comprising a relatively large proportion of the items analyzed, and those yielding five or more narrow-band syndromes comprising smaller proportions of the items analyzed (cf. Achenbach & Edelbrock, 1978). As mentioned earlier, the broad-band syndromes generally represent a contrast between aggressive and delinquent behavior, on the one hand, and anxious, inhibited behavior, on the other, although one or two other broad-band syndromes have also been found in a few studies. The narrow-band syndromes correspond more closely to the level of differentiation characterizing DSM syndromes. The content of some is quite similar to DSM–III child syndromes, whereas others have no clear DSM–III counterparts (see Achenbach, 1980).

There is, of course, no a priori "correct" level of differentiation. The differentiation of the DSM was based on the consensus of committee members, whereas the differentiation yielded by multivariate studies depends on the method of analysis, number of items analyzed, heterogeneity and clinical status of the samples, and decisions about what to retain: Unrotated factor analysis, small item pools, nonclinical samples, and retention only of factors accounting for large proportions of variance militate against finding narrow-band syndromes.

Probably because broad-band factors are simpler to use, their correlates have been more widely researched than those of narrow-band factors (cf. Achenbach & Edelbrock, 1978; Quay, 1979). It appears that the broad-band syndromes represent a least common denominator among ratings of behavior problems, whereas the narrow-band syndromes represent finer-grained differences in patterning, but research with large clinical samples is needed to test the correlates of narrow-band syndromes.

Second-order factor analyses and other assessments of relations between narrow- and broad-band syndromes have shown that many of the narrow-band syndromes can be subsumed by the broad-band syndromes. Thus, for example, our second-order factor analyses have shown first-order Hyperactive, Aggressive, and Delinquent factors to form a second-order Externalizing factor (Achenbach, 1978; Achenbach & Edelbrock, 1979). Similarly, our first-order Depressed, Somatic Complaints, Obsessive-Compulsive, and Uncommunicative factors form a second-order Internalizing factor. Findings of plentiful narrow-band factors by some studies and a few broad-band factors by others are not, therefore, mutually contradictory; they largely reflect different levels in a hierarchy ranging from relatively molecular to relatively molar groupings.

Because we do not yet know which level is most useful for various purposes, it would be prudent to preserve both. This can be done by scoring children simultaneously on narrow- and broad-band taxa derived from the same pool of items. It is possible that the broad-band taxa can guide existing case-management policies, but that the narrow-band taxa may offer the greater discriminative power needed for research on specific etiologies, treatments, and outcomes. As we gain knowledge of specific differences among taxa, management strategies should likewise become more differentiated.

Until we know which differences among taxa can predict other important differences, assessing children on both the narrow- and broad-band syndromes characteristic of their age and sex can provide much more differentiated descriptions than assessing only the broad-band syndromes. If the syndromes can be scored in the form of scales, a child's standing on all the relevant syndromes can be displayed in a profile format. Any narrow-band syndromes that are subsumed by broad-band syndromes can be grouped according to the broad-band syndromes that subsume them. The child can then be viewed simultaneously in terms of two levels of a hierarchy.

DSM–III implies hierarchical relations between certain child-diagnostic categories and their subtypes; it also provides elaborate decision trees to show how some diagnoses preempt others. Yet, neither the relations between types and subtypes nor the preemptive ordering are based on empirical evidence. Although it is possible to compare the predictive power of each subtype of conduct disorder, for example, with the predictive power of all four subtypes lumped together, there is no operational definition for the overarching category that includes them. Nor is there anything to show that the four subtypes are more closely related to each other than to other disorders in the DSM.

Multiaxial or Uniaxial?

Scoring a child simultaneously on several dimensional syndromes in a profile format can preserve more information about the child's overall pattern of behavior than forced-choice categorization in terms of syndromes judged to be present or absent. This *polydimensional* approach (Roth, 1978) maximizes preservation of the information used to describe behavior disorders in syndromal terms. However, other kinds of information may also be needed to describe cases more fully than syndromes can.

Multiaxial Aspects of DSM–III.   DSM–III attempts to formalize additional information by adding four axes to an essentially syndromal nosology. The axes are designated as follows:

1. *Axis I:* Includes clinical syndromes, plus conditions not attributable to a mental disorder that are the focus of attention or treatment (e.g., malingering), and additional codes (e.g., unspecified mental disorder).
2. *Axis II:* Personality disorders and specific developmental disorders.
3. *Axis III:* Physical disorders and conditions.
4. *Axis IV:* Severity of psychosocial stressors.
5. *Axis V:* Highest level of adaptive functioning during the past year.

There appears to have been some ambiguity regarding the use of the five axes, as the principle authors of DSM–III first state (Spitzer, Williams, & Skodol, 1980): "each individual should be evaluated on each axis [pp. 154–155]," but several lines later say: "Axes IV and V are available for use in special clinical and research settings [p. 155]." The DSM itself states that each individual is evaluated only on the first three axes, whereas Axes IV and V are for use in special settings to supplement the official Axes I, II, and III diagnoses.

The multiaxial approach is one way to extend the formalization of diagnosis beyond a syndromal nosology. Although I will not make a detailed critique of the multiaxial aspect of DSM–III, it is nevertheless instructive to consider some of the dilemmas it poses for assessing disorders of childhood and adolescence. Consider the composition of Axes I and II, for example. Mental retardation is included as an Axis-I category with the subtypes mild, moderate, severe, profound, and unspecified mental retardation. The subtypes from mild to profound are based largely on IQ (50–70, 35–49, 20–34, and below 20).

There is no doubt that cognitive functioning as poor as the retarded range needs to be recognized in diagnostic assessments of children. However, the essentially quantitative–dimensional assessment of cognitive functioning is quite different from assessment of the syndromal categories comprising the rest of Axis I: Retarded cognitive functioning per se is not a syndrome, and retarded children may differ greatly as to whether they manifest disorders corresponding to other Axis-I syndromes. The explicit preemption of certain other syndromes—such as Attention Deficit Disorders—by a diagnosis of retardation also seems unwarranted, and implicit preemption may often occur when clinicians feel that a diagnosis of retardation completes their Axis-I work, despite the possible presence of other problems qualifying as Axis-I disorders (cf. Rutter & Shaffer, 1980). The inclusion of stuttering and functional enuresis on Axis I under the heading of Other Disorders with Physical Manifestations likewise seems inconsistent with the notion of a syndromal nosology.

The Specific Developmental Disorders of Axis II raise similar problems. Developmental Reading Disorder and Developmental Arithmetic Disorder, for example, concern academic skills important for all children; but the lack of such skills is not equivalent to a mental disorder. Further ambiguities arise when it is noted that Pervasive Developmental Disorders, such as Infantile Autism, are not on Axis II but Axis I, and that Schizoid Disorder of Childhood or Adolescence is on Axis I but Schizoid and Schizotypal personality disorders are on Axis II.

Two dilemmas posed by the mixing of concepts between Axis I and II are:

1. How can we distinguish aspects of functioning that begin in childhood and can pervasively affect a child's development but are not themselves behavior disorders (e.g., mental retardation) from behavior disorders that are pervasive and chronic (e.g., infantile autism), and behavior disorders that do not seem intrinsically pervasive and chronic (e.g., separation anxiety disorder)?

2. How can we integrate assessment of behavioral syndromes with developmental assessment of cognitive functioning and academic and other skills relevant to all children's adaptation?

Chronicity and Pervasiveness. The dilemmas posed by DSM–III could be better resolved by separating the taxonomic structures dealing with the *descriptions* of behavioral signs and symptoms from those dealing with the questions of *chronicity* and *pervasiveness*. Thus, a polydimensional or profile approach can describe children's current behavior-problem patterns as the basis for a syndromal taxonomy, even though chronicity and pervasiveness are assessed separately.

Cognitive Competence. To integrate a syndromal taxonomy with developmental assessment, separate axes could be provided for cognitive and social competencies. Although it may be hoped that the separate axes will not remain mutually orthogonal but will ultimately converge to define multiaxial taxa, it is important that each be designed to fulfill its primary function well. For example, because little is yet known about the relations between physical and behavioral disorders, a taxonomy of physical disorders accompanying a taxonomy of behavior disorders should be judged primarily in terms of its adequacy with respect to the physical disorders themselves. This is the approach implied by DSM–III's Axis III, which simply draws on the existing medical nosology for physical conditions. By the same token, an axis for cognitive functioning should be designed to assess cognition as accurately as possible.

A cognitive axis could use standardized intelligence tests to provide global indices of functioning as compared to normative samples of agemates. More differentiated assessments of cognitive strengths and deficits can be conveyed via profiles, like those provided by the Wechsler tests. For children of school age, achievement profiles and discrepancies between abilities and achievement would also be important in any comprehensive diagnostic assessment. Note that this approach to cognitive assessment makes it a dimension potentially relevant to all cases rather than a consideration that becomes relevant only when functioning is so poor as to be considered a categorical disorder. Thus, superior ability that is an adaptive strength and indicates a cognitive developmental level exceeding a child's chronological age would receive as much recognition as retardation. So would the specific educational deficits of a child who is of average ability but below average in achievement. The value of a cognitive dimension would be further enhanced by incorporating measures of major cognitive stages, such as those identified by Piaget (1970).

Social Competence. In addition to cognitive assessment, assessment of non-cognitive adaptive skills is also important. The Vineland Social Maturity Scale (Doll, 1965) has long been used to assess the self-help skills of the retarded. Although useful for this purpose, its items do not reflect important adaptive differences among children who are cognitively above the retarded range. After considerable trial and error, we have evolved age- and sex-normed scales of items reflecting the parent-reported quantity and quality of children's participation in activities and social relations. These, in turn, have been found to discriminate well between demographically matched normal and disturbed children (Achenbach & Edelbrock, 1980). Although we originally conceived these social competence scales as part of the same taxonomic structure as our profile of behavior-problem scales, it now appears that they are better viewed as an additional taxonomic structure. A social-competence profile consisting of these or analogous normative–developmental scales is probably a more effective way of assessing adaptive competencies in children than DSM–III Axis V ratings of previous highest level of adaptive functioning. This is especially true because global ratings of children's previous highest level of adaptation are often poor guides to the specific adaptive functioning needed to maintain developmental progress.

Although one could endlessly complicate taxonomies by adding axes, some such additions can simplify a system by reducing the mixing of objectives within and between axes. Thus, if a syndromal axis dealt only with the description of the child's current pattern of signs and symptoms without having to simultaneously reflect chronicity, pervasiveness, and cognitive level, some of the ambiguities inherent in the child and adolescent categories of DSM Axes I and II might be avoided. Furthermore, normative–developmental assessments of cognitive functioning and social competencies may be as informative in the diagnosis of children and adolescents as most syndromes of signs and symptoms. Restraint must be exercised, of course, to keep the number of axes within manageable bounds. Yet, it is not at all clear that the traditional nosological approach should remain at the core of taxonomies of psychopathology or that disorders of children and adults can be optimally conceptualized within the same taxonomic framework. Considerable resourcefulness will be needed to integrate the host of potentially relevant aspects of formal diagnosis into more comprehensive taxonomic systems.

SOURCES OF TAXONOMIC VARIANCE

All taxonomies are vulnerable to unreliability. If a particular phenomenon cannot be consistently classified in the same way on different occasions or by different users, a taxonomy cannot fulfill its intended functions. Problems of reliability are multifaceted, but they all concern consistency in the assignment of phenomena to taxa. Not knowing what phenotypical attributes are the best indices of genotypical differences among disorders makes it hard to stipulate what must remain the same and what can vary in order for an individual to qualify for a particular taxon. In confronting reliability problems, it is helpful to distinguish among potential sources of variance in applying a taxonomic system. Table 5.3 summarizes sources of variance likely to affect taxonomies of child and adolescent psychopathology.

TABLE 5.3
Sources of Taxonomic Variance

Subject Being Assessed	Assessment Process	Taxonomic System
1. Random changes	1. Influence on subject	1. Adequacy of taxa
2. Situational changes	2. Types of data	2. Definitional criteria
3. Occasion changes	3. Sources of data	3. Discrimination among taxa
4. Developmental changes	4. Intraobserver variance	4. Taxonomic format
5. Changes in the disorder	5. Interobserver variance	5. Usability by diagnosticians
	6. Data reduction	

Subject Variability

Some kinds of change listed in Table 5.3 under *Subject Being Assessed* inevitably threaten reliability, whereas the implications of others depend on the taxonomy in question. Random changes in a subject are often a source of unreliability, although the degree of lability might itself be a criterion for defining some disorders. Inconsistent variations from one *occasion* to another over relatively brief intervals that do not reflect either situational changes, developmental changes, or changes in the disorder itself are another common source of unreliability.

Consistent *situational* changes, by contrast, might be criterial attributes in some taxonomies. DSM–III's definition of Attention Deficit Disorder, for example, specifies that the "signs must be reported by adults in the child's environment, such as parents and teachers. Because the symptoms are typically variable, they may not be observed directly by the clinician [p. 43]." Thus, because occurrence of the behavior in school and/or home situations is criterial for the taxon, its absence in clinical settings does not necessarily contribute to unreliability. However, this means that parent and teacher data are crucial for the diagnosis. DSM–III does not formalize the use of parent and teacher data and does not specify the role of such data in other diagnoses, despite the dependence of some—such as conduct disorders—on reports of behavior unlikely to be observed clinically or self-reported. Empirically derived taxa have typically been based on ratings by a single type of informant, such as a parent, clinician, or teacher, although the informant might use information from diverse situations. Further taxonomic progress will require more explicit reconciliation of discrepancies in the occurrence, patterning, and assessment of behaviors in different situations.

The roles accorded developmental changes in the child and changes over the course of a disorder depend on longitudinal findings. For example, if longitudinal data show that a particular disorder typically undergoes certain phenotypic changes as children traverse particular developmental periods, then these changes should be recognized in defining the developmental aspects of the taxon.

Likewise, if longitudinal data show that a particular disorder uniformly undergoes certain changes as a function of time since its onset, *regardless* of the developmental periods being traversed, then these changes should be recognized in defining the (nondevelopmental) course of the disorder. Better longitudinal data on phenotypically well-defined taxa are needed to enable taxonomies to incorporate changes related to children's development and to the nondevelopmental course of disorders.

Assessment Variability

Like subject variability, some kinds of assessment variability almost always contribute error, whereas the effects of other kinds depend on the taxonomic decisions to be made. Inconsistencies in a single observer and between different observers making the same types of judgments almost inevitably contribute error variance, although the inconsistencies may result from the taxonomic system itself rather than from mistakes made by the observers. Likewise, inconsistency in the reduction of data to a form required by a particular taxonomy is a source of error, although the fault may lie with the taxonomy as much as with the assessment process.

Because several types and sources of data may be used to make taxonomic decisions of the DSM kind, differences in these data are another potential source of unreliability. For example, IQ scores and judgments of adaptive behavior are two types of data needed for the diagnosis of retardation. The IQs are obtained from a standardized assessment procedure, normed on age-graded samples and reasonably well documented as to reliability, predictive power, and other parameters. By contrast, the DSM specifies no procedures for assessing adaptive behavior. Although clinical judgments may be essential in all diagnoses, judgments of adaptive behavior require knowledge of a child's coping in everyday situations not likely to be observed by the clinician. For children with IQs in the mildly retarded range (the majority of retarded children), the clinician is unlikely to have a reliable subjective metric for judging adaptive behavior.

Even when adaptive behavior is obviously poor, it may not be easy to ascribe it specifically to retardation versus other factors. Subcultural differences make it especially hard to combine IQ data with clinical judgments into a yes–no diagnosis of retardation. By obtaining behavioral ratings from parents and others in a child's customary environment, Mercer (1975) has sought to formalize the use of culturally relativistic data on adaptive functioning in the diagnosis of retardation. Such data can provide a more explicit basis for judging adaptive behavior, but the reliability of yes–no diagnoses of retardation and other disorders remains vulnerable to discrepancies between different types and sources of data. This may be inevitable until relations between phenotypical indicators and underlying genotypes are definitively established. Yet, because many conditions (including most cases of mild mental retardation) probably lack categorical genotypes, a polydimensional descriptive approach may be more informative than a categorical taxonomy.

Clinical interviews, testing, and many observational procedures affect the variables they are intended to assess. The influence of the assessment procedure need not be a source of error, however, if the procedure's predictive power is well validated. Thus, an IQ test presents unaccustomed tasks but IQ scores predict academic performance reasonably well (cf. Achenbach, 1981). Projective tests are designed to present unfamiliar stimuli in order to elicit behavior not otherwise observable, but validity and reliability are more problematic, because it is often unclear what criteria they should be validated against or how they should be scored. It is therefore hard to determine the reliability of projective data for taxonomic purposes. Direct observations of behavior, on the other hand, are mainly aimed at obtaining representative samples of children's behavior in order to directly ascertain their functioning in important situations. Unless the findings of an observational procedure are representative of the target situations, they will contribute taxonomic error.

Clinical interviews are vulnerable to problems like those of standardized tests, projective tests, and direct observations. Most clinical interviews are intended partly to ascertain factual information, partly to function in a projective fashion, and partly to permit sampling of the interviewee's typical behavior. However, the possibilities for fulfilling any of these functions vary greatly with children's developmental level and other characteristics. Diagnostic interviews are likely to be unfamiliar enough to distort most children's behavior. Even accurate factual information may be hard to obtain from young children; the difficulties of obtaining reliable projective data for taxonomic purposes are compounded by the idiosyncracies of particular interviews and interviewers, as well as the lack of normative standards for comparison. Although clinical interviews are indispensible for most diagnostic workups, and they can elicit reliable factual data from older children (e.g., Reich & Herjanic, 1980), the taxonomic assessment of children is always likely to require other types and sources of data as well.

System Variability

Formal diagnoses cannot be very reliable without good definitional criteria for each taxon. The criteria for each taxon must not only be clear, but must be discriminating enough to prevent confusing overlaps among taxa. The kinds of distinctions and judgments required must also be easy for clinicians to make from the data available to them.

Although problems of reliability in the assignment of cases to predefined taxa have received more attention, the adequacy of the taxa themselves is a more fundamental issue. If taxa do not correspond to important and detectible distinctions among phenomena, reliability is irrelevant. Because there are so many possible distinctions among behavior disorders, the problem is to find those distinctions that are both important and detectible. Determining what is important raises questions of validity, as importance must be judged in relation to other criteria—that is, important with respect to what? Any features that accurately index etiology, appropriate treatment, or prognosis would obviously be important, but few such features have been confirmed as yet. Instead, the tendency has been to reify a disorder and attempt to improve the reliability of diagnosing it without knowing whether "it" is an entity at all or, if it is an entity, how it differentially relates to etiology, prognosis, or treatment.

The Example of Schizophrenia.   An adult example that has been the subject of far more taxonomic research and theory than any disorder of childhood is schizophrenia. Overall and Hollister (1979) have developed the Composite Diagnostic Checklist (CDC–Schizo) for recording all the data needed for diagnosing schizophrenia according to six prominent sets of research criteria. A computer program scores the CDC–Schizo data according to the different sets of research criteria. Thus, once obtained from a clinical interview, the same checklist data are combined by objective rules into yes–no diagnoses of schizophrenia according to each of the six sets of criteria. Unreliability in the diagnostic process cannot, therefore, cause disagreements among the criteria. Yet Overall and Hollister (1979) found mediocre agreement between diagnoses of schizophrenia made by the different criteria. In fact, two versions of the Research Diagnostic Criteria on which the DSM–III is based (the Washington University and New York State Psychiatric Institute versions) agreed on only 49% of their classifications of patients as schizophrenic. Despite well-refined and standardized procedures for obtaining data, plus totally reliable procedures for combining data into diagnoses of an exceptionally well-established taxon, the two taxonomies produced different conclusions about who was schizophrenic. Why?

One source of disagreement is the difference in stringency of criteria for diagnosing schizophrenia. Of the patients clinically diagnosed schizophrenic, only 26.5% were also diagnosed schizophrenic by the Washington University version of the Research Diagnostic Criteria, whereas the other research criteria diagnosed from 73.5% to 91.6% schizophrenic. This reflects major differences in the *base rates* for the diagnosis of schizophrenia according to the different criteria. Yet, the very low base rate yielded by the Washington University criteria is the result of efforts to make the diagnosis both reliable and valid by including only very "pure" cases. Although unreliability does limit validity, efforts to increase the reliability of yes–no diagnoses through strict criteria can also reduce validity—even below chance levels—if the true base rate for the disorder is higher than yielded by the strict criteria (cf. Carey & Gottesman, 1978). To appreciate the paradoxical attenuation of validity through efforts to increase reliability, suppose the true base rate for schizophrenia was 60% in Overall and Hollister's sample: The 26.5% rate yielded by the Washington University criteria would be less accurate than the 60% rate attainable by diagnosing everyone schizophrenic! Higher true base rates would further improve the advantage of diagnosing everyone schizophrenic as compared to the Washington University criteria.

Another study of the diagnosis of adult schizophrenia is especially informative for developmental psychopathology, because it dealt with the impact of different concepts of the taxon on studies of children presumed to be at high risk because their parents had the disorder (Hanson, Gottesman, & Meehl, 1977). It is hoped that such studies will reveal the origins of major disorders as they unfold. However, these hopes can only be fulfilled if the diagnosis of a disorder in the parents indeed predicts rates of the disorder in the offspring high enough to document its unfolding.

Hanson et al. illustrated the diagnostic problem by having five experts judge the psychiatric case histories of parents whose children were assessed in a high-risk study. One expert (Paul Meehl) diagnosed schizophrenia in considerably more parents than did the other experts. There was good agreement on about half the cases diagnosed schizophrenic by Meehl, and there was good agreement on the symptoms occurring in most cases. But disagreements arose from Meehl's use of "qualified" schizophrenic diagnoses (i.e., pseudoneurotic, pseudopsychopathic, and schizoaffective) in cases the other experts diagnosed as nonschizophrenic. Despite agreement on the basic data for each case, disagreements thus arose from different concepts of the schizophrenic taxon. Cases evoking consensus tended to be severely afflicted, chronic state-hospital patients, whereas those diagnosed schizophrenic only by Meehl tended to be mildly afflicted.

Suppose we wish to compare the offspring of parents diagnosed schizophrenic according to the stringent criteria with offspring of other patients, some of whom Meehl calls schizophrenic: If Meehl's broader diagnosis is really a more valid index of the genotype, then differences between the offspring of true schizophrenics and true nonschizophrenics will be blurred by the inclusion of true schizophrenics in the putatively nonschizophrenic group. On the other hand, if we use Meehl's diagnoses and they are, in fact, too broad, differences between the true schizophrenics and nonschizophrenics will be blurred by inclusion of nonschizophrenics in the schizophrenic group. Hanson et al. illustrate the problems created for high-risk studies by uncertainty in the diagnoses of both the parental probands and their offspring. For example, the results of the ambitious Danish high-risk study started by Mednick in 1962 are growing more ambiguous with changes in the symptoms of both the parental probands and their offspring previously diagnosed schizophrenic (Mednick, Schulsinger, Teasdale, Schulsinger, Venables, & Rock, 1978).

If contrasting diagnostic criteria can be made explicit and employed reliably, high-risk studies that include probands receiving different diagnoses may help to test the validity of the diagnoses: If criterion A predicts disorders in the offspring more accurately than criterion B, this would support criterion A. However, this strategy is complicated by the same uncertainty in the diagnoses of the offspring. Until choices among specific categorical criteria can be made with more confidence, it may be preferable to score cases in terms of quantitative–dimensional criteria. Quantitative–dimensional scoring enables us to measure gradations of severity that would be confounded with stringency of criteria if we used categorical taxa. Furthermore, the likely role of polygenic (Hanson et al., 1977) and other multivariate determination in most disorders may make quantitative–dimensional scoring a better index of underlying genotypes than yes–no categorical scoring.

A PROGRAM OF MULTIVARIATE TAXOMETRIC RESEARCH

Meehl (1978) has described his efforts to formalize the diagnosis of schizophrenia as *taxometrics,* which he defines as "the application of psychometric procedures to detection of a taxonic situation and classification of individuals into the taxon or outside of it [p. 825]." From his conjectures about the underlying genotype, Meehl (1978) attempts to:

> derive formulae for estimating the theoretical quantities of interest, such as the proportion of schizotypes in a given clinical population, the mean values of the schizotypal and nonschizotypal classes, the optimal cut ("hitmax") on each phenotypic indicator variable for classifying individuals, and the proportion of valid and false positives achieved by that cut [p. 825].

Meehl's concept of taxometrics thus refers to psychometric approaches to selecting indicators of a priori categorical constructs, such as schizophrenia. However, the application of psychometric procedures to taxonomic problems need not be restricted to preexisting categorical constructs. In fact, the paucity of taxonomic constructs for children's disorders makes taxometric approaches especially attractive for deriving tentative constructs.

A taxometric framework for testing the reliability, validity, discriminative power, and heuristic value of such constructs also offers greater explicitness and quantitative precision than categorical nosologies of the DSM type. Whether important underlying genotypes actually exist in categorical or dimensional form, quantitative–dimensional approaches can generally make more efficient use of multiple indicators than categorical approaches in which the nature of the underlying genotypes is unknown.

To illustrate a taxometric approach to the derivation and quantification of taxa for child psychopathology, I will outline the major stages and findings of our research program. (For further details, see Achenbach, 1978; Achenbach & Edelbrock, 1979, in press; Edelbrock & Achenbach, 1980). It should already be clear from the preceding discussion of dilemmas raised by taxonomic systems that there are no total solutions. Instead, every solution involves trade-offs between potential gains and losses. Yet, until tentative solutions are tested in practice, we cannot determine the relative value of each option.

Instrumentation

In our effort to apply psychometric procedures to the taxonomy of child psychopathology, we selected parents' reports of their children's behavioral problems and competencies as a starting point. Although other sources and types of data are also relevant, parents are crucial to the evaluation of almost all children referred for mental-health services. They must typically participate in clinical evaluations of their children, and they are the chief source of data. Furthermore, their perceptions of their children's behavior are important determinants of what can or should be done about it. Our target subjects were children aged 4 through 16, because few younger children are referred for behavior disorders, and parental involvement typically declines after youths pass the age of 16.

Having chosen parent reports as a starting point, we compiled behavior-problem items that literature searches and our own previous research had shown to be of concern to mental-health professionals and the parents of children referred for mental-health services. After stating these items in easily ratable form, we tried out a succession of pilot editions with parents seeking mental-health services for their children. In the process, we obtained feedback from parents and from paraprofessionals and clinicians who met with the parents in order to improve the wording of items, to add relevant items, and to delete items that parents never reported or that overlapped with other items. We sought broad but nonredundant coverage of problems readily reportable by parents; redundant items would have yielded high correlations with one another, which, in turn, would have produced artifactual groupings in multivariate analyses. Had we wished instead to measure preconceived taxa, we would have begun with redundant items designed to tap a given taxon in overlapping ways. After finalizing the data-collection instrument—dubbed the Child Behavior Checklist (CBCL)—we used it to obtain data from parents of children being seen in some 30 mental-health settings and from 1400 randomly selected parents of normal children.

Although we had also intended to assess children's positive characteristics with items that could then be grouped via multivariate analysis, we found that simple statements of positive characteristics were almost universally endorsed by parents of even the most disturbed children, evidently due to social desirability influences on responses to such items. After considerable trial-and-error testing of other approaches, we found that parental reports of children's sports and nonsports activities, organizations, jobs and chores, number of friends, contacts with friends, relations with other people, quality of play and work alone, and various aspects of school functioning discriminated well between normal and disturbed children. We then assembled these items into three scales entitled Activities, Social, and School.

The nature of the social-competence scales and our cluster-analytic findings (discussed later) dictated that our assessment of social competence be in terms of scores on the linear scales rather than as an integral component of the taxonomy of behavior disorders. This approach resembles that embodied in Axis V of DSM–III, although standard scores based on normative samples make it possible to compare a child's standing on each of our scales with normals of the same age and sex. Lacking norms, Axis V of DSM–III simply reflects the clinician's global judgment about the patient's highest level of functioning in the past year. Another difference is that the items of our scales reflect specific behaviors in various areas as a basis for judging where a child's relative strengths and deficits lie. Although much remains to be done by way of testing the relations between the social-competence scales and other variables, the scales offer a reliable descriptive assessment that validly discriminates between demographically matched normal and disturbed children (Achenbach & Edelbrock, in press).

Derivation of Syndromes

Behavior-problem syndromes were derived by factor analyzing CBCLs filled out by parents of clinically referred children. Clinical samples were used for the factor analyses because many of the problems for which children are referred are too mild or infrequent in normal populations to permit detection of associations among them. Moreover, it is the patterning of behavior occurring in clinical populations that is of primary interest for purposes of a clinical taxonomy.

In order to reflect age and sex differences in the prevalence and patterning of behavior problems, separate factor analyses were performed on CBCLs for each sex within the age ranges 4–5, 6–11, and 12–16. These age intervals were chosen because they demarcate transitions in cognitive, biological, psychosexual, and educational development. If there were in fact age or sex differences in the patterning of behavior problems, combining groups for analysis could produce misleading results by (1) obscuring syndromes peculiar to particular age/sex groups; (2) obscuring age/sex differences in the content of syndromes that may be similar but not identical across age and sex; and (3) exaggerating the generality of syndromes that are not actually present in all groups.

Narrow-Band Analyses.   After an initial principal-components analysis of each sample, we performed orthogonal and oblique rotations of various numbers of factors in order to identify those that remained intact with a substantial number of items loading at least .30 despite changes in rotational criteria. The items loading at least .30 on these factors were then used to define the behavior problem taxa for each age/sex group. Table 5.4 shows the descriptive labels given each of the factor-based taxa derived to date.

The *Somatic Complaints, Delinquent,* and *Aggressive* syndromes recurred with considerable uniformity in all groups. *Withdrawal* and *Schizoid* syndromes also occurred in all groups, but with less uniformity and sometimes mixed with other syndromes. *Depressed, Obsessive,* and *Hyperactive* syndromes were evident in most but not all groups. By contrast, the *Uncommunicative* syndrome was found only for 6–11 and 12–16-year-old boys, whereas the *Cruel* syndrome was found only for 6–11 and 12–16-year-old girls.

The importance of analyzing the groups separately was demonstrated by a comparison of the results of analyzing the 6–11 and 12–16-year-old boys samples

TABLE 5.4
Syndromes Found Through Factor Analysis of the Child Behavior Checklist

Group	Internalizing Syndromes[a]	Mixed Syndromes	Externalizing Syndromes[a]
Boys aged 4–5	1. Social Withdrawal 2. Somatic Complaints 3. Immature 4. Depressed	1. Sex Problems	1. Delinquent 2. Aggressive 3. Schizoid
Boys aged 6–11	1. Schizoid 2. Depressed 3. Uncommunicative 4. Obsessive Compulsive 5. Somatic Complaints	1. Social Withdrawal	1. Delinquent 2. Aggressive 3. Hyperactive
Boys aged 12–16	1. Somatic Complaints 2. Schizoid 3. Uncommunicative 4. Immature 5. Obsessive Compulsive	1. Hostile Withdrawal	1. Hyperactive 2. Aggressive 3. Delinquent
Girls aged 6–11	1. Depressed 2. Social Withdrawal 3. Somatic Complaints 4. Schizoid Obsessive		1. Cruel 2. Aggressive 3. Delinquent 4. Sex Problems 5. Hyperactive
Girls aged 12–16	1. Anxious Obsessive 2. Somatic Complaints 3. Schizoid 4. Depressed Withdrawal	1. Immature Hyperactive	1. Cruel 2. Aggressive 3. Delinquent

[a]Syndromes are listed in descending order of their loadings on the second-order Internalizing and Externalizing factors.

separately and combined: A very robust *Depressed* factor was second only to the *Aggressive* factor in number of high-loading items and total variance for 6–11-year-old boys analyzed separately, but it completely disappeared when we combined the age groups. This does not necessarily mean that the items comprising the *Depressed* factor in the younger group do not occur or are not important in the older group. Some of the items having high loadings on the *Depressed* factor were more prevalent in the older than the younger group, and many of them had high loadings on robust factors in the older group.

What the absence of a *Depressed* factor in the older group does mean, however, is that the items comprising it in the younger group *covary* differently in the older group. Specifically, the numerous items that covaried to form the *Depressed* factor in the younger group were spread across several factors in the older group, with three or more of them loading at least .30 on the *Schizoid*, *Uncommunicative*, and *Hostile Withdrawal* factors. Items indicative of depression are thus associated with a greater variety of other items in adolescent than younger boys. The *Depressed* factor found for 6–11-year-old girls also disappeared when we combined them with 12–16-year-old girls.

Separate analyses for children grouped by age and sex not only provide more precise representations of the actual patterning of behavior problems in each group, but also have heuristic value. They show that the confusion evident in debates over a priori categorical concepts of syndromes like childhood depression (e.g., Schulterbrandt & Raskin, 1977) may arise at least partly from ignorance of age and sex differences. They also suggest that the distinctive features of a particular type of disturbance in one group may be generalized indicators of disturbance in other groups. Such findings can contribute to a conceptual organizing framework for the developmental study of psychopathology and should spur new research and theory as to the reasons for the differences among syndromes.

Broad-Band Analyses. Table 5.4 shows that either eight or nine robust factors were found for each age/sex group. Notice that the factors are grouped under the headings *Internalizing, Mixed,* and *Externalizing.* These represent the results of second-order factor analyses that we undertook to identify broad-band groupings of the relatively narrow-band, first-order factors. We did these analyses because the differences between studies finding a few broad-band factors and those finding more plentiful narrow-band factors seemed worth reconciling by explicitly preserving broad- and narrow-band levels in the taxonomic hierarchy. Our second-order *Internalizing* and *Externalizing* factors are quite consistent with the broad overcontrolled versus undercontrolled groupings found in other studies, although their exact composition varies with the age and sex of the children. Under the *Mixed* heading are listed first-order factors that had moderate loadings on both second-order factors rather than being clearly aligned with one or the other.

Standardization and Profiling of Taxometric Scales

We score individual children in terms of each narrow-band factor by summing each child's raw scores on all the items loading at least .30 on the factor. To put the child's scores into a normative–developmental context, we then convert the scores to normalized T scores based on the distribution of scores obtained on CBCLs filled out for normal (nonreferred) children grouped by sex and age intervals 4–5, 6–11, and 12–16 years. Children are scored for each second-order factor by summing the raw scores of all the items of the first-order scales listed under the second-order factor in Table 5.4 and converting the raw sum to a normalized T score based on the distribution of raw scores in the normative sample. Raw scores on the three social-competence scales are also converted to normalized T scores derived from the normative sample.

In order to display a child's scores simultaneously on all the scales, the scales are organized in a profile format called the Child Behavior Profile. The Profile, available in both hand-scored and computer-scored versions, shows the child's raw score on every behavior problem and social-competence item, the T score and percentile for every narrow-band scale, T scores for the broad-band *Internalizing* and *Externalizing* grouping, and total behavior-problem and social-competence scores. This profile format provides the clinician with a visual image of the concentration and patterning of a child's problems and competencies, as compared to normals of the same age and sex. The quantification of the scales also provides a basis for statistical analysis and the measurement of change over time or in response to treatment.

Intraclass correlations in the .90's have been found for 1-week test–retest and interparent reliabilities in the scoring of individual behavior problems and social-competence items (Achenbach & Edelbrock, in press). Pearson correlations for scores on the behavior-problem and social-competence scales have averaged .88 for 1-week test–retest reliabilities and .68 for interparent agreement, with no more than chance differences in mean scores (Achenbach, 1979).

Profile Typologies

The factor-analytically derived scales reflect covariance among items but not necessarily *types* of children. They are thus analogous to a syndromal nosology like that of DSM–III's Axis I, in that an individual may manifest attributes of more than one syndrome at a time. In fact, the aim of the Child Behavior Profile is to display the particular patterns of high and low points that characterize children in terms of all the robust syndromes found for their age and sex. Do the patterns themselves have any regularity that could enable us to categorize individuals?

To find out, we performed centroid cluster analyses of Child Behavior Profiles scored for large samples of clinically referred children, separately for each sex within age groups 6–11 and 12–16 (Edelbrock & Achenbach, 1980). (Like factor analysis of behavior-problem items, cluster analysis of profiles is affected by many parameters of the method and data—see Edelbrock, 1979, for some relevant parametric comparisons.) Because we found that the consistent negative correlations between the social-competence and behavior-problem scales contributed a built-in configuration to all the profile patterns, we cluster analyzed only the behavior-problem portion of the Profiles.

For each of the boys' groups, we found six profile types that replicated well across two randomly selected clinical samples, and for each of the girls' groups we found seven. Like factor analysis of items, cluster analysis of profiles can be viewed in a hierarchical fashion, moving from relatively numerous, well-differentiated taxa to a smaller number of less differentiated taxa that subsume the more differentiated ones. Fig. 5.1 shows the hierarchical relations among the

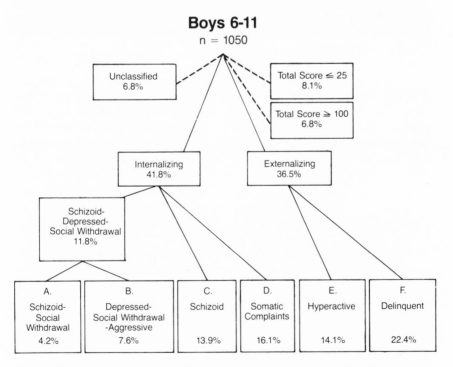

FIG. 5.1.   Distribution of Child Behavior Profile types found for clinically referred 6–11-year-old boys (Edelbrock & Achenbach, 1980).

six differentiated profile types found for boys aged 6–11 and their convergence in two broad *Internalizing* and *Externalizing* types. The lower-level types are designated according to the behavior-problem scales having the highest peaks in each type. Fig. 5.1 also shows what percentage of a sample of 1050 clinically referred boys were classified, and what percentage were excluded from the classification because their total behavior-problem scores were either too high or too low to form meaningful profile patterns.

The results of the cluster analysis make it possible to compare boys who are grouped in a fashion analogous to categorical nosologies. We have found that boys grouped according to the clusters differ on a number of variables, and further work is under way to determine how well the groupings predict important variables such as outcome after mental-health services. However, in moving from quantitative–dimensional taxa of behavior problems to categorical groupings of individuals via cluster analysis, we need not sacrifice the explicitness and quantitative precision of the taxometric approach. The operational definition of each cluster-based category is the profile pattern formed by averaging the profiles of all the members (who were originally grouped on the basis of their profile similarities). This average profile is called the *centroid* of the cluster. The resemblance of any new boy to each of the cluster-based categories can be computed by calculating a coefficient of similarity between his profile and the centroid of each cluster.

Choices must, of course, be made about the type of similarity measure and other options, but the results obtained with different options can be explicitly compared. The one-way intraclass correlation coefficient has proven to be a good measure on many grounds; it provides a quantitative index of how well a subject's profile matches the pattern and elevation of the centroid of each profile type. It can therefore be decided whether a subject is a relatively pure exemplar of a particular profile type (i.e., has a high intraclass correlation with its centroid), or has similar correlations with the centroids of more than one type. Some cases not readily classifiable into one of the six differentiated profile types will nevertheless be classifiable as Internalizers or Externalizers.

We have determined the effects of various cut-off points on the percent of cases classified by the profile types and their discriminative power with respect to some of their correlates (Edelbrock & Achenbach, 1980), but the degree of purity required will vary according to the specific research, theoretical, or clinical purposes. Cluster-based typologies can thus be used as categorical taxonomies, but they have the added advantages of being based on overall patterns of scores for each individual and of preserving taxometric explicitness and quantitative precision.

Parents' reports cannot, of course, provide the only basis for assessing children's behavior disorders. We are therefore exploring the relations among reports by parents, clinicians, teachers, trained observers, and children themselves. Complete agreement among the various informants is unlikely, because they have different perspectives and impacts on the behavior to be reported.

The inevitable interactions between the target behavior and the observer mean that there is no perfectly veridical index of the target behavior. Instead, the value of various data sources needs to be assessed largely in terms of the power of these sources to predict other important variables, such as prognosis, responsiveness to particular treatments, and etiological differences.

Nevertheless, we found from 70 to 95% agreement between profile types scored from CBCLs filled out by mothers and those scored from CBCLs filled out by a clinician who had access to parent, teacher, and child data (Edelbrock & Achenbach, 1980). Although agreement varied according to the age and sex of the children and the level in the hierarchy of profiles, both the percentage of agreement and chance-corrected indices (*kappa* and *kappa/kappa max*) showed much better agreement between the parent-based and clinician-based profile types than between clinicians' DSM-III child diagnoses (Mattison et al., 1979; Mezzich & Mezzich, 1979). It therefore appears that many of our immediate research, clinical, and epidemiological needs can be served at least as well by the taxometric use of parent reports as by a system of the DSM type.

SUMMARY

Although developmental psychology should contribute to our understanding of childhood behavior disorders, little connection is evident between clinical practice and developmental research. Existing theories have not effectively accommodated the growing body of research questions and findings pertaining to child psychopathology. Because no single developmental or clinical theory is likely to subsume all aspects of deviant development, taxonomic and normative-developmental constructs are needed to guide the developmental study of psychopathology.

Efforts to formulate taxonomies of child psychopathology must contend with dilemmas that can be posed in terms of a series of contrasting alternatives. These include the degree to which a system is considered provisional or final; distinctions between the nomothetic functions of formal diagnosis and the idiographic functions of diagnostic formulations; the weight given empirical versus theoretical considerations in the derivation of taxa; the categorical versus dimensional structuring of taxa; the cross-sectional versus longitudinal segmentation of development; the narrow- versus broad-band differentation of taxa; and the multiaxial versus uniaxial portrayal of individuals. Rather than implying mutually exclusive alternatives, many of these dilemmas can be best handled through solutions that combine various alternatives and promote empirical tests of contrasting approaches.

Variance arising in the application of taxonomic constructs is another challenge that all taxonomies face. Subject variability, assessment variability, and variability among taxonomic systems all affect the taxonomic process. Even venerable taxa of adult psychopathology—such as schizophrenia—for which highly formalized diagnostic procedures exist are quite vulnerable to differences in taxonomic procedures.

Considering the lack of well-established taxa for child psychopathology, multivariate and normative–developmental approaches offer possibilities for evolving tentative taxonomies that are more explicit, quantitatively precise, and flexible than traditional nosologies. The term *taxometrics*—which Meehl (1978) coined for the application of psychometric procedures to the detection of categorical taxa—also seems apt for the derivation of taxonomic constructs through multivariate analysis.

A program of multivariate taxometric research has been described wherein factor analysis is used to identify dimensions of covarying behavior problems reported by parents of disturbed children grouped by sex and age. The items loading highest on the most robust dimensions are then used to form behavior problem scales that are normed separately for each sex and age group. These scales are assembled into a profile format that displays a child's scores on specific behavior problems, narrow-band behavior-problem scales, and broadband groupings of the scales. Cluster analysis has been used to derive hierarchical typologies of profile patterns that permit classification of children according to their degree of resemblance to particular profile types. This makes it possible to assess the correlates and predictive power of the groupings in the same fashion as in categorical nosologies, but with the added advantage of classification criteria that can be adjusted according to the purity of groupings desired.

REFERENCES

Achenbach, T. M. The Child Behavior Profile: I. Boys aged 6–11. *Journal of Consulting and Clinical Psychology,* 1978, *46,* 478–488.

Achenbach, T. M. The Child Behavior Profile: An empirically based system for assessing children's behavioral problems and competencies. *International Journal of Mental Health,* 1979, *7,* 24–42.

Achenbach, T. M. DSM–III in light of empirical research on the classification of child psychopathology. *Journal of the American Academy of Child Psychiatry,* 1980, *19,* 395–412.

Achenbach, T. M. *Developmental psychopathology* (2nd ed.). New York: Wiley, 1981.

Achenbach, T. M., & Edelbrock, C. S. The classification of child psychopathology: A review and analysis of empirical efforts. *Psychological Bulletin,* 1978, *85,* 1275–1301.

Achenbach, T. M., & Edelbrock, C. S. The Child Behavior Profile: II. Boys aged 12–16 and girls aged 6–11 and 12–16. *Journal of Consulting and Clinical Psychology,* 1979, *47,* 223–233.

Achenbach, T. M., & Edelbrock, C. S. Behavioral problems and competencies reported by parents of normal and disturbed children aged 4–16. *Monographs of the Society for Research in Child Development,* in press.

American Psychiatric Association. *Diagnostic and statistical manual of mental disorders.* Washington, D.C.: Author, 1st ed., 1952; 2nd ed., 1968; 3rd ed., 1980.

Baltes, P. B., & Nesselroade, J. R. History and rationale of longitudinal research. In J. R. Nesselroade & P. B. Baltes (Eds.), *Longitudinal research in the study of behavior and development.* New York: Academic Press, 1979.

Beitchman, J. H., Dielman, T. E., Landis, J. R., Benson, R. M., & Kemp, P. L. Reliability of the Group for the Advancement of Psychiatry diagnostic categories in child psychiatry. *Archives of General Psychiatry,* 1978, *35,* 1461–1466.

Binet, A., & Simon, T. New methods for the diagnosis of the intellectual level of subnormals. *L'Annee Psychologique,* 1905. (Translated and reprinted in A. Binet & T. Simon, *The development of intelligence in children.* Baltimore: Williams & Wilkins, 1916.)

Carey, G., & Gottesman, I. I. Reliability and validity in binary ratings: Areas of common misunderstandings in diagnosis and symptom ratings. *Archives of General Psychiatry,* 1978, *35,* 1454–1459.

Cattell, R. B. *The scientific use of factor analysis in behavioral and life sciences.* New York: Plenum Press, 1978.

Conners, C. K. Rating scales for use in drug studies with children. *Psychopharmacology Bulletin: Pharmacotherapy with children.* Washington, D.C.: U.S. Government Printing Office, 1973.

Doll, E. A. *Vineland Social Maturity Scale.* Circle Pines, Minn.: American Guidance Service, 1965.

Edelbrock, C. Mixture model tests of hierarchical clustering algorithms: The problems of classifying everybody. *Multivariate Behavioral Research,* 1979, *14,* 367–384.

Edelbrock, C., & Achenbach, T. M. A typology of Child Behavior Profile patterns: Distribution and correlates for disturbed children aged 6–16. *Journal of Abnormal Child Psychology,* 1980, *8,* 441–470.

Freeman, M. A reliability study of psychiatric diagnosis in childhood and adolescence. *Journal of Child Psychology and Psychiatry,* 1971, *12,* 43–54.

Freud, A. *Normality and pathology in childhood.* New York: International Universities Press, 1965.

Greenspan, S. I., Hatleberg, J. L., & Cullander, C. C. M. A developmental approach to systematic personality assessment: Illustrated with the case of a 6 year old child. In S. I. Greenspan & G. Pollock (Eds.), *The course of life: Psychoanalytic contributions toward understanding personality development. Vol. 2: Latency, adolescence, and youth.* Washington, D.C.: DHEW, 1979.

Group for the Advancement of Psychiatry. Psychopathological disorders in childhood: Theoretical considerations and a proposed classification. 1966, *Report No. 62.*

Guzé, S. B. Validating criteria for psychiatric diagnosis: The Washington University approach. In M. S. Akiskal & W. L. Webb (Eds.), *Psychiatric diagnosis: Exploration of biological predictors.* New York: Spectrum, 1978.

Hanson, D. R., Gottesman, I. I., & Meehl, P. E. Genetic theories and the validation of psychiatric diagnoses: Implications for the study of children of schizophrenics. *Journal of Abnormal Psychology,* 1977, *86,* 575–588.

Hobbs, N. (Ed.). *Issues in the classification of children.* San Francisco: Jossey-Bass, 1975.

Kanner, L. Autistic disturbances of affective contact. *Nervous Child,* 1943, *2,* 217–250.

Kessen, W. *The Child.* New York: Wiley, 1965.

Kraepelin, E. *Compendium der Psychiatrie.* Leipzig: Abel, 1883.

Mattison, R., Cantwell, D. P., Russell, A. T., & Will, L. A comparison of DSM–II and DSM–III in the diagnosis of childhood psychiatric disorders. *Archives of General Psychiatry,* 1979, *36,* 1217–1222.

Mednick, S. A., Schulsinger, F., Teasdale, T. W., Schulsinger, H., Venables, P. H., & Rock, D. R.

Schizophrenia in high-risk children: Sex differences in predisposing factors. In G. Serban (Ed.), *Cognitive defects in the development of mental illness*. New York: Brunner/Mazel, 1978.

Meehl, P. E. Theoretical risks and tabular asterisks: Sir Karl, Sir Ronald, and the slow progress of soft psychology. *Journal of Consulting and Clinical Psychology*, 1978, *46*, 806–834.

Mercer, J. R. Psychological assessment and the rights of children. In N. Hobbs (Ed.), *Issues in the classification of children* (Vol. 1). San Francisco: Jossey-Bass, 1975.

Mezzich, A. C., & Mezzich, J. E. *Diagnostic reliability of childhood and adolescent behavior disorders*. Paper presented at the American Psychological Association, New York, September 1979.

Overall, J. E., & Hollister, L. E. Comparative evaluation of research diagnostic criteria for schizophrenia. *Archives of General Psychiatry*, 1979, *36*, 1198–1205.

Piaget, J. Piaget's theory. In P. E. Mussen (Ed.), *Carmichael's manual of child psychology*. New York: Wiley, 1970.

Quay, H. C. Classification. In H. C. Quay & J. S. Werry (Eds.), *Psychopathological disorders of childhood* (2nd ed.). New York: Wiley, 1979.

Rapoport, J. L., Buchsbaum, M. S., Weingartner, H., Zahn, T. D., Ludlow, C., Bartko, J., Mikkelsen, E. J., Langer, D. H., & Bunney, W. E. Dextroamphetamine: Its cognitive and behavioral effects in normal and hyperactive boys and normal men. *Archives of General Psychiatry*, 1980, *37*, 933–943.

Reich, W., & Herjanic, B. *Development of a structured psychiatric interview for children*. Unpublished manuscript. St. Louis: Washington University, 1980.

Roth, M. Psychiatric diagnosis in clinical and scientific settings. In H. S. Akiskal & W. L. Webb (Eds.), *Psychiatric diagnosis: Exploration of biological predictors*. New York: Spectrum, 1978.

Rutter, M., & Shaffer, D. DSM-III—A step forward or back in terms of the classification of child psychiatric disorders? *Journal of the American Academy of Child Psychiatry*, 1980, *19*, 371–394.

Schulterbrandt, J. G., & Raskin, A. (Eds.). *Depression in childhood: Diagnosis, treatment and conceptual models*. New York: Raven Press, 1977.

Spitzer, R. L., Endicott, J., & Robins, E. Research diagnostic criteria: Rationale and reliability. *Archives of General Psychiatry*, 1978, *35*, 773–782.

Spitzer, R. L., Williams, J. B. W., & Skodol, A. E. DSM-III: The major achievements and an overview. *American Journal of Psychiatry*, 1980, *137*, 151–164.

Wainer, H. Estimating coefficients in linear models: It don't make no nevermind. *Psychological Bulletin*, 1976, *83*, 213–217.

Woolf, H. B. (Ed.). *Webster's New Collegiate Dictionary*. Springfield, Mass.: Merriam, 1977.

6 Two Different Principles of Conceptual Organization

Ellen M. Markman
Stanford University

In order to cope with the overwhelming diversity of objects and properties in the world, people must mentally group objects, treating them as instances of a category instead of as unique individuals. Many natural categories are hierarchically organized—that is, they are organized into nested class-inclusion relations (e.g., poodle, dog, animal), with some classes being superordinate or subordinate to others. Because hierarchical classification is such a fundamental cognitive process, it has attracted the attention of psychologists interested in cognition and cognitive development. Models of adult concept formation, natural categories, and semantic memory are all concerned to some degree with class inclusion relations. In these models, questions of how information is accessed and organized are of prime concern.

How children establish and come to use a taxonomic organization has been the focus of much developmental research. Whether or not children have taxonomic organization and whether they can rely on it to solve problems are major questions this research addresses. For reasons that are still poorly understood, young children frequently organize objects in nontaxonomic ways, at least on tasks that supposedly tap classification principles and skills. In classification tasks, for example, children are presented with a variety of objects that fall into one of several common categories—for example, animals, vehicles, furniture, and food. They are then told to put the things that are alike together. Older children sort on the basis of taxonomic category, putting all and only the animals together, all and only the vehicles together, and so on. That is, they perceive the similarity of the objects to each other and find their common taxonomic category to be a natural way of organizing the objects. Younger children, however, sort on some other nontaxonomic basis. Though there is controversy about how to interpret these results (Huttenlocher & Lui, 1979; Markman, Cox, & Machida, in press), traditionally they have been taken as evidence for differences in the organizational principles children use for classification of objects (Bruner, Olver, & Greenfield, 1966; Inhelder & Piaget, 1964; Vygotsky, 1962).

Studies of organization in memory provide another example of developmental changes in classification. In these studies, children are presented with words to learn that, though randomly ordered, can be arranged into taxonomic categories. When older children report the words that they have remembered, they tend to recall the words category by category. Again, these older children find taxonomic category to be a natural, salient principle by which to organize information. Moreover, by exploiting the category structure of the word lists in this way, children improve their memory. Clustering in memory is not so evident in younger children, suggesting developmental differences in the existence or salience of taxonomic organization.

In another well-known developmental task, the Piagetian class-inclusion problem, children view objects that form a small hierarchy with one superordinate set (e.g., flowers) consisting of two mutually exclusive subordinate sets (e.g., roses and daisies). One of the subordinate sets is larger than the other and the child is asked to make a quantitative comparison between the larger subordinate set and the superordinate set. For example, a child might be shown pictures of five roses and two daisies and asked, "Are there more roses or flowers?" Though there are alternative interpretations of what this task entails (Klahr & Wallace, 1972; Trabasso, Isen, Dolecki, McLanahan, Riley, & Tucker, 1978; Wilkinson, 1976), Inhelder and Piaget (1964) argued that the class-inclusion problem was one measure of concrete operations. They argued that to solve the problem, children must simultaneously add two classes (roses + daisies = flowers) and subtract two classes (flowers − daisies = roses). That is, the child must be able to subtract roses from the whole set of flowers and simultaneously include it in the whole set in order to make this part–whole (roses–flowers) comparison. Young children find this to be extremely difficult and quite consistently answer that there are more roses than flowers. Note that failure to solve this problem does not mean that a child does not know that roses are flowers. It is important that children know the inclusion relations because otherwise they could fail the class-inclusion question out of ignorance rather than because they lack concrete operations. Thus, this task does not measure children's knowledge of a hierarchical inclusion relation, but rather their ability to operate upon that relation, adding and subtracting classes and comparing parts to wholes. According to Piagetian theory, the ability to answer the class-inclusion question is one of the major accomplishments of the stage of concrete operations.

Though there is a great deal of evidence like that just described for the young child's failure to use categorical structure when it is appropriate or useful, we still do not have a full appreciation of why such an organization is so difficult for children. Because of the importance and prevalence of class inclusion, it has

overshadowed the investigation of other relations. Though everyone would ac-
knowledge that other types of relations exist, the differences are often left unex-
amined. For example, network models of adults' knowledge incorporate different relations in the network. These models contain nodes that represent
categories or objects, and labeled relations between the nodes. The labels specify
the different types of relations. For example, a node for *hand* would be connected to *arm* by the relation *part of,* and *dog* would be linked to *animal* by the
relation *is a*. Different relations are specified in such models, but little attention
is paid to these differences. Predictions are generated mainly about principles
that are assumed to cut across the various relations—for example, how the
information is accessed, what the distance is between nodes, how many paths
must be traversed, when the same path was last activated, etc. (Collins & Quillian, 1970; Hayes-Roth & Hayes-Roth, 1975)—although the nature of the relations is ignored.

In ignoring the differences between class inclusion and other relations, we
may be overlooking important differences in principles of organization. I have
been studying one type of concept, collections, that differs in its organization
from another type of concept, classes. The organization of collections is of
interest in its own right, but gains additional importance in providing a contrast to
class inclusion. By contrasting with inclusion, collections help us to understand
why children find hierarchical classification so difficult.

THE NATURE OF CLASSES AND COLLECTIONS

Collections are the referents of collective nouns—for example, *forest, pile,
family, army*. To determine membership in a collection, one must consider more
than properties of individual objects; the relationship between objects is also
critical. There are at least four related ways in which classes and collections
differ: (1) the manner in which membership is determined; (2) the nature of their
part–whole relations; (3) their internal structure; and (4) the nature of the whole
that is formed. These differences are discussed in the following sections.

Determining Membership

Membership in a class can be determined (at least in principle) by measuring an
object or an entity against the defining criteria of the class. To know whether an
object is a toy block, for example, one must examine it for its size, shape,
material, or function, etc. In other words, an analysis of the object's intrinsic
properties is required. To know whether an object is a member of a collection,
however, one needs to know something about its relationship to the other possible members of the collection. An analysis of the object's extrinsic relations is
required. To determine whether a block is part of a pile of blocks, for example,

one must examine whether it is under or on top of other blocks in the pile. Although spatial proximity is not needed to determine whether a person is a member of a family, a team, or a club, some type of relationship is still required.

Part-Whole Relations

Collections have more literal part-whole relations than do classes. A dog, for example, is a kind of animal, not part of an animal. In contrast, children are parts of families, not types of or examples of families.

Internal Structure and the Nature of the Whole Formed

The internal structure of collections seems to give them greater psychological coherence. This may be best illustrated by considering physical objects in comparison to classes and collections. To result in a physical object, component parts must be appropriately organized. A random set of body parts does not form a human being. Parts of objects properly assembled result in a whole in a literal sense. Classes do not have anything like the internal organization of objects, nor do they result in a good psychological unit. Collections, however, do have an internal organization that results in a coherent structure. A random set of people does not make a family. To be a family, the people must be related to each other. Intuitively, it seems fairly natural to consider a family, a pile, or a crowd as a single thing. Language captures this intuition in that collective nouns are singular.

The contrast between collections and objects makes it all the more remarkable that collections could have good psychological integrity. Though this certainly is an oversimplified version of object perception, in some sense we perceive and think of objects quite automatically as organized wholes. It seems less natural to think of a person as a set of person parts or a car as a set of car parts, because we tend to perceive them as single entities. If an object were literally divided into parts, then the object parts would become the more natural level of organization and the original object would no longer exist.

What is so interesting about collections is that, unlike objects, they are readily conceptualized as a multiplicity of objects rather than as a single entity, yet we have the ability to think of them as a single aggregate as well. It is not obvious whether the more natural level of organization is trees or forest, soldiers or army, ships or fleet. These levels do not contrast in naturalness to the same extent as person parts versus person. The parts of a collection—for example, the trees, the soldiers, or the ships—can be readily perceived without literally segmenting the perceptual array. Collections impose singularity on an array that can be easily seen as consisting of discrete objects. In so doing, collections reveal that the principles that unify an array are not entirely perceptual. A cognitive act can give object-like properties to highly individualized discrete elements.

It may seem surprising to argue that by being relational collections could simplify hierarchical organization. Having to take relations into account could just as well complicate rather than simplify the problem. But noticing relations should not necessarily be thought of as an additional requirement. It may be that having to ignore the relations rather than notice them is what creates problems. In naturally occurring situations, objects exist in spatial, temporal, and causal contexts. To treat an object solely as a member of a class requires abstraction away from much other information to consider only what is relevant for the category. To treat an object as a member of a collection involves noticing relations that exist between the objects. In this regard, collections are similar to events or themes that also have relational organizations. Such relational structures are likely to be a common way of organizing information. As we move about in our daily life, we observe people interacting or using tools, machines, or other artifacts to accomplish some goal. We view natural occurrences such as storms, and we admire scenery. Much of our perception is interpretive, making sense of what we encounter. Probably little time is spent cataloguing objects, in trying to generate the taxonomies to which objects belong. Thus, these event-like meaningful structures might be a more spontaneous, natural way of organizing information. Because stories embody this type of organization, there are few cross-cultural or developmental differences in the organizational principles people use to understand stories (Mandler, Scribner, Cole, & DeForest, 1980). This is in marked contrast to the cross-cultural and developmental differences found in the use of taxonomic organization. Thus, the relational structure of collections does not necessarily have to be more difficult for children to understand.

Compared to classes, collections form a more literal part–whole structure with greater coherence of the higher-order unit. Moreover, because of the greater coherence of collections, the hierarchy they form might be more stable than that of classes. That is, the levels of the hierarchy should be more easily kept distinct. Both adults and children tend to find the asymmetry of class-inclusion hierarchies difficult to maintain. For example, children find questions such as "Are all the roses flowers?" difficult (Inhelder & Piaget, 1964). They incorrectly answer "no" because there are daisies or other flowers around. This suggests that they are answering a question about the total identity of the classes, a symmetrical relation, rather than about the asymmetrical relation of inclusion.

Even adults can become confused and treat inclusion as a symmetric relation. In syllogistic reasoning tasks, for example, when adults hear a premise such as "All *A*s are *C*s," they erroneously infer that "All *C*s are *A*s" (Bucci, 1978; Ceraso & Provitera, 1971; Chapman & Chapman, 1959; Revlis, 1975). With abstract or unfamiliar material, adults fail to treat inclusion as asymmetrical.

Another way of seeing how the two relations differ is to compare the relations at both levels of the hierarchy. For class inclusion, both levels of the hierarchy can involve the same *is a* relation. A poodle is a dog and is an animal. This may contribute to the confusion of levels and difficulty of keeping track of the asymmetry. For part–whole structures, the relations differ at the two hierarchical levels. A boy *is a* child but is *part of* a family. An oak *is a* tree but is *part of* a forest. If there were less confusion between part and whole than between sub-class and superclass, then the asymmetrical relations of collections would have greater psychological stability and would not so readily degenerate into symmet-rical relations.

To summarize, collections and classes are both hierarchically organized con-cepts, but they differ in their structural principles. The part–whole structure of collections is a type of relational structure that confers psychological coherence on the higher-order aggregate formed. If this analysis is correct, then organizing items into collections should be advantageous for solving problems that depend on psychological coherence. This should be especially true for children, who have more difficulty with class inclusion. There are classic developmental tasks that require children to deal with hierarchical inclusion relations—some ex-plicitly (for example, the Piagetian class-inclusion problem) and some implic-itly (for example, as I argue later, number conservation). The analysis of the relations should help explain why, if class inclusion is so pervasive and so fundamental, it should still be so difficult for children. Some of the results I summarize later demonstrate that children become able to pass some of the milestones of cognitive development—for example, part–whole comparisons and number conservation—when they think of objects as collections. Yet, they typically fail these problems when they think of the same objects as classes. If we understand how the collections simplify the task for the child, then we will better understand what problems hierarchical inclusion relations create.

CLASSES VERSUS COLLECTIONS

Contrasting classes and collections allows us to study organizational differences in a controlled way because it is not necessary to literally rearrange or reorganize the materials. The same set of objects can be thought of as a class (trees) or a collection (forest). Any changes in the conceptual organization that occur would be due to simply relabeling the array and thereby mentally imposing one of two different principles of organization on the identical objects. In this way, the studies reported here explore some of the consequences of organizing materials into class-inclusion relations versus the part–whole structure of collections.

The Piagetian Class-Inclusion Problem

One type of evidence for the greater coherence of collections over classes comes from work on the Piagetian class-inclusion problem described earlier, in which children are asked to make a quantitative comparison between a superordinate set and the larger of its subordinate sets (Inhelder & Piaget, 1964). For example, a child might be shown pictures of four boys and two girls and be asked, ''Are there more boys or more children?'' Until about 7 or 8 years old, children find the class-inclusion problem very difficult (Ahr & Youniss, 1970; Inhelder & Piaget, 1964; Kohnstamm, 1963). Though a part–whole comparison (boys versus children) is asked for, children make part–part (boys versus girls) comparisons instead. To answer the class-inclusion question correctly, children must maintain the whole class in mind while simultaneously attending to its subclasses. This division of the superordinate class into subordinate classes weakens the psychological integrity of the superodinate class. If collections have greater psychological integrity, they should be less vulnerable to this weakening.

In four studies, children have consistently revealed a superior ability to make part–whole comparisons with collections than with classes (Markman, 1973; Markman & Seibert, 1976). In each of the studies, the objects children viewed and the questions they were asked in the two conditions were identical. The only difference in the two conditions was in the description given the higher level of the hierarchy. As one example, for the "boys–children" comparison in the class condition, children were told, "Here are kindergarten children. These are the boys and these are the girls and these are the children. Who would have a bigger birthday party, someone who invited the boys or someone who invited the children?" As usual, young children often answered incorrectly, claiming that there were more boys. The collection version of this question was identical, except that "kindergarten children" was changed to "kindergarten class" (note that *class* is a collection term). So, the question became, "Who would have a bigger birthday party, someone who invited the boys or someone who invited the class?" With this change of just one word in the question, children became able to solve the part–whole comparison that they usually find so difficult.

For comparison, children were asked to make part–whole comparisons on single objects that form quite literal, psychologically real wholes (Markman & Seibert, 1976). For example, children were shown an outline drawing of a butterfly with large wings and a small body. They were then asked, "Who would have more to color, someone who colored the wings or someone who colored the butterfly?" Both objects and collections facilitated performance relative to classes. However, children as young as 4 years old were not better able to make part–whole comparisons on objects than on collections. Although, of course, one cannot conclude that there is no difference between objects and collections, this result highlights the discrepancy in psychological integrity between classes and collections.

Empirical Versus Logical Solutions to Part–Whole Comparison Problems

In the studies of part–whole comparisons just described, children unable to solve the problems with classes were able to solve them with collections. In the studies reported in this section (Markman, 1978), all children who participated were capable of correctly solving the Piagetian class-inclusion problem. These studies addressed whether the children appreciated the logical status of the solution rather than whether they had the ability to solve the problem.

Given a part–whole relation, it follows logically that the whole is larger than one of its parts. To illustrate, suppose that a class-inclusion relation between roses and flowers has been established; then, compare the following questions: (1) Are there more roses or flowers (part versus whole)? (2) Are there more roses or daisies (part versus part)? The answer to the first question follows logically from the class-inclusion relation (as long as the classes are finite). No additional information is needed to be certain that there are at least as many flowers as roses. In contrast, the second question cannot be answered without additional factual information specifying the relative number of daisies and roses.

Children who correctly answer the Piagetian class-inclusion question could do so on empirical rather than logical grounds. They could take the greater numerosity of the superordinate set as compared to its subordinate set to be an empirical fact about the classes rather than a logical consequence of the inclusion relation. In Markman (1978), I reviewed several reasons for believing this to be the case. Let me now suggest that given the hypothesized abstractness of the part–whole relation of class inclusion, children might be expected to have difficulty examining the relation in order to assess its logical consequences.

How could we determine whether children understood the logic of the problem? First, when empirical means of judging the relative numerosity of the classes are withheld from children, they should still be able to answer the question. Second, children should realize that no addition or subtraction of objects could result in the subordinate set having more members than its superordinate set. Third, if a new, unfamiliar class is said to be subordinated to another class, then children should be willing to make the part–whole comparison without any additional information about the classes. A child who does not solve the part–whole comparison problems in these situations can be said to be treating the answers as empirical rather than logical consequences of the classes.

The first study reported in Markman (1978) established that when children initially solve the class-inclusion problem, they do so on empirical rather than logical grounds. Children from grades two through six participated in the study once it was established that they could consistently solve the class-inclusion problem. The experimental items were designed to assess whether or not children thought the answers required empirical confirmation. The items were:

1. After children solved a class-inclusion problem for an array of objects, the array was hidden, thus eliminating empirical data, and the children were told that something had been removed. They were then asked whether they could "tell for sure" whether the superordinate or larger subordinate class had more.

2. After answering the standard class-inclusion question, children were asked if they could modify the relation such that the subordinate had more than the

superordinate—for example, "Could you make it so that there will be more roses than flowers?"

3. A new, unfamiliar class was said to be subordinated to another familiar class and the children were asked the inclusion question without any additional quantitative information about the classes.

Children under about 10 or 11 years old did poorly on class-inclusion problems when empirical means of quantification were not available, and they often allowed for the possibility that a subordinate class could be made larger than its superordinate class. Thus, children who could consistently solve the class-inclusion problem treated the quantitative relationship between the subordinate and superordinate classes as an empirical fact.

If children do not appreciate the logical status of part–whole comparison on classes, the question of a class–collection comparison becomes of interest. The more literal part–whole relation that characterizes collections should promote an appreciation of the logic of the problem. This hypothesis was tested in a replication of the first study that included a condition in which children heard objects described as collections. As before, children from grades two through six participated and only children who demonstrated competence in solving standard class-inclusion problems were included in the study. The findings from the first study were replicated. Children failed to appreciate the logic of the class-inclusion problems. In marked contrast, the collection questions produced significantly superior performance. Though the materials used and the questions asked were identical in all respects except for the collection–class difference, children solving collection problems better appreciated that empirical confirmation of the part–whole comparison is not needed.

In sum, the internal structure and greater psychological integrity of collections compared to classes improves children's ability to solve part–whole comparison problems (Markman & Seibert, 1976) and promotes their awareness of the logical necessity of their answers as well (Markman, 1978).

Imagery

Kosslyn (1978) has demonstrated that the time to construct an image increases with the complexity of the imaged stimulus. One of Kosslyn's findings is of particular interest. Subjects were shown a matrix of letters arranged, for example, in three rows and six columns. After viewing the matrix, subjects were instructed to image either the three rows or the six columns. Subjects forming images, presumably of the same matrix, were faster at forming an image of the three rows of six letters each than of the six columns of three letters each. What this finding suggests is that the time to generate an image increases with the number of units into which the display is parsed.

If imagery is affected by the organization subjects impose on the display, then they might form images of collections more readily than of classes. Given the identical display to image, subjects may find it simpler to form an image of a collection, an organized structured whole, than of a class of many individual elements. In collaboration with Kosslyn, I tested this hypothesis.

Twenty college students participated in the study. Each subject examined 12 pictures, each of which could be readily labeled by either a class or a collection term. The 12 pairs were: *forest, trees; flock, birds; army, soldiers; navy, sailors; gang, delinquents; herd, cows; tribe, Indians; band, musicians; choir, singers; team, players; troop, dancers.* Subjects were provided with a label for each picture and were told to examine the pictures carefully as they would be required to answer questions about them. After the subjects examined the pictures, they were told that they were going to be asked to image the pictures and then be questioned about some detail of the pictures.

Each subject was asked to examine all 12 pictures. Half of the pictures were given class labels and half collection labels, counterbalanced across subjects. When subjects heard the label of the picture they had seen, they were to form an image of it and press a button as soon as they had the image.

As predicted, subjects were able to form images of collections more quickly than for classes. The mean difference in time taken to form an image was 118 msec., with the mean equaling 1.920 sec for the classes and 1.802 sec for the collections. Moreover, the collection advantage held for every picture. If time to form an image is taken as a measure of organization, then the results of this study support the analysis of collections as forming a better organized structure than classes.

PROPERTIES OF SETS VERSUS PROPERTIES OF INDIVIDUALS

Collections should help people reason about a set itself and not just the individuals that make up the set. This hypothesis was tested in the studies that I describe next on collective versus distributive inferences and on cardinal number.

Collective Versus Distributive Inferences

The analysis of part–whole relationships for classes and collections leads to differential predictions about the type of inferences that people will make when provided with information about the whole set. In particular, people should be more inclined to draw *distributive* inferences for classes than for collections for which the possibility of drawing *collective* inferences will be greater. Collective attributions are those that apply to a class or a collection as a whole in contrast to distributive attributions, which are those that apply to each member of the class or collection. For example, when it is claimed that ''there is not enough food to feed the people'' (or the ''family''), one is describing a fact about the people (family) collectively. One does not mean that there is not enough food to feed any given person (family member). As another example, consider the argument: ''Men are numerous. John is a man. Therefore, John is numerous.'' This argument is absurd because ''numerous'' applies to the class ''men'' considered collectively and does not distribute over each of its members. In contrast, the argument ''Men are mortal. John is a man. John is mortal.'' is sensible because ''mortal'' is a distributive attribution, true of the members of the class ''men.'' Analogous examples for collections are the arguments: ''The crowd is growing. Lee is a member of the crowd. Lee is growing.'' and ''The crowd is silent. Lee is a member of the crowd. Lee is silent.''

In summary, collective attributions of either classes or collections are true of the class or collection as a whole, whereas distributive attributions are true of each of their members. It is important to notice that collective and distributive attributions can be used with both collections and classes.

Suppose that the meaning of an adjective were unknown. One would not know whether it should have a collective meaning like *numerous* or a distributive interpretation like *mortal*. In such a situation, if collections are more readily conceptualized as wholes, there should be a greater probability of interpreting attributions of collections collectively as compared to classes. And, if classes are not readily conceptualized as wholes, a distributive interpretation should be a very dominant response.

I addressed this issue by determining what type of inferences people would draw about a member of a class or a collection when an unknown property had been attributed to the class or collection. In addition, subjects were asked to rate their confidence in their responses. The rationale for assessing confidence is as follows: The question asks the subject whether an attribute true of a class or collection is true of a member as well. The question is explicitly asking whether the attribution is distributive (is it true of a member?). Thus, subjects are likely to be primed for distributive responses. Given the hypothesized difference in the salience of the wholes, subjects should be more likely to consider collective interpretations for collections than for classes, even if they decide to make a distributive inference. If so, subjects in the collection condition should be less confident of their answers because they would have thought of more alternative possibilities.

Twenty-four undergraduates served as subjects. Half of the subjects were randomly assigned to the class condition and half to the collection condition.

Each subject received a booklet of true–false questions arranged in a random order. Though there were other filler items included to prevent response biases, there were 44 experimental items for each condition, all of the following form: The first statement attributed a nonsense property to either a collection or a class, depending on the condition. The second statement specified that a given individual was a member of the class or collection. The third statement either asserted or denied that the property was true of the member. Subjects were required to judge whether the third statement was true or false and to rate their confidence in their judgment on a 5-point scale. Twenty-two different collective nouns and corresponding class terms were used in the experimental items. Each term appeared in two different problems, one with a positive conclusion and one with a negative conclusion. Examples of the collective nouns and corresponding class terms used are: *navy, sailors; faculty, professors; choir, singers; crowd, people; forest, trees; band, musicians; flock of birds, birds; team, players; school of fish, fish; swarm of bees, bee; clergy, ministers; class, students; tribe, Indians; family, relatives.* The filler items differed from the experimental items in that the second statement denied that the individual was a member of the collection or class so that no conclusion followed. Each of the questions contained a different CVC nonsense syllable judged to have a low association value to English words (Noble, 1961). An example of a collection item with a positive conclusion and a class item with a negative conclusion is provided here:

The choir is faw.
The soprano is in the
   choir.   True False ____ ____ ____ ____ ____
The soprano is faw.   very   pretty   not at all
                           sure   sure   sure
                           1   2   3   4   5

Singers are pev.
The soprano is a
   singer.   True False ____ ____ ____ ____ ____
The soprano is   1   2   3   4   5
   not pev.

On the filler items, there were no differences between the two conditions. Both groups of subjects lacked confidence in their responses. The mean confidence rating (on a 5-point scale with 1 indicating very confident) was 3.60 for the class condition and 3.33 for the collection condition. Subjects in both conditions were sensitive to the fact that they could not draw certain inferences from the premises provided.

Each of the 44 experimental items was scored as being consistent with a distributive interpretation of the adjective or not. For arguments with a positive conclusion, a ''true'' response reflects a distributive interpretation. For arguments with a negative conclusion, a ''false'' response reflects a distributive interpretation. The mean number of distributive responses for subjects in the class condition was 43.4 out of a possible 44. As predicted, subjects hearing the class arguments are extremely likely to give the adjective a distributive interpretation. The mean for the collection subjects was 37.9. These subjects were also likely to give the adjective a distributive interpretation. However, they were significantly less likely to do so than class subjects.

In addition to drawing somewhat different inferences, subjects in the collection condition were less confident of their responses. Apparently, these subjects considered alternatives to the distributive interpretation and recognized the ambiguity of the situation more often. The overall mean confidence rating for the class subjects was 1.26; for the positive items, it was 1.25, and for the negative items it was 1.27. Thus, on all of the items, the class subjects were extremely confident of their decisions, as if no alternative possibilities were considered. The mean confidence ratings for the collection subjects were 3.02 overall, and 2.89 and 3.15 for the positive and negative items respectively. Overall, the class subjects were far more confident of their answers than the collection subjects.

This study showed that when provided with information about a class, subjects almost invariably assume that information true of the class is true of its members as well. In addition, they are extremely confident of their answers. Only rarely do subjects spontaneously consider classes as wholes unless the meaning of the adjective dictates such an interpretation. Though subjects hearing attributions of collections are quite likely to draw disbributive inferences, they are less likely to do so than class subjects. Moreover, they generally lack confidence in their responses. Taken together, these data support the hypothesis that due to the greater salience of the whole formed by collections, subjects recognize the possibility of collective attributions for collections but not for classes.

Cardinal Number

The cardinal number of a given set of items is not a property of the individual items themselves. Number is a property of the set taken as a whole and not a property of the elements that compose the set. Recall the syllogism presented in the discussion of collective attributions: "Men are numerous. John is a man. Therefore, John is numerous." The syllogism is absurd because numerosity does not distribute over each element of a set, but is a characteristic of sets themselves. To take another example, "There are five apples" does not imply that any one of the apples is five. "Five" applies only to the group, not to the individuals in it. Of course, one cannot ignore individual members when computing the numerical value of a set. Individuals must be counted or otherwise enumerated. But it is not enough just to focus on the individuals. One must also consider the set taken as a whole. Because collections should promote conceptualization of individual objects as aggregates and because cardinal number applies to aggregates, not individuals, collections should facilitate numerical reasoning about discrete objects. There are many well-known problems that young children have in dealing with cardinal number (e.g., number conservation). Young children should be better able to solve these problems when the objects are thought of as collections rather than classes. This hypothesis was investigated in the following studies (Markman, 1979), which focused on different aspects of a full appreciation of cardinal number.

Number Conservation—Understanding the Irrelevance of a Length Transformation. In the standard conservation task (Piaget, 1965), two equal rows of pennies, or other items, are lined up in one-to-one correspondence. A 4- to 5-year-old child will usually judge both rows to be equal. The child watches as one of the rows is spread out, and then typically judges that the lengthened row now has more pennies, though no pennies have been added or subtracted from either row. There are several ways in which the spreading of the pennies could prevent children from judging that the rows still contain the same number of objects. First, it could draw the child's attention to individuals rather than the aggregate as the individuals are moved about. Second, the one-to-one correspondence betwen rows has been disrupted, forcing the child to rely on more abstract notions of numerical equality (Gelman & Gallistel, 1978). Third, other quantitative dimensions, length, and density have been changed, although number remains invariant. A child must correctly interpret the original judgment in terms of number and must attend to number per se throughout the physical transformation in order to override these other misleading factors. By making it easier for children to think about the aggregate and thus about number, collection labels might help them to conserve.

This hypothesis was tested by having children solve conservation problems when the objects were given either class or collection labels. Twenty-two 4 year olds participated in the study. Half received class questions and half collection questions. Each child was given four conservation problems. The only difference between conditions was that a collection label (e.g., *army*) was substituted for a class label (*soldiers*) for the rows. For example, a child in the class condition saw two rows of soldiers lined up in one-to-one correspondence and heard: "These are your soldiers and these are my soldiers. What are more: my soldiers, your soldiers, or are they both the same?" A child in the collection condition saw the identical two rows and heard: "This is your army and this is my army. What's more: my army, your army, or are they both the same?" Then the experimenter spread out one of the rows and asked, "What are more, my army, your army, or are they both the same?" or "my soldiers, your soldiers..." depending on the condition. After responding, children were asked to justify their answer.

Treating the objects as collections was an effective means of helping children to conserve. Children hearing the objects described as classes correctly answered an average of only 1.46 out of 4 problems. Children hearing the objects described as collections correctly answered an average of 3.18 problems.

Children who conserved often gave reasonable justifications for their correct responses. The common types of justifications were: (1) the child explicitly referred to number; (2) the child referred to numerical operations of addition or subtraction (e.g., stated that nothing was added or taken away); (3) the child referred to the irrelevance of the transformation (e.g., "you just spreaded them"). The proportion of justifications that made reference either to number or numerical operations was comparable in the two conditions. Yet, more children in the collection condition than in the class condition justified their response by noting the irrelevance of the transformations—an early form of justification (Botvin & Murray, 1975). Because conservation in the collection condition is an instance of early conservation, this type of justification would be expected to occur relatively often.

To summarize, the children in the two conditions were presented with identical perceptual information and were asked virtually identical questions. Simply relabeling the objects as collections helped children to conserve.

Understanding the Relevance of Addition and Subtraction.   The study reported next addressed whether children who have thought of objects as collections would be better able to judge that number had, in fact, changed with the addition or subtraction of an object.

Children should be very likely to judge that two initially equal rows differ after they have seen someone add or subtract an object from one row. In the standard conservation task, young children judge that the rows are different even when they should judge them to be the same. The conservation procedure leads children to erroneously respond "different" because:

1. Children make an initial judgment that the two quantities are equal, witness a change, and then are requestioned. These demand characteristics call for a "different" response (Hall & Kengsley, 1968; McGarrigle & Donaldson, 1974).

2. There are misleading perceptual differences that the child must resist in order to judge the rows to be equivalent.

3. The rows do in fact differ on other quantitative dimensions (e.g., length).

All of these factors would lead a child to judge that the two rows are not equal. When an object is added or subtracted from a row, all of these factors remain and so still call for a judgment of difference. However, now "different" is the correct answer, so children could respond correctly without attending to number per se. One way of assessing whether or not children base a judgment on number is to examine their justifications for their responses. Though children hearing arrays described as collections are predicted to be more sensitive to numerical change, this difference may appear only when their justifications are taken into account.

This hypothesis was tested by having children solve addition and subtraction problems when the objects were given either class or collection labels. Seventy-two 4 year olds participated in the study; half were in the class condition and half in the collection condition. Each child was asked four problems, two addition and two subtraction. The procedure in this study was identical to the conservation procedure in the previous study, except that instead of lengthening a row, the experimenter added or subtracted an object from a row.

As expected, after witnessing an addition or subtraction, most children correctly judged that the two rows were no longer equivalent. The mean number correct for children hearing class descriptions was 3.14 out of 4 compared to 3.55 for children hearing collection descriptions.

The good performance of children in the collection condition rules out an alternative explanation for the superior performance in the conservation study. Children were not better able to conserve because of any type of "same" bias that a collection term might have introduced. Children hearing collection labels are quite ready to respond "different" when it is appropriate.

The children's justifications for their judgments were scored in order to determine whether or not they were basing their answers on numerically relevant information. Five categories were used to code the children's responses according to whether the child (1) mentioned the numerical transformation (e.g., "you took the other one," "you put that one there"); (2) mentioned number or counted; (3) used one-to-one correspondence to indicate the difference, usually by pointing and saying, for example, "because you have one here"; (4) used a quantity term to refer to the change; (5) provided no explanation (e.g., "because they are") or gave an explanation that was irrelevant to quantity (e.g., "they look green").

The modal justification for correct answers was to say that an item had been added or subtracted. The main difference in the justification between the two conditions was that collection children mentioned number relatively more often whereas class children gave relatively more irrelevant explanations. Considering categories (1)-(4) to be relevant, then, children hearing the objects described as collections provided more evidence that their judgments were in fact made on the basis of number per se. They correctly answered and justified a mean of 3.36 responses compared to 2.53 for children hearing class descriptions.

Children's Initial Judgments of Equality.   Earlier, I argued that there are many factors that could lead children to correctly answer the addition–subtraction questions without basing their judgments on number per se. That is why children's justifications of their judgments were thought to be critical. A similar argument can be made for the pretransformation "same" judgments. These are not the conservation judgments, but rather the first judgments children make when the two equal rows are lined up in one-to-one correspondence. Children could base these initial "same" judgments on the perceptual similarity of the row, on their equal length or density, or even on some nonquantitative, qualitative identity. Because these factors would all lead to a judgment of sameness, a correct answer may not necessarily reflect a judgment of numerical equality.

To test this possibility, children's justifications for these initial pretransformation "same" judgments were coded into the same categories used for the post transformation responses. When only their judgments are taken into account, children in both conditions are close to perfect on these simple "same" judgments. The mean correct out of four was 3.64 for children in the class condition and 3.69 for children in the collection condition.

When children's justifications are taken into account, children in the collection condition can be seen to have been basing their judgments on number more than children in the class condition. Children hearing class labels correctly answer a mean of only 1.14 of 4 problems compared to a mean of 2.33 for children hearing collection labels.

In summary, in this study, children were asked to make two quite simple comparisons. Two equal rows of objects were lined up in one-to-one correspondence and the child judged which was more or whether they were both the same. Then, an object was added or subtracted from one row and the child requestioned. Because children could be correct for a variety of reasons, children's justifications were used to help clarify the basis for their judgments. Children hearing objects described as classes were unable to offer much beyond "they look the same" as explanations for their judgments. Children hearing the identical objects described as collections more often offered numerically relevant explanations, indicating their judgments were in fact based on number.

Selection of Equivalence Based on Number Versus Length.   In another study, children were presented with three rows of items and were explicitly asked to select the two that were numerically equivalent. In each triad, two of the sets of objects were equated for number and differed in length, whereas two were equated for length but differed in number. When length is pitted against number in this way, kindergarten children often base their selection of equivalence on length rather than number, especially for numbers greater than five (Miller & Heller, 1976). This procedure was used to determine whether children would be more likely to select on the basis of number when the sets had been described as collections.

Sixteen kindergarten children participated in the study, half in the collection condition and half in the class condition. Pictures of objects that could be given either collection or class labels (e.g., *forest, trees*) were pasted in horizontal lines onto strips of poster paper. For each object type, four cards were constructed, two with five pictures and two with eight pictures. Each card with five pictures was equated for length with one of the cards of eight pictures. Cards that were numerically identical differed in length. As it was presented, each card was labeled for the child "Here are some trees" or "Here is a forest," depending on the condition. Once the three cards were visible, the children in both conditions were asked, "Which two cards have the same number of things on them?" Each child answered 12 problems.

An answer was considered correct if the child selected on the basis of number and was able to justify that selection with a numerically relevant explanation.

Children hearing class descriptions for the objects correctly answered only 1.25 of the 12 items. In contrast, children hearing collection descriptions correctly answered a mean of 6.63 items. Again, by helping children conceptualize the elements as an aggregate, collections labels helped children to attend to number per se.

The Cardinality Principle.   Three- and 4-year-old children are generally able to count an array of five toys. However, when they are then asked, ''How many toys are there?'' they often count again rather than answering ''five.'' This is a reflection of the child's difficulty with the cardinality principle, the failure to appreciate that the last number counted becomes the cardinal number of the set (Gelman & Gallistel, 1978; Shaeffer, Eggelston & Scott, 1974). If part of the child's problem with the cardinality principle is a difficulty in thinking of the individual items as a set to which cardinal number applies, then helping the child think of the arrays as collections might promote correct use of this principle.

Twenty-six 3 to 4 year olds participated in a study designed to test this hypothesis. Half of the children were assigned to the class condition and half to the collection condition. In both conditions, children were presented with four problems. For each problem, children viewed some objects, were instructed to count the objects, and then were asked how many objects there were.

When children heard a class description, such as ''Here are some pigs, count the pigs,'' they counted ''one, two, three, four, five.'' When they were then asked ''How many pigs are there?'' they tended to count again, ''One, two, three, four, five.'' They correctly gave a cardinal number (the last number mentioned when counting) only 1.85 out of 4 times. In marked contrast, when children in the collection condition heard, for example, ''Here is a pig family, count the pigs in the family,'' they counted. But when asked ''How many pigs are in the family?'' they correctly responded ''five.'' These children gave the cardinal number a mean of 3.46 out of 4 times.

In summary, I argued that number is a characteristic of a set of objects and not of objects themselves. If thinking about individuals as collections helps children focus on the aggregate as well as the individual, it should thus facilitate numerical reasoning. As predicted, thinking of objects as collections helped children solve numerical problems they otherwise would have failed. It helped them conserve number in the face of an irrelevant change. It helped them access and verbalize a numerically relevant basis for their judgments of equality and of difference. It allowed them to judge equivalence on the basis of number rather than length, and it promoted their use of the cardinality principle.

Numerical-Classifier Languages.   I have argued that dealing with number requires a type of part–whole analysis. Individuals in a set must be enumerated, yet number is a characteristic of the set itself. Collections help children by allowing them to maintain the whole set in mind. I would like now to speculate about how this analysis might have some bearing on a linguistic curiosity that occurs in some natural languages called "numerical-classifier" languages.

In English, which is not a classifier language, there is a distinction between count and mass nouns. Count nouns can be counted directly—for example, "one pencil, two pencils, three pencils, etc." Mass nouns cannot be counted directly as in "one milk, two milks, three milks." Instead, some other unit or measure is mentioned and then that unit is counted—for example, "one cup of milk, two cups of milk, three cups of milk." Because mass nouns typically refer to undifferentiated masses—such as milk, clay, rice—they cannot be counted until some individuating unit or measure is imposed on them. What is of interest is that some languages express quantity by using a construction that is similar to the mass construction in English, even when the objects being referred to are not masses (Greenberg, 1972). In fact, they require such a construction for virtually all expressions of quantity. Thus, in these languages, one would have to say something like "two long things of pencil" rather than "two pencils."

If, in these languages, there were no mass–count distinctions, or if all nouns were mass nouns, then that might explain why a classifier, such as "long thing" would be needed to impose units on the mass. However, at least some of these languages do have a mass–count distinction, and do have a singular–plural contrast. For example, the classifiers themselves can be counted, in some of the languages, but then require their own classifiers. What is odd about these languages, then, is that, at least occasionally, something like count nouns must be transformed into mass nouns in order to count them.

Of course, there must be many forces that determine what structure any language has. But I would like to raise the possibility that there is a functional explanation that can help account for the peculiarity of classifier languages. The explanation is related to my argument as to why collections help children conceptualize number.

Though mass nouns and collective nouns differ in some ways (see the discussion of mass nouns in the section on hierarchical organization), they are similar in referring to the whole rather than the individuals that comprise it. By using mass nouns and then requiring a classifier to be used, quantitative expressions in classifier languages provide an explicit representation of both levels of analysis that are needed for cardinal number. "Two long things" refers to the individuals whereas "of pencil" provides a representation of the whole. Greenberg reviewed over 100 classifier languages and found that there was wide variation in the types of linguistic constructions for which use of a classifier was mandatory. Some languages use classifiers in many different constructions, including adjectives and demonstratives, for example, whereas some use them in only one construction. Yet, even with considerable diversity of numerical-classifier languages, all of them required classifiers when mentioning number (Greenberg, 1972).

An historical analysis of the languages indicated that regardless of how many different classifier constructions the modern language contains, classifiers originated for use in quantitative expressions (Greenberg, 1972). What I am suggesting is that they may have originated in order to better express quantity. One untested prediction of this analysis is that one would expect that, if cultural and social differences could be controlled, children learning a classifier language should exhibit accelerated number development.

LEARNING HIERARCHICAL RELATIONS

Children are often faced with having to learn hierarchically organized class-inclusion relations—for example, that chairs are furniture, that poodles are dogs, that oaks are trees. In English, class membership can be expressed by *is a* at any level of the hierarchy. For example, a given object *is a* poodle, *is a* dog, and *is an* animal. In first learning terms, children learn common labels for objects often at the basic level (Anglin, 1977; Brown, 1958; Rosch, Mervis, Gray, Johnson, & Boyes-Braem, 1976). Children hear, for example, "What's this?" "That is a chair." "What's this? That is a dog," with adults tending to be consistent in the labels they give. I suspect that from the child's point of view, this may be tantamount to learning what things are—learning something important and unique about the identity of objects. Once these labels are learned, then, the child must cope with the fact that now the chair will also be labeled "furniture" and the dog, "animal," and so on. As Macnamara (1979) pointed out, children must learn how one object can have multiple labels and must figure out what the relations between them are. Many options are possible, including that the terms be synonomous, overlapping, or hierarchical. If the terms are taken to be hierarchical, one might suppose that class inclusion would be a likely hypothesis, especially for older children, because class terms are far more frequent in the language and children must have encountered many more of them. Yet, the evidence I have reviewed so far demonstrates that when children must solve problems of class inclusion or of cardinal number, the part–whole organization of collections works to their advantage. Collections have a more stable hierarchical structure than classes and form a hierarchy that is easier for children to operate upon than one of class inclusion. Though collective nouns are scarce relative to class terms, it still could be that the collection hierarchy is easier for children to construct. When children are relatively free to impose their own structure on a novel hierarchy, they might prefer a collection to a class organization.

This hypothesis was tested by contriving a situation in which children were presented with only minimal information about a hierarchical relation (Markman, Horton, & McLanahan, 1980). We wanted to see how children would spontaneously interpret the relations when given relative freedom. In actuality, the relations were novel class-inclusion hierarchies, analogous to the relations between oaks, pines, and trees. Ostensive definition (pointing and labeling) was used to achieve a minimal specification of the relationship. To illustrate, imagine that oaks and pines are lined in a row in front of the child. Pointing to the oaks, the experimenter says, "These are oaks"; pointing to the pines, the experimenter says, "These are pines"; and, pointing to the trees, the experimenter says, "These are trees." Describing trees in the plural, "These are trees," means that each individual tree is a tree. Thus, the use of the plural establishes the class-inclusion relation. The singular would have to be used in order to establish a collection—for example, "This is a forest." Though the ostensive definition provides only minimal information, it does establish that the objects presented form a class-inclusion hierarchy.

Suppose children misinterpret the class-inclusion relation as a collection hierarchy. What errors should they make? They should erroneously believe that several of the items together form an instance of the concept at the higher level of the hierarchy (trees in the example) and should not believe that any single item is an instance. To see why, consider what the correct response would be had children actually learned a collection—for example, "forest." If asked to point to the forest, the child should point to many trees, but should deny that a pine or any other single tree is itself a forest.

Under ordinary circumstances, children are able to learn class-inclusion relations, so with enough information constraining their interpretation, they should be able to learn the inclusion relations we are teaching them as well. For this reason, we included a condition in which inclusion relations were specified more explicitly, with statements such as "Oaks and pines are kinds of trees."

Ninety-six children participated in the study. There were 24 children from each of four age levels, the mean ages of which were: 6;8, 11;10, 14;1, and 17;3. Half of the children learned the novel concepts by ostensive definition alone, and half were given the additional inclusion information. Each child learned four novel categories, one at a time, each composed of two subcategories. All of the category exemplars were small construction-paper figures. Some of the categories were novel shapes whereas some were novel animate figures. Twelve nonsense syllables were used as names for the novel figures, and were counter-balanced over the different types of categories.

I summarize the procedure in the following discussion. The two bottom nodes of the hierarchy, the two subcategories, are referred to as A and B. The top node is referred to as C.

In the ostensive learning condition, the experimenter pointed to each of the two subcategories, As and Bs (analogous to oaks and pines), or the entire category Cs (analogous to trees), and simply labeled them. Whether the top node (C) or the bottom nodes (A and B) were mentioned first was counterbalanced over items. In this labeling condition, as in the inclusion condition, the labels taught to the child were always plural. So the procedure is analogous to pointing to oaks and saying "These are oaks," pointing to pines saying "These are pines," and pointing to trees saying "These are trees." The experimenter always pointed to each array from left to right in an identical manner for each. This labeling continued until children could provide the correct labels.

Children were than asked eight questions about the categories. All of the questions used singular terms. Four of the questions were about the entire category (C), and four were about the subcategories (A or B). Two of the questions required a behavioral response—that is, "Show me a C" (analogous to show me a tree). Two required a yes–no answer: "Is this a C?" (pointing to a C). This is analogous to asking "Is this a tree?" while pointing to a tree. Similarly, at the lower nodes, two of the questions required behavioral responses: "Show me an A" (Show me an oak) and two required yes–no answers, "Is this an A?" while pointing to an A ("Is this an oak?" while pointing to an oak).

The procedure for the inclusion condition was identical to the procedure for the ostensive definition conditions. The only difference was in the additional information provided about category membership—for example, As and Bs are kinds of Cs.

The results of this study revealed that children, until a surprisingly late age, tend to misinterpret class-inclusion relations as collections when only minimal information is provided. When given more explicit information, as in the inclusion condition, they had little trouble interpreting inclusion correctly.

The hypothesis that children treat a novel hierarchy as a collection structure predicts that collection errors should predominate in the upper level of the hierarchy. This prediction was strongly supported by the findings. In the ostensive learning condition, children average 3.49 errors at the upper levels compared to only .18 errors at the lower nodes. It is not until children reached 11th grade, until they were 17, that these misinterpretations disappeared.

In summary, when the novel class-inclusion relations are taught by osentive definition, children as old as 14 often mistakenly interpreted the relations as collections. When asked what would be analogous to "Show me a pine," children correctly picked up a single pine. When the experimenter, while pointing to a pine, asked "Is this a pine?" children responded correctly. The errors occurred almost exclusively on the upper level of the hierarchy. When asked to "Show me a tree," children scooped up a handful rather than just one. When the experimenter, while pointing to a tree asked "Is this a tree?" children often said "No." This is exactly what one would expect if children were answering questions about a collection.

Because collections form more stable hierarchies, it may be easier for children to keep the two levels of the hierarchy distinct. At least in the somewhat artificial conditions of the present study, children apparently found it simpler to impose a collection structure on a novel hierarchy than to correctly interpret it as inclusion. This is true despite the fact that children must certainly have more experience learning inclusion relations, because collective nouns are relatively rare. Because this was an unusual way to learn novel concepts, collection errors may be unlikely in natural situations. However, there is some anecdotal (Valentine, 1942) and experimental (Macnamara, 1979) evidence suggesting that such errors may be found in a naturalistic context. Maureen Callanan and I have conducted a more controlled study to further investigate this possibility (Callanan & Markman, 1980). Our preliminary data suggest that in first acquiring superordinate terms, young children distort some class inclusion-relations into collections. They agree, for example, that a set of toys are toys, but deny that any single toy (a ball, for example) is itself a toy. Thus, even in naturally occurring contexts, very young children may find it simpler to impose a collection structure on what are actually inclusion hierarchies they are trying to learn.

Superordinate Terms and Mass Nouns

I have noticed something puzzling about many superordinate terms in English that this work on the learning of hierarchical relations may help explain. There are many common superordinate terms in English that are mass nouns yet should not be. Ordinary mass nouns in English typically refer to relatively homogeneous masses—for example, clay, water, grass. In contrast to count nouns, mass nouns cannot be counted directly; one cannot say "one or two clays." Instead, one must speak of "pieces of clay," "drops of water," "blades of grass," when referring to individual components or parts of the more or less homogeneous substance. Some terms that refer to categories of discrete objects are nevertheless mass nouns. These include: furniture, clothing, money, jewelry, silverware. One cannot speak of one or two furnitures, silverwares, jewelrys, and so on. Rather, one must say, a piece of furniture, a piece of jewelry, a piece of silverware. Yet, the objects to which these mass terms refer are not masses. Even though we must say "A fork is a piece of silverware," "A chair is a piece of furniture," "A bracelet is a piece of jewelry," certainly these are class-inclusion relations. Chairs *are* furniture, forks *are* silverware, and bracelets *are* jewelry. The relation between chairs and furniture, forks and silverware, bracelets and jewelry is no different conceptually, as far as I can tell, than the relationship between hammers and tools, cars and vehicles.

I would like to speculate about why these categories would be referred to by mass terms. In the study just reported, we argued that the part–whole organization of collections may be more stable than that of class inclusion. It is easier to keep the two levels of the hierarchy distinct when the higher level has greater psychological coherence. Superordinate categories, such as furniture, in contrast to basic-level categories such as chairs, are at the top node (or relatively high node) of a given natural language hierarchy (Rosch et al. 1976). I am suggesting that mass nouns may serve a function similar to collective nouns in helping to keep that top node more stable and distinct. In a sense, mass nouns can be viewed as a compromise between collections and classes, or, to be more precise, as a compromise between part–whole and *is a* relations. Consider a typical mass such as clay. A piece of clay is part of the whole mass of clay. This is similar to the part–whole organization of collections in which each tree, for example, is part of the forest. On the other hand, each piece of clay is itself clay. This is more like the *is a* relation of class inclusion, in which each oak is a tree.

Though collective nouns reflect more stable hierarchical structures, they could not themselves serve as superordinate terms for the very reason that they express a different relation. However, by referring to discrete objects with mass terms, a language might be able to provide some of the stability that the part–whole organization of collections would have achieved, yet remind the speaker that an inclusion relation is still involved.

There are empirical consequences of this analysis. First, the analysis predicts that this peculiarity should not be limited to English. Other languages with a count–mass distinction should also have this type of aberration. Second, if these aberrations serve the purpose of helping to give stability to hierarchically organized categories, then such "inappropriate" mass terms should occur only on what speakers would judge to be superordinate levels, not on basic or lower levels of the hierarchy. That is, languages should contain terms that require one to say "a piece of furniture" or "a piece of vehicle" when what one means is "a furniture" or "a vehicle." But they should not require speakers to say "a piece of chair" or "a piece of car" when what one means is "a chair" or "a car."

There are parallels with these speculations about language and those I made earlier about classifier languages. In both cases, I am suggesting that languages distort count nouns into mass nouns in order to serve some psychological function. In both cases, evidence from developmental studies indicates that the part–whole structure of collections serves a valuable function for children in those domains in which the languages contain some peculiarity. Collections help children conceptualize number (Markman, 1979) and classifier languages use the classifier construction for number. Hierarchical relations of collections seem to be in some respects simpler for children compared to class-inclusion relations (Markman et al., 1980) and it is in the designation of some hierarchical relations that this peculiarity with mass nouns arises. The common speculation is that in both cases, the compromise structure of mass terms may serve a function related to that of collections. If these speculations have validity, then they would demonstrate a novel and interesting way in which psychological functions contribute to the forces that bear on the evolution of linguistic structure.

DISCUSSION

Summary

I argued that the part–whole organization of collections results in a more coherent structure than does the inclusion relation of classes. When collection terms, such as *army* or *forest*, are used to label objects, people conceptualize the same objects differently than when class terms, such as *soldiers* or *trees*, are used.

When viewed as forming a collection, objects are related to each other, thereby forming a higher-order aggregate with good psychological integrity. Once they organize objects into collections, people, especially children, become better able to solve problems that require attending to the set of objects as well as the individuals in the set. This was demonstrated in a variety of different tasks, each of which required some analysis of the higher-order aggregate. In the Piagetian class-inclusion problem, children were better able to compare part to whole for the part–whole organization of collections than for the inclusion relation of classes. Children were also better able to see the logic of the problem—they understood that the whole must be larger than any of its parts more readily for collections than for classes. The ease of constructing an image has been previously related to the unity of the display being imaged. When objects were thought of as collections, they were imaged more readily than when the same objects were thought of as classes. Adults were more likely to recognize the possibility of collective attributions (such as "Men are numerous") for collections than for classes. For classes, only distributive attributions (such as "Men are mortal") were considered. I argued that number is a property of sets themselves and not just members of the sets and that therefore collection organizations should help children solve numerical problems. Younger children were better able to conserve number, to evaluate when a transformation changed the number of objects, to judge equivalence on the basis of number rather than length, and to use the cardinality principle when arrays of objects were thought of as collections rather than classes. When trying to learn a novel hierarchical relation, children erroneously impose a part–whole structure of collections on the inclusion relation of classes.

Though, in most of these studies, collection terms and class terms were applied to the identical displays, they nevertheless induced different organizations. When success on a task depends on the unity or coherence of an array, or requires keeping two levels of a hierarchy in mind at once, collections helped children solve the problem.

Implications for Children's Cognitive Capacity

In several of the studies reported here, when the objects were described as collections, children became able to solve tasks they could not otherwise have solved. This is, of course, by no means the first demonstration that children's performance can be improved during an experimental session. However, when training, feedback, modeling, or other types of practice are used, it is less surprising that children improve. Or, when the problems are modified so as to simplify the task demands, improvement would be expected. In the present work, however, there is no obvious way in which the problems, such as conservation tasks, for example, would be simplified by relabeling trees as a forest, or soldiers as an army. There is certainly no way in which we trained children or induced any abilities or knowledge that they did not already possess before they participated in the studies. To take the clearest case of this, consider the study in which young children counted an array of objects and then were asked how many objects there were. Children hearing the objects described as classes tended to count again whereas children hearing the objects described as collections correctly gave the cardinal number. Relabeling trees as forest could not possibly have taught children that the last number in a count series becomes the cardinal number of the set. They must have already possessed this principle, yet were prevented from accessing it. The general point that young children's abilities may be underestimated by traditional procedures has been forcefully argued by Gelman and her colleagues (Gelman, 1978; Gelman & Gallistel, 1978).

What, then, is preventing children from conserving number, from using the cardinal principle, from solving the class-inclusion problem? Children possess some knowledge or skills, at least in rudimentary form, yet they are not using them. The relabeling from classes to collections, the only manipulation used in this work, helped children impose a hierarchical organization on the material, thus allowing them to attend to and maintain the higher-order level of organization. Apparently, children do not establish the hierarchical organization themselves. They tend to view the objects at one level of classification, as individuals or members of subclasses, but cannot simultaneously view them as belonging to the higher-level category. I have argued that this hierarchical organization and part–whole analysis is needed to deal with cardinal number, as in number conservation, as well as in the class-inclusion problem.

These findings suggest that, for children especially, it may be important to have a fit between the prior conceptualization or organization of information and the processing required for problem solution. It seems as if a prerequisite for initiating the appropriate processes or accessing relevant knowledge may be to establish the hierarchical organization. Otherwise, the part–whole comparison problems and number problems cannot be solved. Because part–whole organization of collections is a simpler hierarchical organization for children than that of class inclusion, it allows children to solve these problems, thus revealing incipient abilities that would ordinarily have been obscured.

Class Inclusion Versus Relational Structures in General

One of the major contrasts between collections and classes is that collections are defined by interrelationships of their elements whereas classes are not. This section presents hypotheses about several diverse domains: syllogistic reasoning, imagery as a mnemonic aid, word associations, and classification, each of which provides a relational contrast to inclusion. I do not mean to argue that these different domains have an organization that is tantamount to the organization of collections. Rather, they suggest that the collection–class contrast is part of a more general difference between relational and class-inclusion organizations. In particular, there is evidence that relational organizations unify arrays and that they are simpler for children to use.

Linear Versus Classical Syllogisms.   The distinction between linear and classical syllogisms may in some ways be analogous to the collection–class distinction. For both collections and linear syllogisms, elements that are explicitly related to each other become organized into a unified representation.

Consider the following two arguments:

1. *A* is smaller than *B*.
   B is smaller than *C*.
   Therefore, *A* is smaller than *C*.
2. All *A*s are *B*s.
   All *B*s are *C*s.
   Therefore, all *A*s are *C*s.

The first, a linear syllogism (also referred to as a three-term-series problem) contains a relational term (*smaller*) in both premises. The two premises provide information from which a simple transitive inference is made to deduce the conclusion. The second is a classical syllogism that specifies class-inclusion relations in both of the premises. This too is a transitive relation, and a simple transitive inference is sufficient to deduce the conclusion. Both types of arguments can be extended indefinitely by adding additional terms, and the same points about the nature of the relations and inferences hold except that a greater number of inferences are involved.

Despite this similarity, subjects usually represent and solve these two problems in very different ways. There is considerable evidence that people use some type of linear ordering to represent the information given in the premises of linear syllogism (Potts, 1972; Trabasso, 1975). One of the main arguments used to make this point relies on a contrast between what one would expect if people were storing the premises specifying pairwise comparisons and then drawing transitive inferences to judge the truth of a conclusion, versus what one would expect if subjects were constructing a linear ordering to represent the information and then "reading" the answer off this ordering. If subjects stored information about adjacent pairs and then made transitive inferences when questioned, they should be faster at comparing the adjacent items they had learned and memorized (e.g., *B* is smaller than *C*) than at comparing more remote elements that would require them to draw inferences (e.g., *A* is smaller than *C*). In fact, however, for adults, the verification of transitive inferences is faster the more distant the items (Potts, 1972). This inverse distance effect is very reliable and is obtained with both concrete and abstract dimensions (Kerst & Howard, 1977) and with diverse procedures and material (Moeser, 1979; Moyer & Bayer, 1976; Woocher, Glass, & Holyoak, 1978). Trabasso (1975) and his colleagues have demonstrated that if precautions are taken to ensure that children have learned and stored the original information, then their reaction times show a similar pattern to the adults. In summary, when individual items are explicitly related to each other via relational terms (such as *smaller* or *friendlier*), they appear to be represented as a linear ordering rather than as discrete pairs.

Performance on syllogisms involving class inclusions contrasts markedly with the pattern just described. In a direct comparison of the two types of relations, Carroll and Kammann (1977) presented subjects with paragraphs that contained either linear orderings or class-inclusion relationships. The paragraphs were identical in all respects except for the relationship that was expressed. This was accomplished by pairing each relational sentence—for example, "... atmospheric planets are found to be warmer than life-supporting planets"—with something like "... all atmospheric planets are found to be life-supporting planets." Thus, they held all factors constant except for the nature of the relation expressed. For the most part, the findings on the linear ordering replicated that of previous work (e.g., Potts, 1972). That is, accuracy increased and latency decreased with the distance of the two elements being compared. The pattern of errors and latencies was markedly different for the class-inclusion relations. First, subjects were significantly less accurate in their judgments of class-inclusion comparisons than of the relational comparisons. This is consistent with much other work showing high error rates on class-inclusion problems (e.g., Griggs, 1976; Potts, 1976). Second, accuracy *decreased* and latency *increased* with remoteness for the true items. For false items, these patterns reversed. Though Mynatt and Smith (1979) claimed that their subjects used linear orderings to represent inclusion, they found this only when inclusion was expressed as "*A is in B*" rather than as "All *A*s are *B*s." However *is in* specifies a literal spatial relation between two objects and is not class inclusion. Across several studies, the evidence indicates that most untrained subjects do not spontaneously represent classical syllogisms as linear orderings (Griggs, 1976; Mynatt & Smith, 1979; Potts, 1976).

Despite Carroll and Kammann's (1977) and Potts' (1976) attempts to keep inclusion and linear-ordering paragraphs identical, there are differences between the two types of problems. Class-inclusion relations require quantifiers whereas the relational problems do not. The class-inclusion relations in these studies involved universal quantification, "All *A*s are *B*s." With "Some *A*s are *B*s," a linear representation would not be so appropriate. The syllogisms in these studies could have easily been represented in a linear ordering, but other syllogisms could not be represented in this fashion. Consequently, no firm conclusions regarding the source of the differences in mode of representation can be made on the basis of existing data. Nevertheless, there may be an interesting analogy between the collection–class differences and linear versus classical syllogisms. Subjects do not construct unified representations for classical syllogisms. Classes were not represented as ranked on a unified continuum of inclusiveness although in principle they could have been. In contrast, just as the relational structure of collections results in a coherent representation of the whole, the relational structure of linear syllogisms results in a unified representation of the ordering.

Imagery as a Mnemonic. The analysis of collections implies that a collection structure confers unity on an array by emphasizing the interrelationship of the elements. A similar principle explains why interactive imagery is such an effective mnemonic. An example of an interactive image would be for someone who had to remember the word pair *bandaid–shoe* to image the bandaid encircling the shoe. People's memory for paired associates or lists of unrelated words or objects improves, sometimes dramatically, when they form interactive images of the items to be remembered (Bower, 1970, 1972). Such imagery is effective apparently because it organizes unrelated items into an integrated unit.

Alternative hypotheses for the advantage of interactive imagery have been considered and largely rejected. One hypothesis is that imagery is beneficial because it increases the memorability of the individual items. However, instructions to image each object separately do not result in the same improvement as do instructions to form an interactive image (Bower, 1972; Morris & Stevens, 1974). Further evidence comes from comparing free recall to cued recall of the items. If interactive imagery were simply increasing the memorability of each item, then it should promote free recall of the items as well as cued recall. Yet, subjects who form interactive images have been found to remember no more items when tested by a free recall procedure than subjects who form separate images (Begg, 1973). Also, if the interactive image promoted unitization of the separate items, then even in free recall there should be some evidence that the items are recalled as a unit. One measure of such unity is the degree to which the items are remembered together and, as expected, high rates of clustering have been found in the free recall of subjects forming interactive images (Bower, Lesgold, & Tieman, 1969; Morris & Stevens, 1974).

For the most part, the developmental findings parallel the findings with adults. Children told to form interactive images show clear improvements in cued recall (Begg & Anderson, 1976; Danner & Taylor, 1973). Again, this effectiveness seems due to the relational organization because forming separate images does not lead to improved recall for children (Begg & Anderson, 1976). Also, as with adults, the effectiveness of interactive imagery is greater in cued recall than in free recall (Begg & Anderson, 1976). Thus, there do not seem to be major developmental differences in whether these relational principles promote unitization. Even kindergarten children have been trained to use interactive imagery with resulting improvement in their memory (Yuille & Catchpole, 1973). The developmental differences lie in the extent to which children spontaneously form such images as a mnemonic device, and how explicit the instructions must be before children will follow them (Rohwer, 1970). These studies with adults and with children support the hypothesis that imagery helps because it imposes a unitary structure on previously unrelated items that results in better memory for the items.

In addition, there are procedures that, though they do not require subjects to form images, in other ways establish relations between the objects to be remembered with comparable effects on memory. For example, one can directly vary the degree of organization of the material to be recalled. Horowitz, Lampel, and Takanishi (1969) predicted that a unitized scene should allow for better detection of a deleted element than a poorly organized scene. They argued that the remaining elements of an organized scene, but not a poorly organized one, would elicit the whole unit, thus allowing for good recall of the missing element. To manipulate the unity of a scene, Horowitz et al. (1969) presented objects either simply lined in a row or arranged into a salient configuration. For example, if the objects were a doll, a chair, and a ball, the doll could sit in the chair with a ball in its lap. As predicted, Horowitz et al. (1969) and also Lampel (1973) found that nursery-school children were better able to recall the missing element in unitized scenes. Related studies have been done with adults with similar results (e.g., Epstein, Rock, & Zuckerman, 1960).

Relational information is also readily conveyed through certain linguistic constructions, and studies have found that such constructions similarly result in better paired-associate memory. Use of verbs and prepositions improves memory for paired associates over simple conjunctions for both adults (Rohwer, 1966) and children (Rohwer, 1970). Verbs and prepositions explicitly relate one object to another, either in terms of action on an object or the spatial relations between two objects. Again, it appears to be the interactive component and resulting unitization that improves memory.

Word Associations.   There is a developmental change that occurs in the types of responses given in word-association tasks (Emerson & Gekoski, 1976; Entwistle, 1966; Entwistle, Forsyth, & Muus, 1964; Lippman, 1971; Masters, 1969; Palermo, 1971). Adults and older children tend to give what have been termed *paradigmatic* responses as associations—for example, *boy-girl, hot-cold, add-subtract.* Younger children tend to respond with *syntagmatic* associations—for example *boy-runs, hot-bath,* and *add-numbers.* Paradigmatic ic responses maintain the form class of the target word; that is, nouns are given in response to nouns, adjectives in response to adjectives, and so on. Clark (1970) has constructed a set of rules that can account for many of the data regarding adult word associations. The general form that the rules take is based on what Clark terms the "minimal contrast rule," which involves modifying the sign of only one of the word's semantic features. In other words, paradigmatic associations involve accessing the criteria that define a term. To form the association, one of the criteria is modified in a minimal way. In syntagmatic responses, the form class of the word is not maintained, nor are children concerned about maintaining similarity between the target word and the associate. Rather, it is as if the children are attempting to complete a phrase or a sentence with their associate.

The contrast between paradigmatic and syntagmatic associations provides one example of a contrast between inclusion or similarity and other types of relations. In paradigmatic responding, the form class is maintained, and the words, though contrasting, still refer to very similar objects, events, or attributes. In contrast, in syntagmatic associations, some causal, temporal, or thematic relation forms the association.

This difference has been made even more apparent by Petry (1977) who offered an interpretation of the word-association shift that relies on Tulving's (1972) distinction between episodic and semantic memory. Consider some of the associations that children gave to "happen" (from Entwistle, 1966, as cited by Petry, 1977): *accident, and we all fall down, bruise, cut yourself, damn, get mud throwned in my face*. According to Petry, the children are recalling the catastrophies that occurred on the specific occasions on which they might hear the question "what happened?" Petry argues that although paradigmatic associations tap semantic memory (in accord with Clark's analysis), syntagmatic associations tap episodic memory—memory of personally-experienced events or episodes.

What I would like to suggest is that the internal structure of events or episodes is not class inclusion but rather is in some ways similar to the collection structure. For example, consider the event of coming home. Events and actions may be hierarchically organized—for example, the relation of turning the key in the lock, to opening the door, to entering the house—but the hierarchy is not one of class inclusion; rather, it is of part–whole relations. (Note that this analysis of episodes and events is not meant to be an analysis of the relations of, say, walking, to running, or to moving. This type of relation—for example, walk to run—is an instance of a paradigmatic, not a syntagmatic, association.)

Developmental changes in word associations have been interpreted as representing major changes in the organization of concepts (see Nelson, 1977, for a review and critique of the theories). This interpretation is probably unwarranted. A more conservative interpretation is that the shift reflects differences in the saliency of one type of organization over another.

Thus, the changes in word associations suggest that children may find it easier, or more preferable, to establish event-like interrelationships among concepts rather than to categorize concepts based on an analysis of criteria or features. This suggests that organizations that rely on the form class of words or the similarity of their referents may become salient at a later time than organizations that rely instead on specification of interrelationships of elements with each other.

Classification.   As a means of studying how children form concepts, psychologists have presented children with a variety of objects and have asked them to group together the things that are alike or to describe how various objects are similar. Though the assumption that these are valid measures of conceptual organization may be unwarranted (cf. Huttenlocher & Lui, 1979; Markman, Cox, & Machida, in press; Smiley & Brown, 1979), many investigators using such procedures have found similar developmental changes in the basis children use for grouping diverse objects (Bruner et al., 1966; Goldman & Levine, 1963; Inhelder & Piaget, 1964; Vygotsky, 1962; Wei, Lavatelli, & Jones, 1971). In a relatively immature type of classification, children group together things that form a single object, a pattern, or a theme. For example, a child might place a triangle on top of a square to form a house. Or a child might place a child, a dog, a house, and a tree together because the child is taking the dog for a walk down the street. Like collections, these "graphic" or "thematic" categories are characterized by the relationships of the objects with each other as parts of wholes. For items to compose a story, an event, or a theme, they must be causally or temporally related. For items to form an object or pattern, they must be spatially related.

In a somewhat more advanced form of classification, children use similarity criteria for forming groups, but the basis of the classification is unstable in that children keep shifting criteria. Though the children are attempting to categorize items on the basis of common properties, their attention is diverted by additional relationships among objects.

Finally, adult-like classification results when children form classes in which each item is accepted in the class only if it fulfills the requisite criteria. So, for example, instead of grouping a child, a dog, a house, and a tree together as younger children might, older children would group by taxonomic category, placing people, animals, buildings, and plants in separate categories.

In these object-sorting tasks, children are explicitly asked to group the material. A more indirect measure of organization is to ask children to recall lists of words that can potentially be grouped into taxonomic categories. Though I cannot review the huge number of such studies that have been conducted (cf. Lange, 1978; Moely, 1977), the typical finding is that young children do not take advantage of the taxonomic structure of the list to organize their recall. There is some suggestion that their recall may be organized thematically and that they may in fact cluster material that can be readily organized by a thematic structure (Lange & Jackson, 1974).

In summary, when children are presented with diverse objects to classify, they initially use the relationships between objects rather than taxonomic category as a basis for classification.

The results from these various domains suggest that class inclusion is in some ways more difficult to deal with than the relational structures that linear syllogisms, syntagmatic associations, or thematic groupings exemplify. Moreover, relational organizations, as in linear syllogisms and interactive imagery, appear to help unify separate items. Against this background, the class–collection contrast may be viewed as an instance of a more general distinction with wide-ranging implications for cognitive functioning.

Development of Taxonomic Organization

Even if taxonomic organization is not the simplest or most natural way of viewing objects, it becomes extremely important and useful for adults. Under some circumstances, it may even become the dominant or preferred mode of organization. We still do not fully understand what developmental changes in taxonomic organization actually occur or how they take place.

Early theorizing about this problem suggests that the formation of categories, especially more general one, requires abstraction away from individuals. Concepts are grounded in experience, but one must abstract away from idiosyncratic details of a given experience to form rules that define categories (Bruner, Goodnow, & Austin, 1956). Current research has discovered that concept acquisition may be less abstract than the earlier theories proposed. Concepts may be organized around prototypes or exemplars, and how concepts are acquired depends on their categorical structure and level of generality (e.g., Horton & Markman, 1980; Kossan, 1978; Rosch et al., 1976). Yet, on these later accounts, abstraction away from individuals to form a representation of the category is still required, even if an abstract rule is not part of the representation.

Until recently, there had not been much analysis of the way in which the initial experiential base is built up. Recently, many investigators have begun to characterize the experientially based, meaningful knowledge. Though different in many respects, theoretical notions of scripts (Schank & Abelson, 1977) and story grammars (Rumelhart, 1975) share an emphasis on characterizing knowledge that has a causal, temporal, thematic, or spatial structure. Developmental accounts of the abstraction process are now beginning to incorporate a more complete description of these experiential bases (Nelson, 1978, and this volume). With a more elaborated set of principles to describe the original knowledge base, we may be in a better position to understand the abstraction process by which taxonomic organizations are eventually formed.

There is also evidence that taxonomic organization develops as a function of education. Cross-cultural comparisons show large differences between schooled and unschooled populations in whether or not taxonomic organization is used. This finding about the role of education raises the question of the utility of taxonomic organization. Why should it become more salient or more prevalent in school?

The question of schooling is in turn a question about knowledge and the dissemination of knowledge. A major purpose of categorization must be to provide knowledge that goes beyond the information one has about an individual.

Given that one knows that an object is a bird, for example, a great many other facts about that object can be deduced with a fair amount of certainty—facts about its appearance, method of locomotion, means of reproduction, internal organs, etc. So, one purpose of a taxonomic system is to provide a rich deductive network. For the purpose of scientific understanding, one wants to be able to view an object not just as an individual, but as a member of a more general category. Categories are used to establish and express the law-like generalizations of scientific knowledge.

Taxonomic organizations are likely to be especially useful for organizing large amounts of information. Because hierarchically organized class inclusion is transitive, it could be an efficient means of keeping track of information. One can move up or down the hierarchy deleting and supplying details as necessary. One has ready access to properties of an object based on all of the more general categories to which it belongs. As a consequence, it could be very useful for domains in which a culture or an individual has many distinctions to encode. In Western societies, for example, there are enormous numbers of artifacts (tools, vehicles, machines) that require systematic organization. In those domains in which we have little knowledge, a much less elaborated system, even knowledge of isolated objects, would be sufficient. I personally have a fairly elaborate hierarchy in which to place a chocolate chip cookie. I can move down the hierarchy to various brands and types or up the hierarchy through cookies, baked goods, or desserts, and food in general. Yet, it is only with some difficulty that I could construct a hierarchical organization in which to place an electrical outlet, for example, though I suspect that electricians could do so with ease.

During school, when educators attempt to impart knowledge of the culture to children, taxonomic systems will be used and practiced more, and as a consequence children will find them more salient. Another way in which schooling could help is that children may for the first time find the categorical structure effectively used as a means of organizing knowledge rather than just as an alternative label for something. Prior to entering school, children may well know that oaks and pines are trees. But it may only be after schooling that they discover there are general properties of trees that apply to oaks and pines and any other tree they will ever learn about. They also discover that there are unique properties of oaks and pines, and for any new tree they hear about, they must discover its unique characteristics. So, though children know that oaks are trees, that hierarchical information serves little purpose until children begin to acquire substantial knowledge about a domain. This will not be left entirely to formal education. There is already evidence that young children will use categorical structures to a limited degree (Carey, 1978; Harris, 1975; Smith, 1979). But the point still remains that as more and more information must be learned, there may be greater pressure to systematize knowledge in this way. If children discover how well a taxonomic system can manage large amounts of information, they could promote it to a more prominent principle of organization.

ACKNOWLEDGMENTS

This work was supported by PHS research grant MH 28154. I would like to thank Susan Carey, Herbert Clark, John Flavell, David Klahr, Geoffrey Loftus, Elissa Newport, and Barbara Tversky for their helpful comments on an earlier draft of this chapter.

REFERENCES

Ahr, P. R., & Youniss, J. Reasons for failure on the class-inclusion problem. *Child Development,* 1970, *41,* 131–143.

Anglin, J. M. *Word, object, and conceptual development.* New York: Norton, 1977.

Begg, I. Imagery and integration in the recall of words. *Canadian Journal of Psychology,* 1973, *27,* 159–167.

Begg, I., & Anderson, M. C. Imagery and associative memory in children. *Journal of Experimental Child Psychology,* 1976, *21,* 480–489.

Botvin, G., & Murray, F. The efficiency of peer modeling and social conflict in the acquisition of conservation. *Child Development,* 1975, *46,* 796–799.

Bower, G. H. Analysis of a mnemonic device. *American Scientist,* 1970, *58,* 496–510.

Bower, G. H. Mental imagery and associative learning. In L. W. Gregg (Ed.), *Cognition in learning and memory.* New York: Wiley, 1972.

Bower, G. H., Lesgold, A. M., & Tieman, D. Grouping operations in free recall. *Journal of Verbal Learning and Verbal Behavior,* 1969, *8,* 481–493.

Brown, R. *Words and things.* New York: Free Press, 1958.

Bruner, J. S., Goodnow, J. J., & Austin, G. A. *A study of thinking.* New York: Wiley, 1956.

Bruner, J. S., Olver, R. R., & Greenfield, P. M. *Studies in cognitive growth.* New York: Wiley, 1966.

Bucci, W. The interpretation of universal affirmative propositions. *Cognition,* 1978, *6,* 55–78.

Callanan, M., & Markman, E. M. On the learning of hierarchically organized concepts. Manuscript in preparation, 1980.

Carey, S. *The child's concept of animal.* Paper presented at the Psychonomics Society, San Antonio, Texas, October, 1978.

Carroll, M., & Kammann, R. The dependency of schema formation on type of verbal material: Linear orderings and set inclusions. *Memory and Cognition,* 1977, *5,* 73–78.

Ceraso, J., & Provitera, A. Source of errors in syllogistic reasoning. *Cognitive Psychology,* 1971, *2,* 400–410.

Chapman, I. J., and Chapman J. P. Atmosphere effect re-examined. *Journal of Experimental Psychology* 1959, *58,* 220–226.

Clark, H. H. Word associations and linguistic theory. In J. Lyons (Ed.), *New Horizons in linguistics.* London: Penguin, 1970.

Collins, A. M., & Quillian, M. R. Facilitating retrieval from semantic memory: The effect of repeating part of an inference. *Acta Psychologica,* 1970, *33,* 304–314.

Danner, F. W., & Taylor, A. M. Integrated pictures and relational imagery training in children's learning. *Journal of Experimental Child Psychology,* 1973, *16,* 47–54.

Emerson, H. F., & Gekoski, W. L. Interactive and categorical grouping strategies and the syntagmatic–paradigmatic shift. *Child Development,* 1976, *47,* 1116–1121.

Entwistle, D. *Word associations of young children.* Baltimore: Johns Hopkins Press, 1966.

Entwistle, D., Forsyth, D. F., & Muus, R. The syntagmatic–paradigmatic shift in children's word associations. *Journal of Verbal Learning and Verbal Behavior,* 1964, *3,* 19–29.

Epstein, W., Rock, I., Zuckerman, C. B. Meaning and familiarity in associative learning. *Psychological Monographs*, 1960, *74*(No. 491).

Gelman, R. Cognitive development. *Annual Review of Psychology*, 1978, *29*, 297–332.

Gelman, R., & Gallistel, C. R. *The child's understanding of number*. Cambridge, Mass.: Harvard University Press, 1978.

Goldman, A. E., & Levine, M. A developmental study of object sorting. *Child Development*, 1963, *34*, 649–666.

Greenberg, J. H. Numerical classifiers and substantial number: Problems in the analysis of a linguistic type. *Working Papers on Language Universals*, 1972, *9*, 1–39.

Griggs, R. A. Logical processing of set inclusion relations in meaningful text. *Memory and Cognition*, 1976, *4*, 730–740.

Hall, V. E., & Kingsley, R. Conservation and equilibration theory. *The Journal of Genetic Psychology*, 1968, *113*, 195–213.

Harris, P. Inferences on semantic development. *Journal of Child Language*, 1975, *2*, 143–152.

Hayes-Roth, B., & Hayes-Roth, F. Plasticity in memorial networks. *Journal of Verbal Learning and Verbal Behavior*, 1975, *14*, 506–522.

Horowitz, L. M., Lampel, A. K., & Takanishi, R. N. The child's memory for unitized scenes. *Journal of Experimental Child Psychology*, 1969, *8*, 375–388.

Horton, M. S., & Markman, E. M. Developmental differences in the acquisition of basic and superordinate categories. *Child Development*, 1980, *51*, 708–719.

Huttenlocher, J., & Lui, F. The semantic organization of simple nouns and verbs. *Journal of Verbal Learning and Verbal Behavior*, 1979, *18*, 141–162.

Inhelder, I., & Piaget, J. *The early growth of logic in the child*. New York: Norton, 1964.

Kerst, S. M., & Howard, J. J., Jr. Mental comparisons for ordered information on abstract and concrete dimensions. *Memory and Cognition*, 1977, *5*, 227–234.

Klahr, D., & Wallace, J. C. Class-inclusion processes. In S. Farnham-Diggory (Ed.), *Information processing in children*. New York: Academic Press, 1972.

Kohnstamm, G. A. An evaluation of part of Piaget's theory. *Acta Psychologica*, 1963, *21*, 313–356.

Kossan, N. E. *Structure and strategy in concept acquisition*. Unpublished doctoral dissertation, Stanford University, 1978.

Kosslyn, S. M. Imagery and internal representation. In E. Rosch & B. Lloyd (Eds.), *Cognition and categorization*. Hillsdale, N.J.: Lawrence Erlbaum Associates, 1978.

Lampel, A. K. The child's memory for actional, locational, and serial scenes. *Journal of Experimental Child Psychology*, 1973, *15*, 266–277.

Lange, G. Organization-related processes in children's recall. In P. A. Ornstein (Ed.), *Memory development in children*. Hillsdale, N.J.: Lawrence Erlbaum Associates, 1978.

Lange, J., & Jackson, P. Personal organization in children's free recall. *Child Development*, 1974, *45*, 1060–1067.

Lippman, M. Correlates of contrast word associations: Developmental trends. *Journal of Verbal Learning and Verbal Behavior*, 1971, *10*, 392–399.

Macnamara, J. Unpublished manuscript, McGill University, 1979.

Mandler, J. M., Scribner, S., Cole, M., & DeForest, M. Cross-cultural invariance in story recall. *Child Development*, 1980, *51*, 19–26.

Markman, E. M. Facilitation of part–whole comparisons by use of the collective noun "family." *Child Development*, 1973, *44*, 837–840.

Markman, E. M. Empirical versus logical solutions to part–whole comparison problems concerning classes and collections. *Child Development*, 1978, *49*, 168–177.

Markman, E. M. Classes and collections: Conceptual organization and numerical abilities. *Cognitive Psychology*, 1979, *11*, 395–411.

Markman, E. M., Cox, B., & Machida, S. The standard object sorting task as a measure of conceptual organization. *Developmental Psychology*, in press.

Markman, E. M., Horton, M. S., & McLanahan, A. G. Classes and collections: Principles of organization in the learning of hierarchical relations. *Cognition*, 1980, *8*, 227–241.

Markman, E. M., & Seibert, J. Classes and collections: Internal organization and resulting holistic properties. *Cognitive Psychology*, 1976, *8*, 561–577.

Masters, J. C. Word associations and the functional definitions of words. *Developmental Psychology*, 1969, *1*, 517–519.

McGarrigle, J., & Donaldson, M. Conservation accidents. *Cognition*, 1975, *3*, 341–350.

Miller, P. H., & Heller, K. A. Facilitation of attention to number and conservation of number. *Journal of Experimental Child Psychology*, 1976, *22*, 454–467.

Moely, B. E. Organizational factors in the development of memory. In R. V. Kail, Jr. & J. W. Hagen (Eds.), *Perspectives on the development of memory and cognition*. Hillsdale, N.J.: Lawrence Erlbaum Associates, 1977.

Moeser, S. D. Acquiring complex partial orderings in comparison with acquiring similar-sized linear orderings. *Memory and Cognition*, 1979, *7*, 435–444.

Morris, P. E., & Stevens, R. Linking images and free recall. *Journal of Verbal Learning and Verbal Behavior*, 1974, *13*, 310–315.

Moyer, R. S., & Bayer, R. H. Mental comparison and the symbolic distance effect. *Cognitive Psychology*, 1976, *8*, 228–246.

Mynatt, B. T., & Smith, K. H. Processing of text containing artificial inclusion relations. *Memory & Cognition*, 1979, *7*, 390–400.

Nelson, K. The syntagmatic–paradigmatic shift revisited: A review of research and theory. *Psychological Bulletin*, 1977, *84*, 93–116.

Nelson, K. How children represent knowledge of their world in and out of language: A preliminary report. In R. S. Siegler (Ed.), *Children's thinking: What develops?* Hillsdale, N.J.: Lawrence Erlbaum Associates, 1978.

Noble, C. E. Measurements of association value, rated associations and scaled meaningfulness for the 2100 CVC combinations of the English alphabet. *Psychological Reports*, 1961, *8*, 487–521.

Palermo, D. S. Characteristics of word association responses obtained from children in grades one through four. *Developmental Psychology*, 1971, *5*, 118–123.

Petry, S. Word associations and the development of lexical memory. *Cognition*, 1977, *5*, 57–71.

Piaget, J. *The child's conception of number*. New York: Norton, 1965.

Potts, G. R. Information processing strategies used in the encoding of linear orderings. *Journal of Verbal Learning and Verbal Behavior*, 1972, *11*, 727–740.

Potts, G. R. Artificial logical relations and their relevance to semantic memory. *Journal of Experimental Psychology: Human Learning and Memory*, 1976, *2*, 746–758.

Revlis, R. Two models of syllogistic reasoning: Feature selection and conversion. *Journal of Verbal Learning and Verbal Behavior*, 1975, *14*, 180–195.

Rosch, W., Mervis, C. B., Gray, W. D., Johnson, D. M., & Boyes-Braem, P. Basic objects in natural categories. *Cognitive Psychology*, 1976, *8*, 382–439.

Rowher, W. D., Jr. Constraint, syntax and meaning in paired-associate learning. *Journal of Verbal Learning and Verbal Behavior*, 1966, *5*, 541–547.

Rowher, W. D., Jr. Images and pictures in children's learning: Research results and educational implications. *Psychological Bulletin*, 1970, *73*, 393–403.

Rumelhart, D. E. Notes on a schema for stories. In D. B. Bobrow & A. M. Collins (Eds.), *Representation and understanding: Studies in cognitive science*. New York: Academic Press, 1975.

Schaeffer, B., Eggelston, V. H., & Scott, J. L. Number development in young children. *Cognitive Psychology*, 1974, *6*, 357–379.

Schank, R. C., & Abelson, R. P. *Scripts, plans, goals, and understanding*. Hillsdale, N.J.: Lawrence Erlbaum Associates, 1977.

Smiley, S. S., & Brown, A. L. Conceptual preference for thematic or taxonomic relations: A nonmonotonic age trend from preschool to old age. *Journal of Experimental Child Psychology,* 1979, *28,* 249–257.

Smith, C. L. Children's understanding of natural language hierarchies. *Journal of Experimental Child Psychology,* 1979, *27,* 437–458.

Trabasso, T. Representation, memory, and reasoning: How do we make transitive inferences? In A. D. Pick (Ed.), *Minnesota symposium on child psychology* (Vol. 9). Minneapolis: University of Minnesota Press, 1975.

Trabasso, T., Isen, A. M., Dolecki, P., McLanahan, A. G., Riley, C. A., & Tucker, T. How do children solve class-inclusion problems? In R. S. Siegler (Ed.), *Children's thinking: What develops?* Hillsdale, N.J.: Lawrence Erlbaum Associates, 1978.

Tulving, E. Episodic and semantic memory. In E. Tulving & W. Donaldson (Eds.), *The organization of memory.* New York: Academic Press, 1972.

Valentine, C. W. *The psychology of early childhood.* London: Methuen, 1942.

Vygotsky, L. S. *Thought and language.* Cambridge, Mass.: M.I.T. Press, 1962.

Wei, T. T. D., Lavatelli, C. B., & Jones, R. S. Piaget's concept of classification: A comparative study of socially disadvantaged and middle-class young children. *Child Development,* 1971, *42,* 919–972.

Wilkinson, A. Counting strategies and semantic analysis as applied to class inclusion. *Cognitive Psychology,* 1976, *8,* 64–88.

Woocher, F. D., Glass, A. L., & Holyoak, K. J. Positional discriminability in linear ordering. *Memory and Cognition,* 1978, *6,* 165–173.

Yuille, J. C., & Catchpole, M. J. Associative learning and imagery training in children. *Journal of Experimental Child Psychology,* 1973, *16,* 403–412.

Author Index

Numbers in *italics* indicate pages with complete bibliographic information.

Subject Index